Irene Rüngeler

SCTP - A Next Generation Transport Protocol

Irene Rüngeler

SCTP - A Next Generation Transport Protocol

Evaluating, Improving and Extending the Protocol for Broader Deployment

Südwestdeutscher Verlag für Hochschulschriften

Impressum/Imprint (nur für Deutschland/ only for Germany)
Bibliografische Information der Deutschen Nationalbibliothek: Die Deutsche Nationalbibliothek verzeichnet diese Publikation in der Deutschen Nationalbibliografie; detaillierte bibliografische Daten sind im Internet über http://dnb.d-nb.de abrufbar.

Alle in diesem Buch genannten Marken und Produktnamen unterliegen warenzeichen-, marken- oder patentrechtlichem Schutz bzw. sind Warenzeichen oder eingetragene Warenzeichen der jeweiligen Inhaber. Die Wiedergabe von Marken, Produktnamen, Gebrauchsnamen, Handelsnamen, Warenbezeichnungen u.s.w. in diesem Werk berechtigt auch ohne besondere Kennzeichnung nicht zu der Annahme, dass solche Namen im Sinne der Warenzeichen- und Markenschutzgesetzgebung als frei zu betrachten wären und daher von jedermann benutzt werden dürften.

Verlag: Südwestdeutscher Verlag für Hochschulschriften Aktiengesellschaft & Co. KG
Dudweiler Landstr. 99, 66123 Saarbrücken, Deutschland
Telefon +49 681 37 20 271-1, Telefax +49 681 37 20 271-0
Email: info@svh-verlag.de
Zugl.: Essen, Universität Duisburg-Essen, Diss., 2009

Herstellung in Deutschland:
Schaltungsdienst Lange o.H.G., Berlin
Books on Demand GmbH, Norderstedt
Reha GmbH, Saarbrücken
Amazon Distribution GmbH, Leipzig
ISBN: 978-3-8381-1517-7

Imprint (only for USA, GB)
Bibliographic information published by the Deutsche Nationalbibliothek: The Deutsche Nationalbibliothek lists this publication in the Deutsche Nationalbibliografie; detailed bibliographic data are available in the Internet at http://dnb.d-nb.de.

Any brand names and product names mentioned in this book are subject to trademark, brand or patent protection and are trademarks or registered trademarks of their respective holders. The use of brand names, product names, common names, trade names, product descriptions etc. even without a particular marking in this works is in no way to be construed to mean that such names may be regarded as unrestricted in respect of trademark and brand protection legislation and could thus be used by anyone.

Publisher: Südwestdeutscher Verlag für Hochschulschriften Aktiengesellschaft & Co. KG
Dudweiler Landstr. 99, 66123 Saarbrücken, Germany
Phone +49 681 37 20 271-1, Fax +49 681 37 20 271-0
Email: info@svh-verlag.de

Printed in the U.S.A.
Printed in the U.K. by (see last page)
ISBN: 978-3-8381-1517-7

Copyright © 2010 by the author and Südwestdeutscher Verlag für Hochschulschriften Aktiengesellschaft & Co. KG and licensors
All rights reserved. Saarbrücken 2010

Abstract

The Stream Control Transmission Protocol (SCTP), originally designed for the transport of signaling messages over IP based telephony signaling networks, is a general transport protocol with features suitable for a variety of applications that can benefit from multihoming, multiple streams, or one of SCTP's numerous extensions. To date, SCTP has found its way into all kernel implementations of UNIX derivatives and a Windows prototype, but there are still flaws, which have to be identified and corrected.

In this thesis, first, a suite of tools consisting of an SCTP simulation and testing environment is provided to lay the groundwork for further studies. Starting from comparing and analyzing kernel implementations, several aspects of the protocol that lead to undesirable behavior are examined. Congestion and flow control that are adopted from the Transmission Control Protocol (TCP), although using the same mechanisms, need a special treatment because of SCTP's message orientation. The analysis of the SCTP specific characteristics with the help of the simulation will finally result in solutions that lead to a better performance.

The deployment of SCTP will be another concern that can be improved by introducing a specific Network Address Translation (NAT) for SCTP.

Keywords:

SCTP, Simulation, Analysis, Deployment, NAT, Message orientation

Zusammenfassung

Das Stream Control Transmission Protocol (SCTP) wurde ursprünglich für den Transport von Signalisierungsnachrichten über IP basierte Netze konzipiert. Inzwischen hat es sich jedoch zu einem allgemeinen Transportprotokoll entwickelt, das einzigartige Eigenschaften besitzt. Daher ist es besonders für Anwendungen interessant, die von mehreren Netzwerkadressen pro Verbindung (Multihoming), mehreren unabhängigen Nachrichtenströmen oder einer der zahlreichen Protokollerweiterungen profitieren können. Mittlerweile hat SCTP in die Betriebssystemkerne aller UNIX-Derivate und eines Windows Prototyps Einzug gehalten, aber es gibt noch Mängel, deren Ursachen es zu entdecken und zu korrigieren gilt.

In dieser Dissertation wird zunächst eine Reihe von Werkzeugen bereitgestellt, um die Grundlage für weitere Untersuchungen zu schaffen. Ausgehend von der Analyse und dem Vergleich von Implementierungen im Systemkern verschiedener Betriebssysteme werden einige Aspekte des Protokolls untersucht, die zu unerwünschtem Verhalten führen. Die Prinzipien der Überlast- und Flusskontrolle wurden vom stream-orientierten Transmission Control Protocol (TCP) übernommen und benutzen daher dieselben Mechanismen. SCTP als nachrichtenorientiertes Protokoll benötigt jedoch eine diesem Unterschied Rechnung tragende Implementierung der Algorithmen. Die Analyse von SCTP-spezifischen Charakteristika mithilfe der Simulation wird schließlich zu Lösungen führen und zu einer Verbesserung des Durchsatzes.

Ein weiteres Anliegen dieser Arbeit ist die Verbreitung von SCTP. Sie kann durch die Einführung einer SCTP-spezifischen Methode zur Umsetzung von Netzwerkadressen (Network Address Translation (NAT)) verbessert werden.

Schlüsselwörter:

SCTP, Simulation, Analyse, Verbreitung, NAT, Nachrichtenorientierung

In Erinnerung an

Andreas,

meinen geliebten Mann.

Acknowledgment

This thesis is the result of my research work during my employment at the Department of Electrical Engineering and Computer Science at Münster University of Applied Sciences. At this point, I want to express my acknowledgment to everyone who has supported me during my research.

In particular, I want to thank Prof. Dr. Erwin P. Rathgeb for his willingness to supervise this thesis and his invaluable comments on my written works. My thanks also go to Prof. Dr. Bruno Müller-Clostermann for the review of this thesis.

I am very grateful to my advisor at Münster University of Applied Sciences, Prof. Dr. Michael Tüxen, for our long, interesting, and profitable discussions. Through his expertise and his enthusiasm, he inspired me for the topic.

Last but not least, I want to thank Prof. Dr. Doris Danziger, who brought up the idea to do a doctorate, and my family for their moral support.

Contents

Contents		**ix**
1 Introduction		**1**
1.1	Fields of Research Regarding SCTP	2
1.2	Outline of this work	3
2 The Stream Control Transmission Protocol (SCTP)		**7**
2.1	History	7
2.2	Main Features of SCTP	9
	2.2.1 Message orientation	9
	2.2.2 Establishing and Shutting down an Association	11
	2.2.3 Reliable Data Transfer	14
	2.2.4 Multihoming and Path Supervision	16
	2.2.5 Congestion Control	18
	2.2.6 Flow Control	19
2.3	Protocol Extensions	20
	2.3.1 Partial Reliability (PR-SCTP)	20
	2.3.2 Stream Reset	20
	2.3.3 Dynamic Address Reconfiguration (Add-IP)	21
	2.3.4 Authenticating Chunks (AUTH)	21
	2.3.5 Packet Drop Reporting (PKTDROP)	22
2.4	SCTP Implementations	23

3	**Computer Simulation**		**25**
	3.1 Modeling and Simulation		25
	3.2 Network Simulators		27
		3.2.1 The OPNET Modeler	27
		3.2.2 The Network Simulator 2 (NS-2)	28
		3.2.3 OMNeT++	30
		3.2.4 INET - an OMNeT++ Framework	35
4	**Analyzing Protocols**		**37**
	4.1 Packet Capturing		37
	4.2 Text-based Packet Analyzers		40
		4.2.1 Tcpdump	40
		4.2.2 Snoop	41
		4.2.3 TShark	41
	4.3 Introduction to Wireshark		41
	4.4 Graphical Analysis of SCTP in Wireshark		42
		4.4.1 Assigning Packets to Associations	44
		4.4.2 Statistics of the Chunk Types	47
		4.4.3 Graphical Representation of the Data Transfer	48
		4.4.3.1 Analyzing TSNs and `SACK` chunks	49
		4.4.3.2 Analyzing the Advertised Receiver Window and transmitted Bytes	50
5	**Extending the Simulation Framework**		**53**
	5.1 Connecting the INET Framework with Real Networks		53
		5.1.1 Simulation - Emulation - Real Network	53
		5.1.2 Preliminary Considerations	55
		5.1.2.1 Requirements	55
		5.1.2.2 Receiving and sending real packets	56

		5.1.2.3	Scheduling Events	57
	5.1.3	Realization of the Requirements		58
	5.1.4	Examples to Connect the ExtInterface with Real Networks		61
		5.1.4.1	Connecting a Simulated with a Real Network . .	62
		5.1.4.2	Capturing on two ExtInterfaces	65
5.2	Using Xgrid to Parallelize Simulations			67
	5.2.1	Overview of Xgrid		67
	5.2.2	Generating Batch Jobs with OMNeT++		69

6 Integration of SCTP in INET 77

6.1	Extensions to the INET Framework		77
6.2	Simulation Architecture		78
	6.2.1	Messages	79
	6.2.2	Association Setup and Take-down	82
	6.2.3	Data Sender	83
	6.2.4	Data Receiver	86
	6.2.5	Congestion Control	87
	6.2.6	Flow Control	88
	6.2.7	Simulation Structure	91
6.3	Implemented Protocol Extensions		93
	6.3.1	Partial Reliability (PR-SCTP)	93
	6.3.2	Stream Reset	93
	6.3.3	Dynamic Address Reconfiguration (Add-IP)	94
	6.3.4	Authenticating Chunks (AUTH)	94
	6.3.5	Packet Drop Reporting (PKTDROP)	95
6.4	Additional Modules		95
	6.4.1	SCTP Applications	95
	6.4.2	Dump Module	97
6.5	Validating the Simulation		98

		6.5.1	Testing Flow Control	98

      6.5.2 Testing Congestion Control 100

            6.5.2.1   SCTP fairness 100

            6.5.2.2   Testing Congestion Control on Lossy Links . . . 101

      6.5.3 Analyzing Trace Files 102

      6.5.4 Validating the Simulation by Using External Sources . . . 102

      6.5.5 Measuring the Throughput against Real Implementations . 103

7 Calculating the Theoretical Throughput of SCTP Associations 107

  7.1 Term Definitions 107

  7.2 Message Orientation versus Byte Stream Orientation 108

  7.3 Calculating the Maximum Throughput under Ideal Conditions . . 109

  7.4 A Rule of Thumb for the Calculation of the Throughput 111

      7.4.1 Mathis' Formula to Calculate the Throughput for TCP . . 112

      7.4.2 Model Assumptions 112

      7.4.3 Calculating the Throughput without Considering the Headers 113

      7.4.4 Including the Headers in the Calculation of the Data in Flight 115

      7.4.5 Verifying the Rule of Thumb for the Calculation of the Throughput 116

8 Validating and Improving the Protocol 119

  8.1 Comparing Kernel Implementations 119

      8.1.1 The Test Scenario 119

      8.1.2 Measuring the Throughput 120

      8.1.3 Identifying Path Failures 127

      8.1.4 Detecting Association Failures 130

      8.1.5 Handling Flow Control 131

  8.2 Reducing the Network Load by Adjusting the Advertised Receiver Window 135

	8.2.1		Simulating the Behavior of the Implementations	135
	8.2.2		Simulation Results	135
	8.2.3		Solutions	140
8.3	The Influence of Byte-Counting on the Network Load			141
	8.3.1		Counting Outstanding Bytes	141
	8.3.2		TCP-friendliness	144
	8.3.3		Simulation Scenario	145
	8.3.4		Fairness on the Transport Layer	146
	8.3.5		Fairness on the Application Layer	148
8.4	Improving the Handling of Acknowledgments			149
	8.4.1		Kernel Initiates the Use of the I-Bit	150
		8.4.1.1	Fairness Considerations	150
		8.4.1.2	The sender has reduced its RTO	153
		8.4.1.3	Short-term associations	154
	8.4.2		Application Initiates the Use of the I-Bit	155
		8.4.2.1	Sending is prevented due to the Nagle algorithm	155
		8.4.2.2	Sending is prevented due to DRY events	156
		8.4.2.3	API and Implementation Considerations	156
8.5	Benefitting from Packet Drop Reporting on Lossy Links			157
	8.5.1		One Association over a Lossy Link	158
	8.5.2		Applying PKTDROP in a fairness scenario	159
	8.5.3		Fairness when Lossy Link is not the Bottleneck	160
8.6	Decreasing Duplicates by Reducing the Number of Fast Retransmissions			161

9 Supporting Deployment through Network Address Translation for SCTP — 165

9.1	Introduction to NAT	165
9.2	NAT for other Transport Protocols	167

	9.2.1 NAT for TCP and UDP	167
	9.2.2 Using Common NAT Middleboxes for Processing SCTP Associations	167
9.3	Specific NAT for SCTP	169
	9.3.1 State of the Art	169
	9.3.2 Using Verification Tags instead of Ports	170
	9.3.3 Creating and Modifying the NAT Table	171
	9.3.4 Code of Behavior for the Endpoints	173
	9.3.5 Code of Behavior for the NAT Middleboxes	174
	9.3.6 New SCTP Protocol Elements	174
9.4	Associations with Stable Routing Conditions	175
	9.4.1 Single homed Client to Multihomed Server	175
	9.4.2 Multihomed Client and Server	176
9.5	Client-Server Communication with Changing Routing Conditions	177
	9.5.1 Adding New NAT Middleboxes	177
	9.5.2 Client using Transport Layer Mobility	178
	9.5.3 Multihomed Transport Layer Mobility	179
9.6	Peer-to-Peer Communication	179
	9.6.1 Single homed Peer-to-Peer Communication	180
	9.6.2 Multihoming with Rendezvous Server	181
9.7	Implementation of NAT for SCTP in INET	182
	9.7.1 Simulation of the NAT Middlebox	182
	9.7.2 Changes on the Application Layer	183

10 Conclusion and Outlook   **187**

10.1 Achieved Results 187

10.2 Future Work 190

List of Figures   **193**

List of Tables		**197**
Bibliography		**199**
A Configurable Parameters of the Simulation		**213**
A.1 Protocol Parameters		213
A.1.1 Parameters for the basic SCTP functionality according to RFC 4960		213
A.1.2 Parameters for special purposes		215
A.2 Application Parameters		217
B Configuration Examples		**221**
B.1 Fairness Test of Section 8.3		221
B.1.1 Setting up the network		221
B.1.2 Configuring the Parameters		224
B.2 Changing Error Rate and Delay		226

Chapter 1

Introduction

The Stream Control Transmission Protocol (SCTP) has its origin in the telephony signaling environment. To meet the strict performance and reliability requirements necessary for this vital medium, SCTP has been designed as a reliable message oriented transport protocol. New features like the support of multi-homing and multiple streams have been added, and finally SCTP has first been specified in 2000 in the RFC 2960 of the Internet Engineering Task Force (IETF).

Although its main field of application is still the telephony signaling environment, SCTP has evolved into a general transport protocol, which is now specified in RFC 4960. SCTP has been integrated in the kernels of the major UNIX-like operating systems. Furthermore, numerous extensions have been added to handle the dynamic reconfiguration of addresses, authenticate messages, support partial reliability, or provide packet drop reporting to improve the throughput on lossy links.

Often, SCTP is compared to the Transmission Control Protocol (TCP) as the main reliable transport protocol and fairness towards TCP is demanded. SCTP has adopted major features from TCP, most important are the congestion and the flow control mechanism. Although the principles used are the same, some issues arise from the fact that SCTP operates message oriented whereas TCP operates byte stream oriented. In addition, SCTP supports the bundling of small messages, common in the telephony signaling environment, which can lead to a large amount of header bytes compared to the payload in a packet. Detailed studies revealed that these differences in the protocol design have an impact on the fairness towards TCP and the number of unnecessary retransmissions.

1.1 Fields of Research Regarding SCTP

As the most outstanding new feature of SCTP is multihoming, the majority of research projects address this topic.

Based on the works of Maximilian Riegel and Michael Tüxen about Mobile SCTP [73, 74] numerous groups are investigating the applicability of SCTP in mobile environments. Some researchers focus on the improvement of the handover mechanism in wireless networks [23, 24], while others choose SCTP as transport protocol to improve the behavior of existing mobility protocols [66].

Another aspect of multihoming is the use of multiple links at the same time. Concurrent Multipath Transfer (CMT), first introduced at the University of Delaware [43], is still an ongoing research topic there and at other institutions. At the University of Duisburg-Essen a project funded by the Deutsche Forschungsgemeinschaft (DFG) focusses on the improvement of load sharing in SCTP multihomed heterogeneous environments.

Using multiple independent streams alleviates the risk that a message is blocked because an earlier one has not arrived yet. This positive effect is taken advantage of when the performance of application layer protocols like the Hypertext Transfer Protocol (HTTP) [60] is improved. A DFG project at Münster University of Applied Sciences concentrates on the applicability of several stream scheduling algorithms and their impact on flow and congestion control.

Securing messages is a prerequisite to deploy SCTP in areas where security considerations are vital. Studies have been conducted to secure SCTP on different layers [6, 21, 49], yet each solution had a disadvantage [33] that prevented its implementation. Datagram Transport Layer Security (DTLS) was the only protocol that could be implemented to secure SCTP with all its features [99]. At Münster University of Applied Sciences it has been integrated in the OpenSSL sources [64].

A research team at the University of British Columbia concentrates on the behavior of Message Passing Interface (MPI) applications. They have chosen SCTP as transport level protocol for MPI [50, 51] and ported the FreeBSD SCTP stack in a userland version. Ongoing research focusses on the influence of network characteristics on MPI application performance.

1.2 Outline of this work

One goal of this thesis is the validation of protocol features, the improvement of SCTP's behavior concerning performance, and the interaction with TCP regarding fairness. Misbehavior shall be discovered and suitable solutions for its correction found. To enhance the deployment of SCTP, a new concept for a specific NAT for SCTP shall be introduced.

To obtain a solid research basis, a suite of tools shall be developed to enable the simulation and an easy testing of the protocol behavior.

This thesis will be organized as follows. After a short introduction to the main features of SCTP in Chapter 2 and its protocol extensions with an emphasis on those that are relevant for the course of this work, computer simulation models will be briefly explained and some network simulators presented in Chapter 3. The OMNeT++ simulation environment and the INET framework, which were chosen for further use, will be described in more detail.

Chapter 4 introduces packet capturing and then focuses on Wireshark as the most popular open-source network analyzer. The integrated graphical representation of message flows and statistical data related to the associations will be presented extensively.

Another invaluable tool for testing is the ExtInterface, a network interface that makes the connection between the simulation environment and real networks possible. Its structure and necessary modules will be described in Chapter 5. To make performing hundreds of runs more efficient, OMNeT++ has been extended to support the generation of specification files that are needed as input for Xgrid, a tool provided by Mac OS X to distribute tasks.

The implementation of SCTP in the INET framework is the subject of Chapter 6. The simulation architecture is outlined together with the necessary new modules and messages that are needed to realize the functionality of SCTP. Implemented protocol extensions, application modules, and a section about the validation of the simulation round the chapter off.

For the course of this thesis the performance characterized by the throughput plays an important role. Therefore, formulae for the throughput under ideal conditions and for lossy links are developed in Chapter 7.

Chapter 8 concentrates on the improvement of SCTP. Starting from the comparison of real kernel implementations, topics related to the message orientation of SCTP are examined. Thus, the fairness towards TCP can be improved and unnecessary retransmissions can be avoided. A new flag is introduced that informs the data receiver that an acknowledgment should be sent as soon as possible. This feature can lead to an increase in the throughput for long term and a shortening of the life time of short term connections. Lossy links, which are typical for wireless LANs, often result in spurious retransmissions. To mitigate this effect, the packet drop extension is applied to the effect that the negative impact of error-prone links can be almost fully compensated. Finally, an advice is given for the handling of retransmissions when dealing with handovers from long to short delay links.

Chapter 9 is dedicated to the deployment of SCTP, which should be realized by a specific Network Address Translation (NAT) for SCTP. It is explained why the traditional NAT is not applicable for SCTP, and the concept for a new NAT is introduced. Examples that explain the message flow of the NAT transversal are outlined for all relevant scenarios including multihoming and peer-to-peer networks.

The final chapter provides a conclusion and an outlook on future work.

Chapter 2

The Stream Control Transmission Protocol (SCTP)

2.1 History

The Stream Control Transmission Protocol has its origin in the telephony environment. In the late nineties the need arose to send signaling data over Internet Protocol (IP) based networks. Up to that time most telephony signaling messages were sent with the protocols of the Signaling System No. 7 (SS7) suite over networks with a link bandwidth of 64 kbps. With the growing traffic a faster means of transportation became necessary.

As the requirements for the SS7 network concerning reliability and availability are very high, the transport protocol, which was to deliver the signaling data over IP, was to meet those demands, too. Neither the reliable Transmission Control Protocol (TCP) nor the message oriented User Datagram Protocol (UDP) was considered suitable to fullfill the rigid standards [91].

The Internet Engineering Task Force (IETF) solved this problem by setting up the Signaling Transport (SIGTRAN) working group that created a new protocol suite called SIGTRAN that adapts the SS7 messages for the transport over SCTP. First, SCTP was part of the SIGTRAN suite, until it was used as transport protocol directly over IP. The responsibility for its further development was taken over by the IETF Transport Area Working Group (tsvwg). According to the three higher levels of the SS7 protocol suite, corresponding application layers were designed to run over the new transport protocol SCTP:

- MTP Level 2 User Adaptation (M2UA) defined in [55] to transport messages from MTP 2 to MTP 3 over IP,

- MTP Level 2 Peer Adaptation (M2PA) defined in [27] to transport messages between MTP 2 layers over IP,

- MTP Level 3 User Adaptation (M3UA) defined in [56] to transport MTP 3 messages to the application,

- SCCP User Adaptation (SUA) defined in [52] for the SCCP message transport, and

- ISDN User Adaptation (IUA) defined in [57] to transport ISDN Q.931 messages.

A special node called Signaling Gateway (SG) was introduced and placed at the border between the signaling network and the IP based network to terminate the SS7 network and transport the messages to an IP based node.

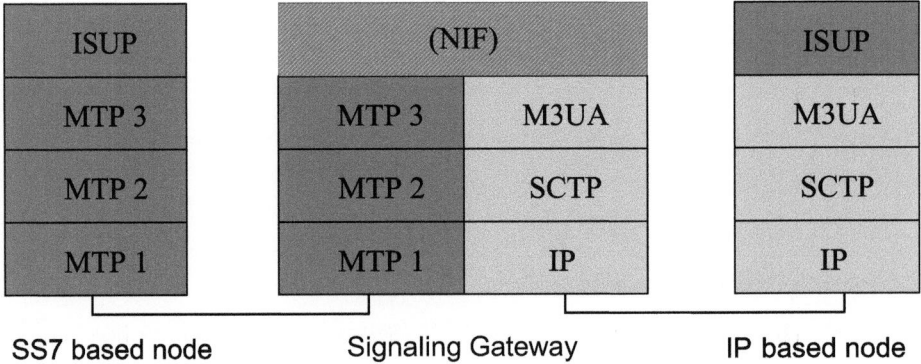

Figure 2.1: Transport of SS7 messages over SCTP

An example of the architecture for M3UA, the most popular of the SIGTRAN protocols, is shown in **Figure 2.1**. The Nodal Interworking Function (NIF), which was not specified by the IETF, is responsible for the conversion of the protocol formats. For further information on SS7 see the International Telecommunication Union (ITU) Recommendations [35–41]. The SIGTRAN protocol suite is specified in [27, 52, 55–57, 63], an overview on all protocols is given in [18].

2.2 Main Features of SCTP

In 2000, SCTP was defined in the RFC 2960, which was updated to RFC 4960 [85] in 2007. Although designed for a special application, SCTP evolved into a general purpose transport protocol.

SCTP is a reliable connection oriented transport protocol, which supports multihoming and multiple streams. A connection, which is called an *association* in SCTP, is set up between a client and a server. The user messages have to be sent reliably and some of them also in the correct sequence. The algorithms for congestion and flow control prevent overutilization of the links and lead to fairness towards TCP. Supervising the availability of the paths and changing to an alternative one in the case of a failure adds to the robustness of this protocol.

The main features of SCTP which are relevant for the course of this thesis are discussed in the following subsections.

2.2.1 Message orientation

SCTP is a message oriented protocol. To keep the message boundaries, all messages are organized in so-called *chunks* (Figure 2.2).

To distinguish between the different types of chunks, e.g. control chunks to set up or shut down an SCTP association or chunks that carry application layer messages, a **Chunk Type** field is introduced. Mostly the **Chunk Flags** value is set to

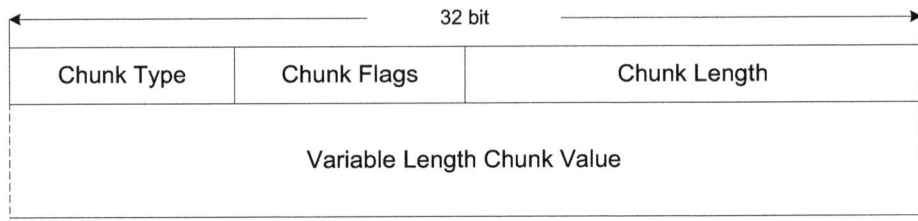

Figure 2.2: SCTP chunk format

zero, but there are cases, like in the DATA or ABORT chunk, where these flags are very important. In Section 8.4 a new DATA chunk flag will be suggested the use of which can save resources and improve the performance of an association. The Chunk Length field features the length of the complete chunk in bytes including the just mentioned fields.

The Chunk Value is type dependent and even optional in some cases. The only requirement is its 32-bit alignment, which is achieved by adding up to three padding bytes. The number of these bytes is not included in the Chunk Length field. Besides mandatory fields and parameters, optional parameters can be added which follow the so-called TLV format. It consists only of a two bytes type field, a two bytes length field and a variable length value.

Signaling data feature relatively small single messages that are, for instance, in the case of ISDN User Part (ISUP) traffic typically only between 17 and 48 bytes long (see [80]). However, the maximum size of a packet to be transferred without fragmentation is limited by the maximum transmission unit (MTU), which is defined as the maximum size of a datagram that can be transmitted through the next network [69]. It is dependent on the underlying hardware, e.g. for an Ethernet link it is 1500 bytes. To be able to utilize the full size of a packet, SCTP chunks can be bundled, which means that smaller chunks can be combined into one packet (see Figure 2.3). With the exception of some combinations, an SCTP message can also be composed of different types of chunks.

Figure 2.3 shows a complete SCTP message that consists of the common header

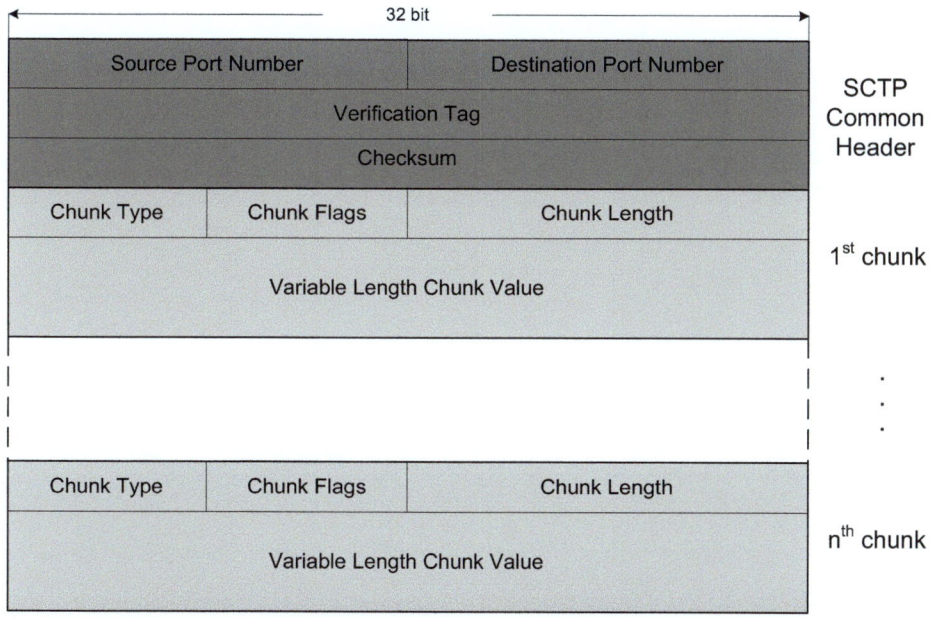

Figure 2.3: SCTP message format

and a number of chunks. The common header includes information about the source and destination port like the headers in other transport protocols. In addition, a **Verification Tag** is introduced that identifies all the chunks that belong to the same direction of an association (see Subsection 2.2.2). A **Checksum** that is calculated according to the CRC32c algorithm introduced by Castagnoli et.al. in [12] verifies the integrity of the SCTP message.

2.2.2 Establishing and Shutting down an Association

SCTP is a connection oriented protocol. Therefore, before sending data, an association has to be established. In contrast to TCP, SCTP uses a four way handshake that can protect the server against blind Denial-of-Service (DoS) attacks according to the guidelines of RFC 4732 [31].

In Figure 2.4 three variants of four way handshakes are drawn. The most

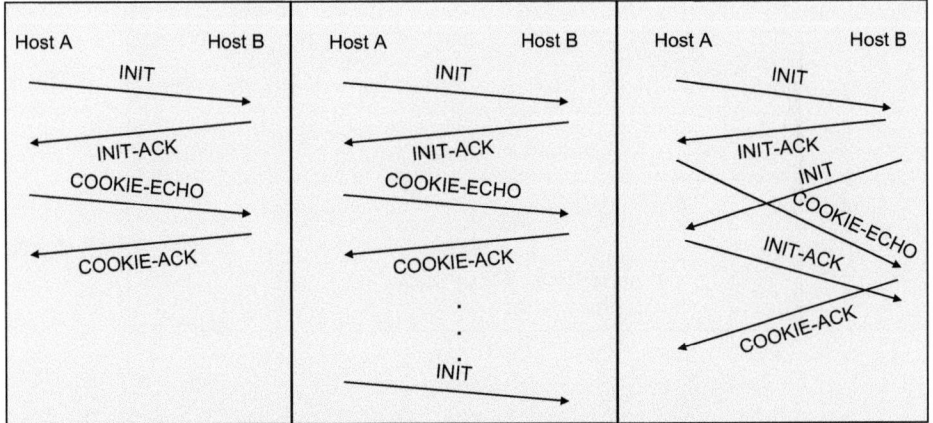

Figure 2.4: Variants of SCTP handshakes

common flow (left hand side of Figure 2.4) will be described in more detail.

The client starts by sending a packet containing an INIT chunk, whose parameters inform the server about:

- The initiate tag, which is going to be the verification tag that the server will use in each common header.

- The maximum advertised receiver window (arwnd) that indicates, how many bytes the client can accept without delivering data to the application.

- The initial 32-bit transmission sequence number (TSN), i.e. the TSN of the first DATA chunk that the sender of the INIT chunk will use. The following DATA chunks are numbered consecutively to obtain a unique identification.

- The number of outbound and inbound streams the client wants to set up.

The server accepts the INIT chunk by sending an INIT_ACK chunk of the same format. To mitigate the risk of a successful DoS attack, the server does not reserve resources for a future association, but includes a State-Cookie parameter that contains all the information that is needed to create the future association. For further information about the advantage of a four way handshake concerning DoS attacks refer to the results in [71].

Besides the `State-Cookie` parameter, additional ones can be included in the `INIT` or `INIT_ACK` chunk to inform its receiver about implemented protocol extensions, addresses etc.

The `State-Cookie` parameter is reflected in the `COOKIE_ECHO` chunk that is acknowledged in the `COOKIE_ACK` chunk.

The handshake in the middle of Figure 2.4 can happen, if one endpoint starts the association procedure again while the peer is still in the established state. A reason for this behavior could be that one side rebooted without tearing down the association and then restarted the association setup procedure. The four way handshake will succeed and for the server side the association will restart.

SCTP does not only support the client-server model for association setup, but also the more general peer-to-peer model. Both endpoints can start the four way handshake at about the same time and the SCTP setup procedure will ensure that exactly one association is established. This is called an INIT collision. An example message flow is given on the right hand side of Figure 2.4. Detailed descriptions of the handling of all the possible scenarios are given in the SCTP reference guide [91].

After the association is established, the data transfer may start, which will be decribed in the next section.

One of the hosts initiates the closing of an association by sending a shutdown primitive to the transport layer. SCTP will send a `SHUTDOWN` chunk, after the local send queues have been emptied. The receiver answers with a `SHUTDOWN_ACK` chunk, which is acknowledged with a `SHUTDOWN_COMPLETE` chunk. This three way handshake terminates an association gracefully, while an `ABORT` chunk can be sent any time on reception of a packet for which no association can be looked up, or when a critical error occurs, to close the association abruptly.

Error conditions can be signaled by sending an **ERROR** chunk that can include the causes of the error in order to provide more detailed information for the receiver.

2.2.3 Reliable Data Transfer

All messages that are handed down from the upper layer are encapsulated as payload into the **DATA** chunk (Figure 2.5).

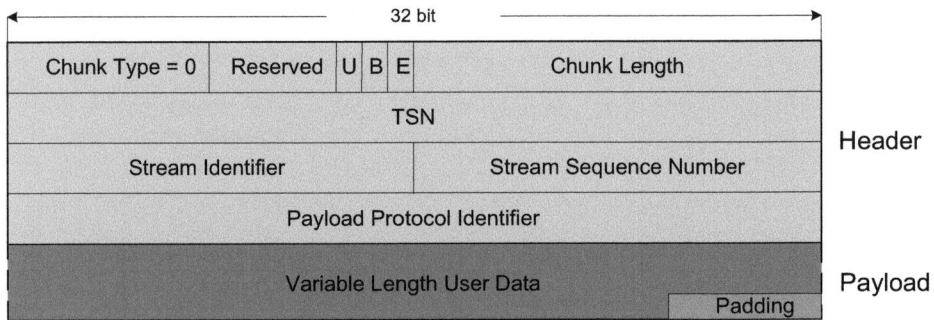

Figure 2.5: SCTP DATA chunk format

The **DATA** chunk is divided into a fixed length header of 16 bytes and the variable length application data (payload), which have to be padded at the end to become 32-bit aligned. The **DATA** chunk is identified by the **TSN** that it will keep for its lifetime. If user data does not fit into an MTU and has to be fragmented, each fragment will be assigned a distinctive TSN. Three of the eight possible flags are in use indicating whether a series of fragments begins (B-Bit) or ends (E-Bit) or data should be sent unordered (U-Bit). Unordered **DATA** chunks must be dispatched to the upper layer by the receiver without any attempt to reorder. In Section 8.4 another flag will be introduced that initiates the immediate sending of an acknowledgment and thus improves the performance in some situations.

One unique feature of SCTP are streams, unidirectional logical channels within an association. In TCP, as a reliable transport protocol, all data is delivered to the application in the same order as it was sent. This implies that the absence of one packet at the beginning of a series of data to be delivered results in the blocking of the other already received data. This phenomenon is called *Head-of-Line* (HOL) blocking. To overcome these undesirable delays, the streams in SCTP are independent from each other in that the sequence has to be kept only within a stream and not within the overall message flow. Furthermore, only the user messages which are marked as ordered have to keep the sequence. The user can choose the stream for a particular message by setting its **Stream Identifier** (SID). The SCTP layer assigns a **Stream Sequence Number** (SSN) to define the order within a stream. SCTP can handle a great number (up to 65536) of streams that can be filled according to special needs of the application, sending, for instance, important data unordered to be delivered immediately.

Finally, the **Payload Protocol Identifier** (PPID) informs about the protocol of the encapsulated message. This is needed, for example, in the case of all SIGTRAN protocols that are transported over SCTP. In case the payload does not contain data of another protocol, the PPID is set to zero.

As SCTP is a reliable transport protocol, all data have to be acknowledged. In SCTP a selective acknowledgment (**SACK**) chunk is sent for every second packet. The **Cumulative TSN Ack** (CumTSNAck) field (Figure 2.6) carries the TSN up to which all TSNs have been received. In case that TSNs have arrived out of order, the receiver fills gap ack blocks with the first and the last sequenced TSNs of a block. Thus, the sender will be informed about the missing TSNs, i.e. those between the Cumulative TSN Ack and the first block and those between the blocks. If a TSN arrives although it has been acknowledged in a previous **SACK** chunk, this TSN is added to the list of duplicate TSNs.

The **Advertised Receiver Window Credit** (arwnd) plays an important part in the flow control mechanism and will be discussed in Subsection 2.2.6.

Packet loss due to queue exhaustion or error-prone links leads to gap reports,

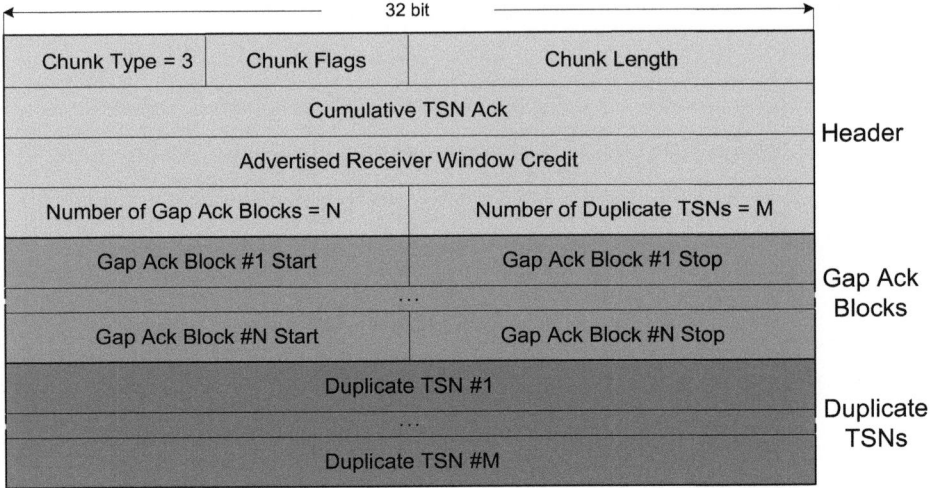

Figure 2.6: SCTP SACK chunk format

i.e. a TSN higher than the one missing has been acknowledged and announced in a gap ack block. If a specific TSN has been reported missing for three successive times, it will be marked for retransmission to be re-sent as soon as possible. In most scenarios this mechanism is sufficient so that packet loss has no negative influence on the performance.

In the case of error-prone links or heavy traffic, one fast retransmission per TSN might not be enough to fill the gap. When a DATA chunk leaves the sender, a timer is started to expire after a retransmission timeout (RTO). If the TSN has not been acknowledged before, a timer-based retransmission is triggered.

2.2.4 Multihoming and Path Supervision

A feature that is unique to SCTP is multihoming, which means that an endpoint may have several IP addresses that can be used as destination addresses to reach this endpoint.

During the association setup the endpoints announce their addresses in the address parameter of the INIT or INIT_ACK chunk, respectively. One address is selected as primary path, either explicitly by the upper layer or the destination address of the first message is used.

The availability of the paths is supervised by sending HEARTBEAT chunks every ($HB_{Interval} + RTO$) seconds to all known endpoint addresses. If the corresponding HEARTBEAT_ACK chunk arrives, this path is stated *confirmed*. The value for $HB_{Interval}$ is usually 30 secs. The first value for RTO is RTO_{Min} which is one second by default. The next values are calculated by taking the round trip time (RTT) into account. The RTT is measured by either calculating the time difference between the sending of a HEARTBEAT chunk and the arrival of the corresponding HEARTBEAT_ACK chunk, or the first transmission of a user message and its acknowledgment in the SACK chunk, considering only the DATA chunks that have not been retransmitted. The computation of RTO in SCTP follows closely the rules for TCP in RFC 2988 [67].

HEARTBEAT chunks are only sent when the path has been idle for some time. In case the acknowledgment does not arrive, RTO is doubled and a path error counter is increased. The maximum number of trials for the path supervision is configured in the Maximum Path Retransmission ($RTX_{Max}^{(P)}$) parameter. After $RTX_{Max}^{(P)}$ fruitless trials, the path is declared *inactive*. All regular traffic is transmitted via the primary path, but in case of a timer based retransmission or a path failure, i.e. the path becomes *inactive*, the next confirmed path is used.

As the properties and the usage of the paths are different from each other, the calculation of the RTO has to be done for each path individually.

Up to date multihoming is used for redundancy purposes only, however, the utilization of the additional paths for load-balancing has been the topic of several research projects [42, 43, 46, 47].

2.2.5 Congestion Control

Congestion control, which is also adopted from TCP, is a mechanism to control the traffic on a link between two endpoints of a connection. The goal is to prevent senders from blocking links by forcing them to reduce the rate of sending packets.

The most important parameter is the congestion window (cwnd). It limits the number of bytes the sender is allowed to transmit before waiting for a new acknowledgment. That means that not more than cwnd bytes may be outstanding, i.e. sent, but not acknowledged yet.

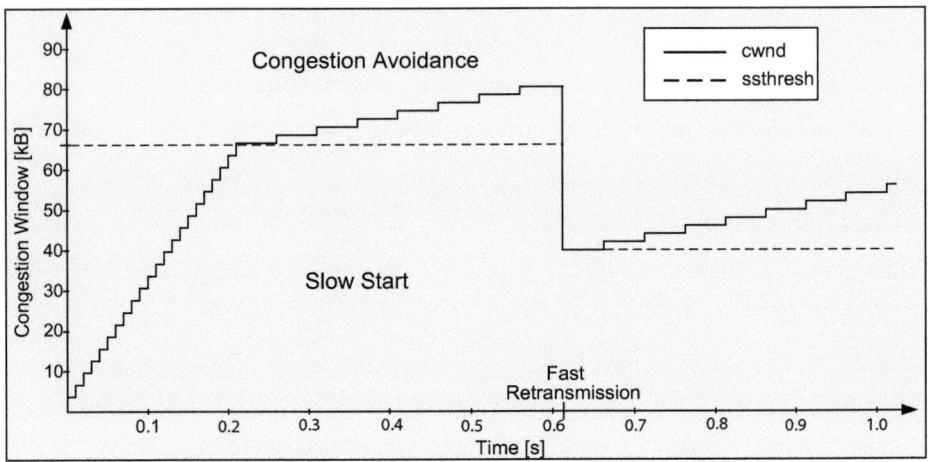

Figure 2.7: Evolution of the congestion window

The congestion control mechanism is divided into two phases (see Figure 2.7). The first one is called *slow start*. It operates for cwnd values less than or equal to the slow start threshold (ssthresh), which is set to an arbitrary value (mostly the advertised receiver window of the peer during association setup) at the beginning of an association. *Slow start* is characterized by an exponential increase of the congestion window. Every time an incoming SACK chunk announces that the Cumulative TSN Ack parameter has advanced and the cwnd is fully utilized, i.e. the number of outstanding bytes is greater than cwnd, the minimum of the path

MTU and the acknowledged bytes is added to cwnd.

When cwnd exceeds the slow start threshold, *congestion avoidance* results only in a linear increase of cwnd. As cwnd indicates the upper bound for the amount of data that may be sent, its growth can lead to an excessive injection of data into the network which will result in packet loss. While fast retransmissions result in halving the congestion window, a timer based retransmission leaves cwnd at the size of the path MTU and in *slow start* again. Thus cwnd follows usually a zigzag curve in the lifetime of an association. It has to be calculated for each path separately.

2.2.6 Flow Control

Flow control like congestion control is a mechanism to influence the amount of data injected into the network. Whereas congestion control protects the network from a fast sender, flow control should prevent the receiver from being overloaded.

To achieve this, the advertised receiver window parameter is used to announce the amount of data that the receiver is willing to accept. During the setup of the association the hosts exchange their initial arwnd in the `INIT` and `INIT_ACK` chunk. Upon arrival of a `DATA` chunk, arwnd is decremented by the message size. After the delivery of the data to the upper layer, arwnd can be incremented again. When the receiver sends a `SACK` chunk to acknowledge data, it includes the actual value of the arwnd. The sender attempts to keep track of the size of its peer's arwnd by trying to predict the window size. It takes the value of the announced arwnd as basis, reduces it by the number of outstanding bytes, i.e. the data that are assumed to be in flight.

In case of large gaps or a very slow application, the peer's arwnd might reach zero. In this situation only one `DATA` chunk may be sent to probe the window, which is similar to the Zero Window Probing mechanism in TCP described in RFC 793 [70]. The intervals between the sending of the probes are increased exponentially. As soon as the receiver is ready to accept new data, it will send a `SACK` chunk stating the updated size of the arwnd.

But before zero is reached the silly window syndrome (SWS) avoidance algorithm (see RFC 813 [14]) has to be applied. This algorithm uses a threshold, usually 3000 bytes, below which no arwnd is announced. Sending a window update only when more than 3000 bytes can be accepted prevents the sending of small messages that would only result in a re-closing of the window. Research results to the benefit of the SWS avoidance algorithm will be discussed in Section 8.2.

2.3 Protocol Extensions

Since the basic properties of SCTP were first published in RFC 2960, several SCTP extensions have been developed and have already been standardized or are in the process of standardization.

2.3.1 Partial Reliability (PR-SCTP)

The partial reliability extension PR-SCTP, specified in RFC 3758 [84], allows the sender to control the level of reliability. There are different ways of specifying the reliability: by limiting the time a message is considered worth being (re-)transmitted, by specifying a priority, or by just limiting the number of retransmissions. This provides a service to the user which is not available when using UDP or TCP. With UDP as an unreliable and TCP as a reliable transport protocol, the user can benefit from both when applying PR-SCTP.

2.3.2 Stream Reset

Several groups using SCTP have requested to be able to switch back individual SCTP streams to the state they had directly after association setup. An extension called STREAM-RST has been developed to provide this functionality and is specified in the draft [86].

2.3.3 Dynamic Address Reconfiguration (Add-IP)

Only being able to negotiate the IP addresses of the SCTP endpoint during the setup of an association is a severe restriction for long term SCTP associations. Therefore, an extension called ADD-IP has been specified in RFC 5061 [92]. It allows SCTP endpoints to change the set of IP addresses being used during the lifetime of an SCTP association. Special chunk types called `ASCONF` and `ASCONF_ACK` are sent to ask the destination host to add or delete an address, or to use it as primary path.

A special rule that will be of importance in Chapter 9 specifies that in case the address to be added is the wildcard address (0.0.0.0 for IPv4 or ::0 for IPv6), the source address of the packet containing the `ASCONF` chunk is added. If the address to be deleted is the wildcard address, all addresses except the source address of the packet containing the `ASCONF` chunk are deleted.

Not only in mobile networks and other scenarios, where a host moves and changes its addresses over time, Add-IP can be beneficially applied, but also in the creation of Network Address Translation (NAT) tables, which will be described in Section 9.4.2.

2.3.4 Authenticating Chunks (AUTH)

As security is of prime importance, the possibility to hijack an association has to be inhibited. Especially when Add-IP is applied and addresses are transmitted in plain text, the risk to be successfully attacked rises. Therefore, a security extension called SCTP-AUTH, has been specified in RFC 4895 [101]. It allows the sender to authenticate chunks using shared keys that have been exchanged during the association setup. Thus the receiver can verify that the chunks have been sent by the sender and not by an attacker.

The `AUTH` chunk that holds the result of the authentication code calculation precedes one or more encrypted chunks. The chunk types to be encrypted can be chosen by the host, however, `ASCONF` and `ASCONF_ACK` must be included in the `Chunk-List` Parameter of the `INIT` or `INIT_ACK` chunk.

2.3.5 Packet Drop Reporting (PKTDROP)

The need to deal with lossy links is growing as the number of wireless networks increases. Links with high bit error rates lead to spurious retransmissions. In TCP and SCTP, a packet loss is considered a congestion indication, which leads to reducing the number of transmitted packets and, hence, the throughput. Packet drop reporting (PKTDROP) [87] is an extension of SCTP to report packets that have been dropped by middle boxes or the host due to a false checksum or an exhausted receiver window. If PKTDROP is supported by both hosts, which they announce in the `INIT` or `INIT_ACK` chunk, the host receiving a corrupted packet will send a `PKTDROP` chunk back. This chunk includes the complete packet that was corrupted. In case that the resulting packet is larger than the maximum segment size, the corrupted message is truncated, which is announced by setting the T-bit and the `Truncated Length` field in the header. The receiver of the `PKTDROP` chunk tries to figure out, which TSNs were included. To identify the TSNs the 4 byte `TSN` field and the 2 byte `Length` field have to be uncorrupted. The retrieved TSNs have to be marked for retransmission to be re-sent as soon as possible. In addition to this faster way of retransmission, compared to the three necessary `SACK` chunks reporting the TSN missing, the congestion window will not be decreased and the fast recovery status will not be entered. This is justified by the fact that the packet was not lost due to congestion but because of a lossy link.

The impact of the PKTDROP extension on the performance will be examined in Section 8.5.

2.4 SCTP Implementations

SCTP has gained quite some acceptance since its beginning. As its first goal was the use as transport protocol for SIGTRAN, it is deployed in signaling networks of telephone network operators and in IP-based signaling for Universal Mobile Telecommunication System (UMTS) networks.

As an all-purpose transport protocol, it is integrated in the Linux 2.6 kernel, Solaris 10 and FreeBSD release 7. An SCTP kernel implementation for 32 bit Windows XP and Vista has recently been developed by a Japanese research team and can be downloaded from [110].

To provide the user with a uniform interface between the application and the transport layer, a Socket Application Programming Interface (API) [88] was developed, which is to a great extent integrated in the kernel implementations.

Except for Stream Reset and Packet Drop Reporting, which is only available in FreeBSD, the other extensions are implemented in all operating system (OS) kernels.

Very early in the development of the protocol, the userland implementation *sctplib* has been realized for UNIX-like platforms. It has been the result of a cooperation between the Siemens company, the University of Duisburg-Essen, and Münster University of Applied Sciences. Later is has been ported to Windows and is available at [44].

Chapter 3

Computer Simulation

The performance analysis and the testing of new features are major issues in the development and validation of new protocols. As the behavior of real implementations is not always predictable and the integration of new features for testing purposes requires a great effort, simulations are the method of choice. The advantages of simulations lie in the abstraction from details which are not relevant, the possibility to easily debug the model and reproduce tests because everything can be run in a deterministic way.

3.1 Modeling and Simulation

A simulation is the imitation of the operation of a real-world process or system over time. To study the behavior of this system, it has to be modeled. Therefore, assumptions have to be made about the operation of the system, properties have to be gathered that are suitable to describe the behavior of the real system. The output data from the simulation should correspond to the outputs of the real system. Thus the simulation helps to gain a better understanding of the system.

Reasons to develop and exploit simulations are manifold [4]:

- A simulation study can help to understand how a system works.

- New policies or features can be tested without disrupting the ongoing operations of the real system.

- New hardware designs can be tested without committing resources for their acquisition.

- "What if" questions can be answered.

- Insight can be obtained into the interactions of variables and their importance to the performance of the system.

There is a wide range of possible applications for simulations. Some examples are [7]:

- Education and training

- Engineering design

- Performance evaluation

- Prototyping and concept evaluation

- Risk/safety assessment

Systems can be characterized as continuous or discrete depending on whether the state variables change at a discrete set of points in time or continuously. A queuing system is an example for a discrete system, whereas the changing level of water behind a dam can be subject to a continuous system. The decision, which model is used, is a function of the characteristics of the system [5]. In the following the main focus will be on discrete-event simulation.

Discrete-event simulation models are analyzed by numerical methods, which means that they are not "solved", but "run". The operations are represented by a chronological sequence of events that occur in certain system states or change them. A scheduler inserts the events into a list where they are sorted in chronological order according to their execution time. A clock keeps track of the simulation time and can jump to the start time of the next event. Thus, simulation runs with rare events can be processed faster than real time runs. Typical for discrete-event simulators are also random-number generators which enable the user to apply some randomness to selected input variables.

3.2 Network Simulators

The diversity in the range of applications is reflected in the number of simulation programs available. As the main focus is the simulation of network traffic, a short introduction to three network simulators and their pros and cons will be given which led to the decision for OMNeT++.

3.2.1 The OPNET Modeler

The OPNET Modeler [65] is a commercial simulation tool, which was originally developed at the Massachusetts Institute of Technology (MIT). It provides discrete-event, hybrid, and analytical simulations, as well as grid computing support for distributed simulations.

The Modeler provides three editors for the user to configure his network simulation:

- The Project Editor helps to create the topology of a communications network.

- The Node Editor depicts the flow of data between the functional elements, which can be protocols or algorithms.

- Protocols, resources, algorithms, and queuing policies are specified in the Process Editor by assigning states and specific events using a finite state machine.

OPNET offers a variety of protocol models like TCP, SIP, UMTS, and VoIP. To analyze the simulation runs, built-in statistics are offered, as well as tools to visualize the packet routes between source and destination.

Nevertheless, the OPNET Modeler was no option, although SCTP had been implemented by Andreas Jungmaier as part of his PhD thesis [45]. As the OPNET Modeler is a commercial tool, licensing was an issue. The available funds did not allow the renewing of the current license, and therefore, only a free network simulator came into consideration. Furthermore, a commercial tool normally lacks the possibility to change code in the simulator itself, which might be of importance in the case of bugs or when features in the protocol make changes to the modeler necessary.

3.2.2 The Network Simulator 2 (NS-2)

The Network Simulator 2 (NS-2) is an open-source discrete-event simulation environment developed at the University of California, Berkeley [61]. It provides support for the simulation of TCP, routing, and multicast protocols over wired and wireless networks.

NS-2 is an object oriented simulator in C++ with an OTcl [109] interpreter as a frontend. OTcl is used for the configuration and setup of simulation scenarios, whereas the detailed protocol implementation is written in C++. NS-2 supports a class hierarchy in OTcl and C++ with a one-to-one correspondence between a C++ class and one in the OTcl hierarchy [22].

A simple network with two nodes could be configured as follows [58]:

1. Define the nodes

   ```
   set n1 [$ns node]
   set n2 [$ns node]
   ```

2. Connect them

   ```
   $ns duplex-link $n1 $n2 100Mb 10ms DropTail
   ```

3. Assign an agent to a node

```
set udp [new Agent/UDP]
$ns attach-agent $n1 $udp
set null [new Agent/Null]
$ns attach-agent $n2 $null
```

4. Generate traffic

```
set app [new Application/Traffic/CBR]
$cbr set packetSize_ 1000
$cbr set interval_ 0.005
$cbr attach-agent $udp
```

5. Connect agents

```
$ns connect $udp $null
```

6. Configure events

```
$ns at 0.5 "$cbr start"
$ns rtmodel-at 1.0 down $n1 $n2
$ns rtmodel-at 1.5 up $n1 $n2
$ns at 2.0 "$cbr stop"
```

To make the setup of large networks easier, an editor is included which enables the interactive generation of scenarios. The outcome can be stored in a script file.

To be able to analyze the simulation results, a trace file can be recorded in a special format that can be read by the Network Animator (nam). This file contains information about the topology, the layout, and the traffic. Nam interprets the file, visualizes the network and replays the simulation.

There are already a variety of network components available, for instance several schedulers, queues with different strategies, routing and transport protocols. TCP is supported with different flavors, and even an SCTP agent is implemented.

As NS-2 is open-source software, its source code is available, and hence, new protocols can be added. This might be the reason why is it very popular in the academic world.

Although the NS-2 SCTP module has been available as a patch since 2003, and release 3.5 has afterwards been integrated in the NS-2 release, it was decided to implement an independent solution for SCTP. One disadvantage of NS-2 was that multihoming was only possible via an agent that consisted of several nodes, another reason not to opt for NS-2 was that the desired implementation of the IP-stack was supposed to be closer to reality.

3.2.3 OMNeT++

OMNeT++ [105, 106] encompasses all the properties which are important and are not present in the other simulators. OMNeT++ is a public-source discrete event simulation environment, which means that the source-code is available, but the public cannot participate in submitting updates and changes to the source code. But as the code can be compiled, it can be changed for testing purposes, and in case of bugs, patches can be provided to the author. OMNeT++ is a modular component based architecture written in C++. Types of components are channels (described by the parameters delay, bit or packet error rate, and data rate), network definitions, simple and compound modules. The components can be assembled into more complex modules via connected gates. Networks are the result of combined module types that communicate through messages. One message can be encapsulated into another one, thus being able to simulate the transmission of information via layered protocol stacks.

The events are ordered according to their start or stop times using a scheduler. This scheduler was extended to realize the real-time-scheduling needed for the external interface that will be discussed in Section 5.1.

The network topology is described using a special high-level language (ned).

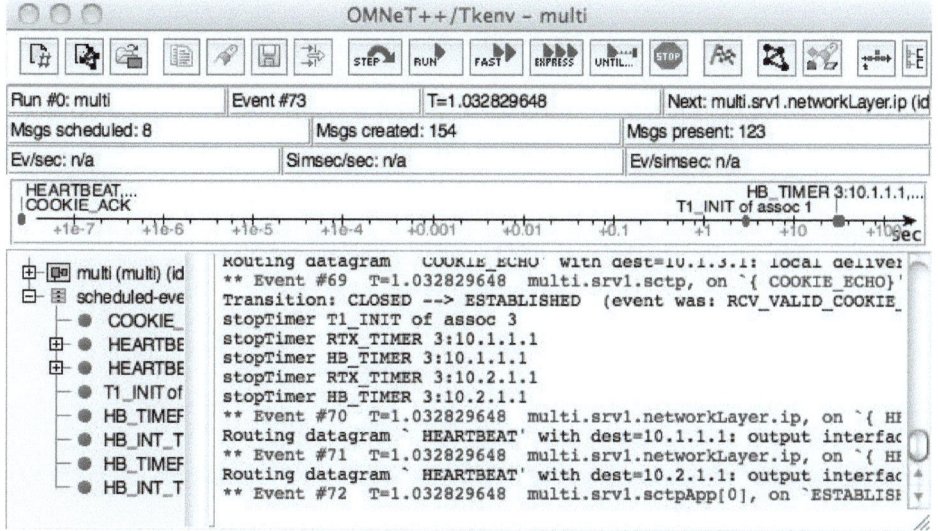

Figure 3.1: OMNeT++ simulation environment

Parameters can be assigned to modules and easily defined in configuration files.

A powerful Graphical User Interface (GUI) is implemented that helps to follow the simulation process. Each packet is animated and its contents can be shown just by double-clicking on it. Furthermore, debug output can be examined for each module individually. Figure 3.1 shows the OMNeT++ GUI. In the left part of the main window the scheduled events are listed, which can be found again in the timeline below the menu. Status information is constantly updated above the timeline. The windows in Figure 3.2 show only a small collection of the possible 'insides' of the simulated network. Clicking on **router2** in the network topology of the top window pops up the right window, which shows the compound module **Router**. Selecting the outgoing link of **ppp[1]** leads to the lower left window showing the gates of the channel between **router2** and **srv1**. The channel parameters can be seen and one message just arriving at **router2**. Further information is available by selecting other modules.

Different speed rates for the simulation can be selected from the toolbar (see

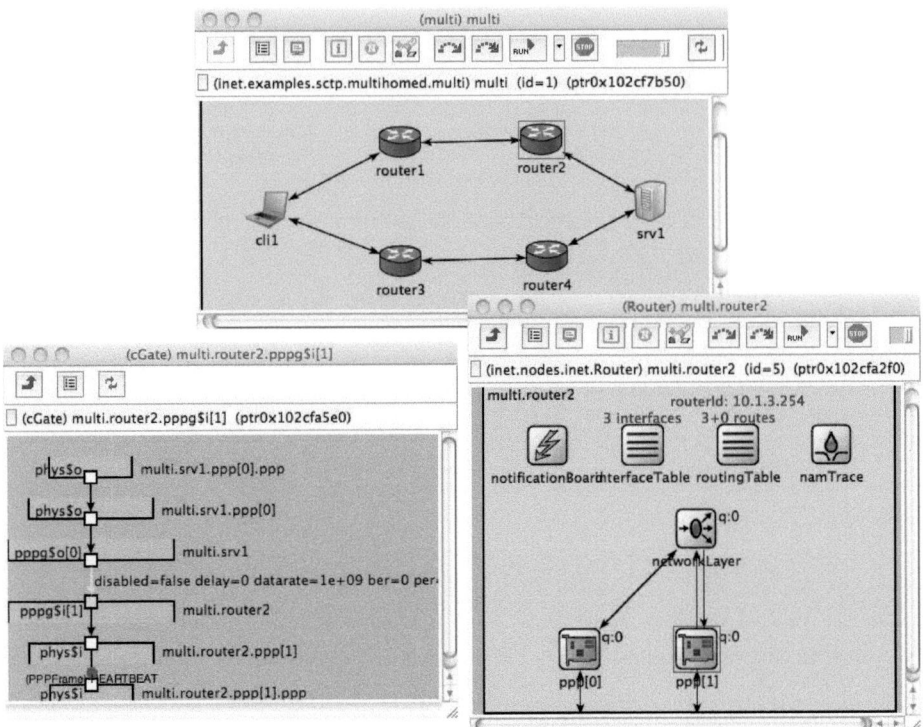

Figure 3.2: Inside the modules

Figure 3.1). Every movement of a message can be inspected by stepping through the simulation. The velocities *Run* and *Fast* provide a normal and less detailed animation than the *Step* mode whereas in the *Express* mode the displayed information is updated only in long intervals.

Sometimes the assistance of the GUI is not necessary, especially when a series of runs with just one varying parameter has to be performed. Then the simulation can be started from the command line with the command environment option set. Thus, no GUI output will slow down the activity.

Since version 4.0, OMNeT++ is integrated in the Eclipse Integrated Development Environment (IDE) [19]. Hence, the complete process from building new

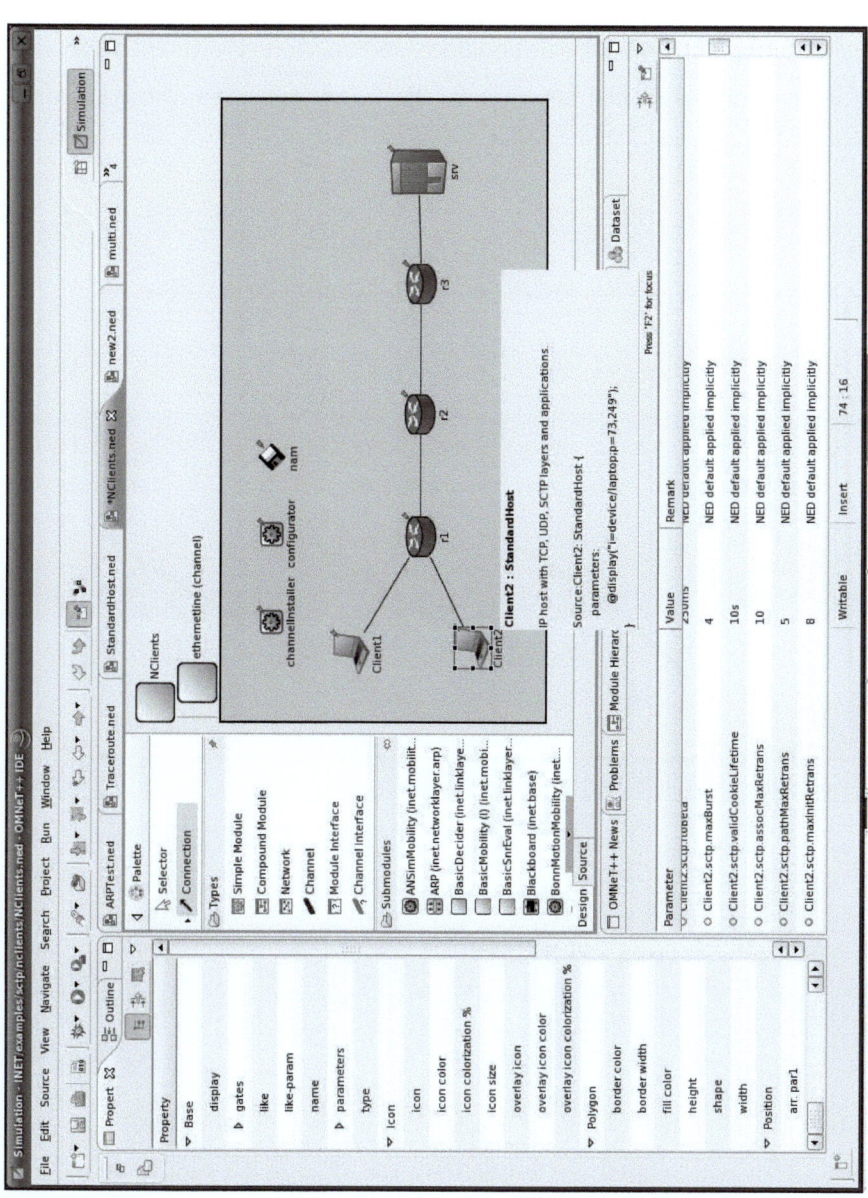

Figure 3.3: OMNeT++ integrated in the Eclipse IDE

networks, coding and debugging the sources to analyzing the results is supported in one tool. Figure 3.3 shows the IDE with the tool to set up a new network. Via drag-and-drop submodules can be added and connected with channels, the possible connection points can be selected. Then the properties of the modules can be set, e.g. name, icon, color, size, gates.

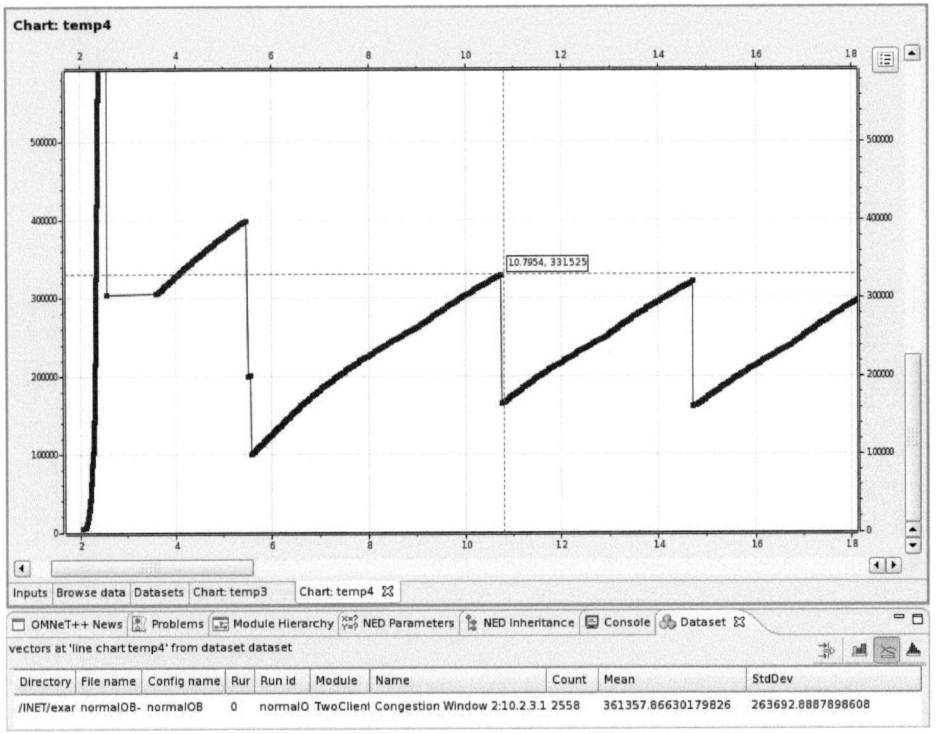

Figure 3.4: Analyzing results of a vector file

Simulation results are collected for a later analysis in vector (.vec) or scalar (.sca) files. They can be analyzed in the IDE, too. Figure 3.4 depicts one of the charts generated from one dataset. In the lower window the dataset properties including the number, the mean, and the standard deviation are shown.

3.2.4 INET - an OMNeT++ Framework

As OMNeT++ is a very versatile tool, there are a great number of ready-made simulation models provided for download. One of those is the INET framework [104].

The INET framework is ideal for simulating IP-based networks. The different network layers can be distinguished and layer specific protocols are provided. On the link layer Point-to-Point Protocol (PPP), Ethernet and wireless Local Area Network (WLAN) interfaces can be configured, the network layer features IPv4 and IPv6, routing protocols like Open Shortest Path First (OSPF), and IP control protocols like the Internet Control Message Protocol (ICMPv4 and ICMPv6), and the Resource ReSerVation Protocol (RSVP). On the transport layer TCP and UDP are implemented. In addition, a lot of protocol independent modules like routing tables, routers, switches, and hubs are available. They are all configured as simple modules and can be combined to form compound modules and networks.

One of those compound modules for instance is the *StandardHost* (Figure 3.5) which consists of a complete IP stack with PPP or Ethernet interfaces, a network layer, a Ping application, TCP or UDP as transport layer protocols and corresponding applications. This host has been complemented with the transport protocol SCTP, a suitable application, a dump module and external interfaces. These modules will be specified in Section 5.1 and Chapter 6.

Another important feature of INET is the ability to use real network addresses and do the routing according to rules derived from routing tables. Although the *FlatNetworkConfigurator* can be used to automatically distribute addresses among the hosts of a network, the preferred configuration mode is setting up routing tables where routes to other hosts or networks can be configured. Especially for multihomed hosts, where each IP address has to belong to a different subnet, this feature helps to keep the network scenarios close to reality.

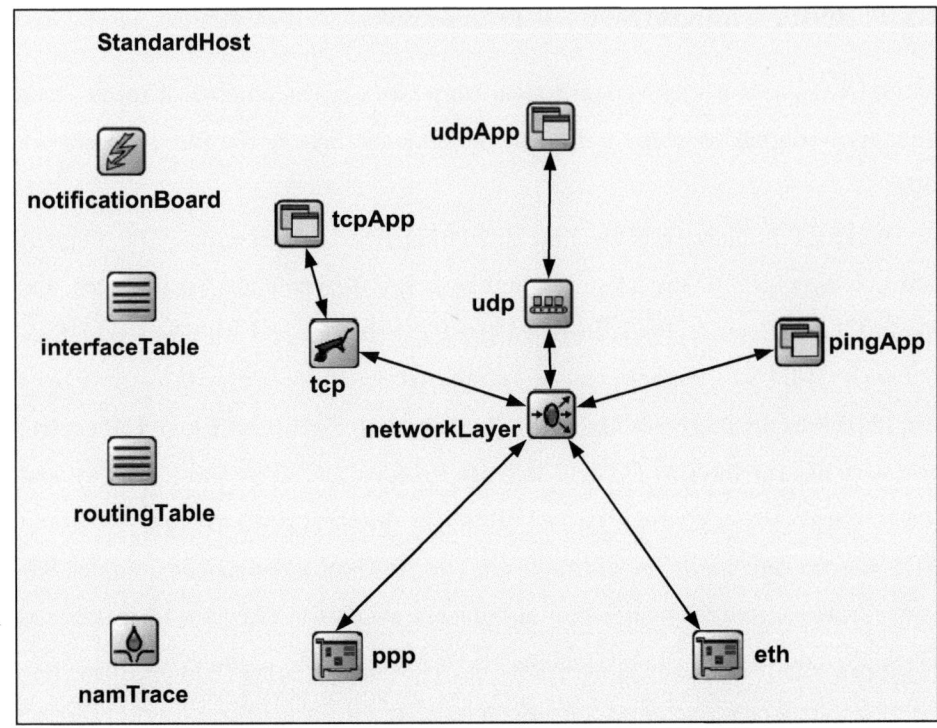

Figure 3.5: Compound Module StandardHost

Together with OMNeT++, INET provides an ideal basis for the implementation of another transport protocol. Since OMNeT++ is public-source, it is free for academic institutes, as long as it serves a strictly noncommercial purpose.

Chapter 4

Analyzing Protocols

Evaluating the functionality of a protocol implies the ability to control whether the parameters are set properly and the message flow is correct. Therefore, the packets arriving at the network adapter have to be traced, i.e. the byte sequence has to be recorded and analyzed according to the protocol specifications.

In this chapter first methods to filter packets are explained and text-based network analyzers introduced, before Wireshark is presented in more detail. Wireshark is the most popular GUI-based network analyzer, which has been expanded, as part of this thesis, by adding a feature to draw graphs of the SCTP message flow.

4.1 Packet Capturing

To be able to analyze the network traffic, an application needs access to the link layer. There are three methods, which are used depending on the operating system.

The BSD Packet Filter (BPF), also known as Berkeley Packet Filter, was introduced in [54]. It is supported by most Berkeley-derived implementations, e.g. FreeBSD. Figure 4.1 shows the mechanism to capture packets with a BPF device as described in [83]. Each packet that arrives at the link layer, i.e. which is destined for that computer, is filtered by the BPF device according to the

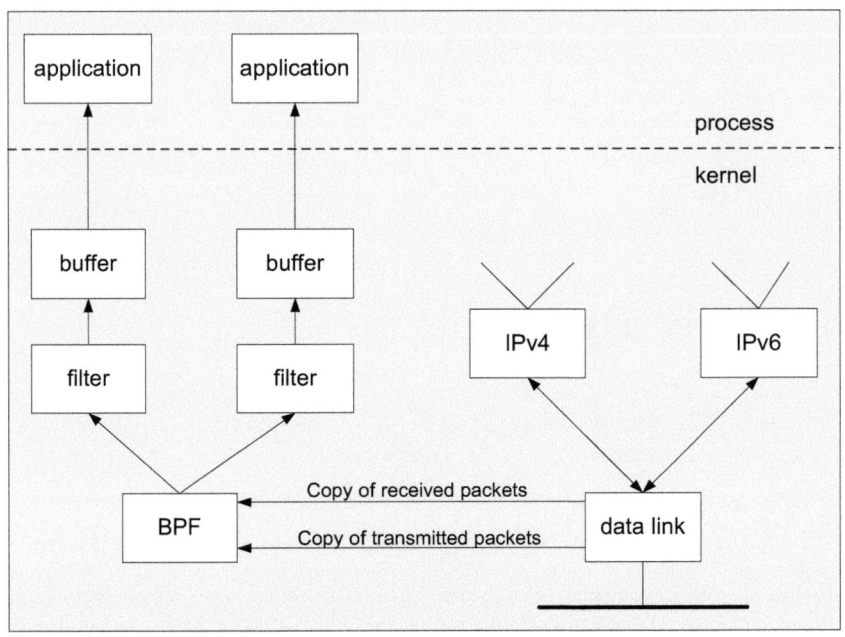

Figure 4.1: Data link access with a BPF device

application's needs. A filter could be an expression like

`sctp and dst host 10.1`

which would result in the extraction of packets that have SCTP as transport layer and are bound to hosts, which belong to the 10.1.0.0 subnet. Thus, not all of the received packets are copied to the application. In addition, applications specify a *snaplen*, which means that only the beginning snaplen bytes of a packet are needed, which again reduces the load. A third possibility to reduce the overhead lies in the organization of the buffer. In fact, there are two buffers, one of which is filled, while the contents of the other is copied to the application. As only full buffers are copied, the number of system calls is decreased. Further information about the configuration of BPF devices is given in [112].

In the Solaris operating system the Data Link Provider Interface (DLPI) is integrated, which was designed by AT&T. The access to DLPI is provided by sending and receiving STREAMS messages. The process of filtering is similar to the BPF filtering, but the BPF filtering is done before copying the data, while with DLPI, all packets are copied first. Both devices work with pseudomachines, BPF with a register machine and DLPI with a stack machine. Stevens states that BPF is 3-20 times faster [83].

Linux takes a different approach. The user can choose between two kinds of sockets to create:

1. A socket of type SOCK_PACKET

```
fd = socket(AF_INET, SOCK_PACKET, htons(ETH_P_ALL))
```

2. A socket of family PF_PACKET

```
fd = socket(PF_PACKET, SOCK_RAW, htons(ETH_P_ALL))
```

ETH_P_ALL specifies the frame type, which could also be ETH_P_IP (to get only IPv4 packets) or others. In the second call SOCK_RAW could be substituted by SOCK_DGRAM if the application is only interested in the link layer.

The second kind of call is more advanced than the first one, as the socket can be bound to a device, and thus a filtering per device is made possible. In contrast to BPF the number of system calls is much higher, as several frames cannot be bundled for one call.

To provide the user with an implementation-independent access to the link layer, the *libpcap* packet capture library was designed by McCanne and Van Jacobson in 1994 [103]. It features an API between the packet capture facility provided by the operating system and the application. It even includes a filtering mechanism in case it is not supplied by the OS. The libpcap will be used by the ExtInterface described in Section 5.1.

4.2 Text-based Packet Analyzers

4.2.1 Tcpdump

The same team that designed BPF and the libpcap also implemented the text-based packet analyzer *tcpdump* [102]. The user can start the sniffer from the command line and choose from numerous options to specify the filter he wants to apply.

`tcpdump -i em1 -s 1000 sctp`

for instance, starts the capturing of SCTP packets on interface *em1* with a snaplen of 1000 bytes. The result is seen in Figure 4.2. Form feeds have been added for better readability.

```
20:11:22.373842 IP 10.4.3.1.65254 > 10.4.4.1.5001: sctp
     (1)   [INIT] [init tag: 3493527747] [rwnd: 233016] [OS: 10]
           [MIS: 2048] [init TSN: 3369758830]
20:11:22.373913 IP 10.4.4.1.5001 > 10.4.3.1.65254: sctp
     (1)   [INIT ACK] [init tag: 544448621] [rwnd: 233016] [OS: 10]
           [MIS: 2048] [init TSN: 3924307499]
20:11:22.374215 IP 10.4.3.1.65254 > 10.4.4.1.5001: sctp
     (1)   [COOKIE ECHO]
20:11:22.374317 IP 10.4.4.1.5001 > 10.4.3.1.65254: sctp
     (1)   [COOKIE ACK]
20:11:22.374595 IP 10.4.3.1.65254 > 10.4.4.1.5001: sctp
     (1)   [DATA] (B)(E) [TSN: 3369758830] [SID: 0] [SSEQ 0] [PPID 0x0]
20:11:22.374635 IP 10.4.4.1.5001 > 10.4.3.1.65254: sctp
     (1)   [SACK] [cum ack 3369758830] [a_rwnd 232260] [#gap acks 0]
           [#dup tsns 0]
20:11:22.374642 IP 10.4.3.1.65254 > 10.4.4.1.5001: sctp
     (1)   [DATA] (B)(E) [TSN: 3369758831] [SID: 0] [SSEQ 1] [PPID 0x0]
     (2)   [DATA] (B)(E) [TSN: 3369758832] [SID: 0] [SSEQ 2] [PPID 0x0]
20:11:22.374661 IP 10.4.3.1.65254 > 10.4.4.1.5001: sctp
     (1)   [DATA] (B)(E) [TSN: 3369758833] [SID: 0] [SSEQ 3] [PPID 0x0]
     (2)   [DATA] (B)(E) [TSN: 3369758834] [SID: 0] [SSEQ 4] [PPID 0x0]
20:11:22.374681 IP 10.4.4.1.5001 > 10.4.3.1.65254: sctp
     (1)   [SACK] [cum ack 3369758834] [a_rwnd 229992] [#gap acks 0]
           [#dup tsns 0]
20:11:22.374840 IP 10.4.3.1.65254 > 10.4.4.1.5001: sctp
     (1)   [SHUTDOWN]
20:11:22.374856 IP 10.4.4.1.5001 > 10.4.3.1.65254: sctp
     (1)   [SHUTDOWN ACK]
20:11:22.374965 IP 10.4.3.1.65254 > 10.4.4.1.5001: sctp
     (1)   [SHUTDOWN COMPLETE]
```

Figure 4.2: *tcpdump* output for an SCTP association

The trace is quite detailed, as the headers with all parameters are listed. Bundling is supported, listing an entry for each `DATA` chunk.

Tcpdump also allows to save capture files in the pcap format that can be read with any analyzer that supports this format.

4.2.2 Snoop

While tcpdump runs on all platforms, *snoop* [81] is exclusively available for the Solaris OS. Applying this command line tool is similar to tcpdump. The capture files are stored in a proprietary format that is RFC1761-compliant [10]. Yet, the Wireshark packet analyzer that will be introduced in the next section, can read this format.

4.2.3 TShark

TShark [94] is the command line version of Wireshark, which will be introduced in the next section. Like the other text-based analyzers, capture files can be printed to stdout or saved to files, previously captured files can be read. It is noteworthy, that traces can even be saved in human-readable form, which allows the analysis of the output without special tools, like finding and counting protocol properties.

4.3 Introduction to Wireshark

The *Wireshark* [111] packet analyzer was developed in 1998 by Gerald Combs under the name *Ethereal*. It changed its name to Wireshark in 2006, because of a trademark conflict.

Wireshark is licensed under the GNU General Public License (GPL) [28], which implies that the sources can be downloaded, extended and redistributed again. Wireshark is developed by a community of more than 500 contributing authors.

Wireshark can capture packets in real-time from devices, including Ethernet, loopback, wireless LAN or PPP, or read from a trace file. The captured data is temporarily stored on the hard disk to enable the further examination of the protocols. The capturing and filtering is supported by the libpcap.

The captured packets are handed to the dissectors that analyze the protocol headers to display their contents and send the payload to the dissector responsible for the encapsulated protocol. Michael Tüxen implemented the dissector for SCTP, some of the protocols of the SS7 and most of the SIGTRAN suite.

Figure 4.3 shows the main window of Wireshark. It is divided into three parts:

- The top window shows the frames, their arrival time, which can be displayed in different formats, source and destination address, the protocol type, and an information field. In the case of SCTP, the chunk types are listed here. Bundling is visualized by itemizing each one.

- The window in the middle allows a look inside the packets. The protocol hierarchy is visible, and a click on one of the small triangles opens a more detailed description of the item. Thus, a complete analysis of a packet with a thorough explanation of the parameters is possible.

- The frame as seen "on-the-wire" is shown in the bottom window. The variables are in hexadecimal, whereas the "readable" version in the middle window is in decimal notation.

In addition, display and coloring filters can be set, and the user can choose between a variety of protocol specific features.

4.4 Graphical Analysis of SCTP in Wireshark

Large trace files can easily become unmanageable, so that analyzing them to find faulty behavior is almost impossible. Therefore, a graphical tool to visualize the data transfer is very helpful. Besides the visualization of the data flow, statistical

Figure 4.3: Wireshark main window

data like the number of chunks can lead to a better understanding, too. Therefore, Wireshark has been extended to provide these features to the user. The graphical tool is integrated in the publicly available Wireshark distribution.

After having captured the traffic, there are two possibilities to start the analysis. To get information about all associations traced, the menu entry *Telephony - SCTP* leads to the choices

- Analyse this Association

- Chunk Counter...

- Show All Associations...

Via the context menu of an SCTP packet the actual association can be directly analyzed (*SCTP - Analyse this Association*) or a filter can be prepared (*SCTP - Prepare Filter for this Association*) that can be applied to the trace to see only association related frames.

In the following, after a short explanation how packets can be assigned to associations, the different ways to analyze the traffic will be discussed.

4.4.1 Assigning Packets to Associations

To be able to study the data transfer, the packets have to be assigned to associations. The usual way to do this is to match source address and source port with destination address and destination port. As a tool like Wireshark is also used to develop protocols and detect bugs, the data sent often stem from testcases, where the same port numbers are chosen for each association.

Figure 4.4 shows a trace, where only `INIT` chunks were transmitted. Source and destination ports and addresses are the same in all packets. Therefore, it is not possible to make a statement concerning the association, to which they belong, based on the port-address combination.

An SCTP specific variable is the verification tag that is unique for either side of an association. Thus the combination of local verification tag, source address to remote verification tag and destination address is a good way to identify an association.

chunk type	source address	local v_tag	destination address	remote v_tag
INIT	10.0.0.1	0	10.0.0.2	12345
INIT_ACK	10.0.0.1	**56789**	10.0.0.2	12345

Table 4.1: Assigning addresses and verification tags to associations

The SCTP handshake is the basis for the association. In the INIT chunk the initiation tag informs the receiver, which verification tag it has to send. In Table 4.1 an entry reflects the necessary combination of verification tags and addresses to identify an association. With the arrival of an INIT chunk already four fields can be filled. The remote verification tag (remote v_tag) is equal to the initiate tag of the INIT chunk. Only the local verification tag (local v_tag) is not known yet. This information is provided by the initiate tag of the INIT_ACK chunk. All other chunks can be easily assigned, as all necessary values are present.

The situation is more difficult, when only part of a trace is available or the handshake is not complete like in the example in Figure 4.4. Assuming two DATA chunks arriving from opposite directions, the first one provides source address, local verification tag and destination address. From the second one the addresses fit, but it is not known whether the verification tag is the right one. In this case it can be helpful to also compare the port numbers to exclude the possibility that the chunks belong to different associations. This heuristic proved to be very useful in real test traces.

When the SCTP graphical analysis is called the trace is dissected once more. The dissector stores information like ports, addresses, verification tags, the num-

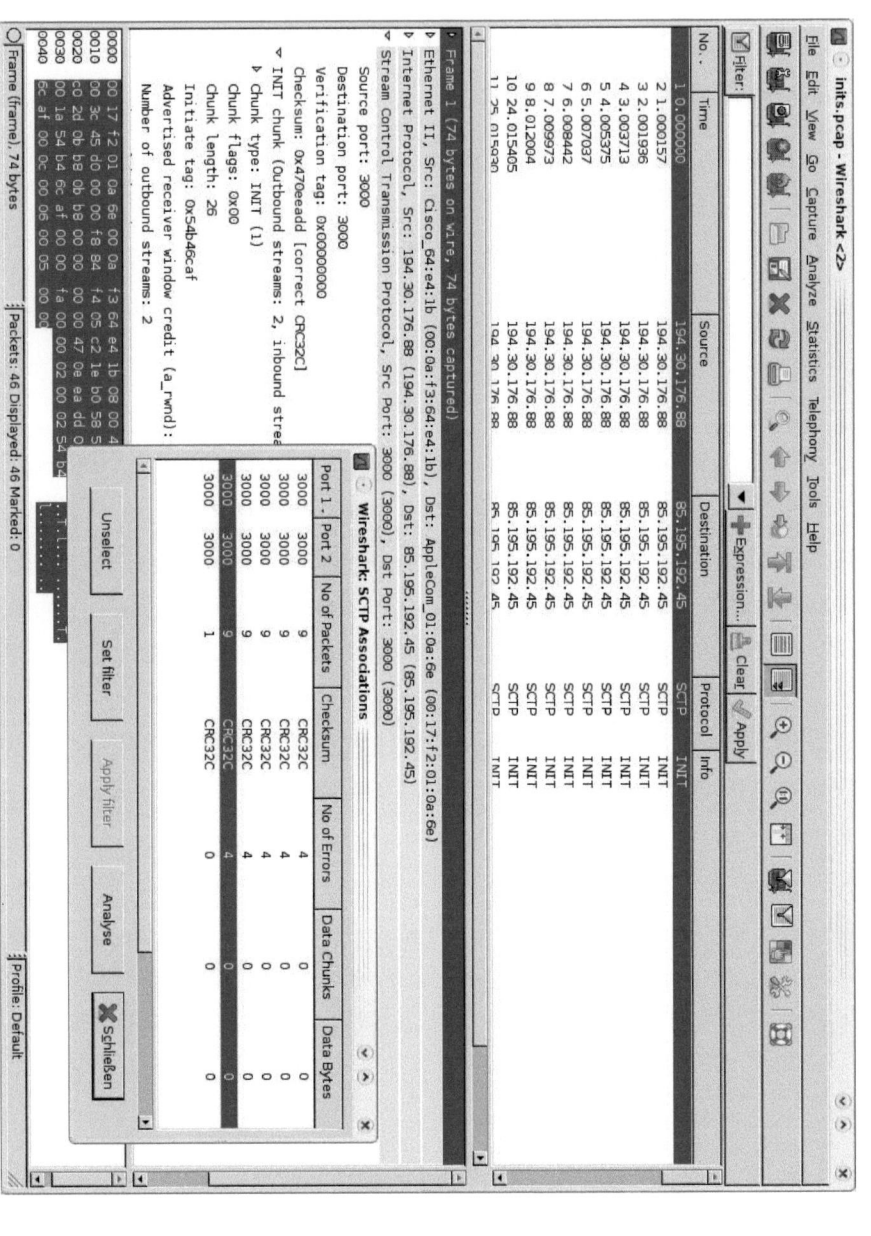

Figure 4.4: Trace with several associations

ber of chunks and the chunks themselves in a file, which is then processed. All information necessary for later analysis, like the maximum and minimum values for TSNs and time, number of bytes and chunks, etc, is stored in a structure, which is kept per association. The different associations are organized in a list that can be accessed within all SCTP functions.

4.4.2 Statistics of the Chunk Types

There are two different chunk statistics implemented for SCTP in Wireshark. One is reached via the main menu and the other one from the *SCTP Analyse Association* window.

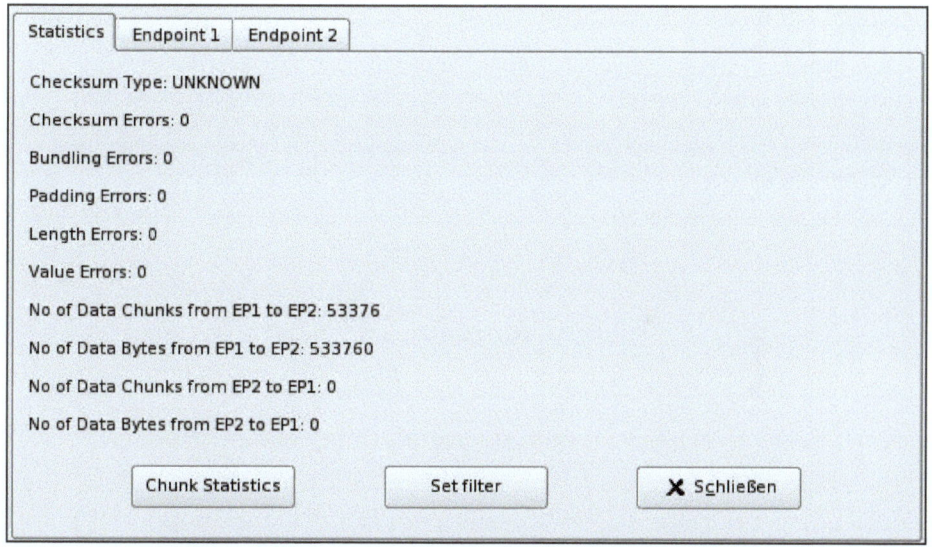

Figure 4.5: *SCTP Analyse Association* window

As the first one was implemented by another author, only the statistics that can be reached from the *SCTP Analyse Association* window will be described. To open this window, either an association of the entries in the *SCTP Associations* window can be chosen (see Figure 4.4), *Analyse this Association* can be called from the main menu or the context menu of an SCTP packet. The first dialog window that appears is the one in Figure 4.5. It lists some statistical data that are relevant for the association, like errors and the number of DATA chunks and bytes in either direction.

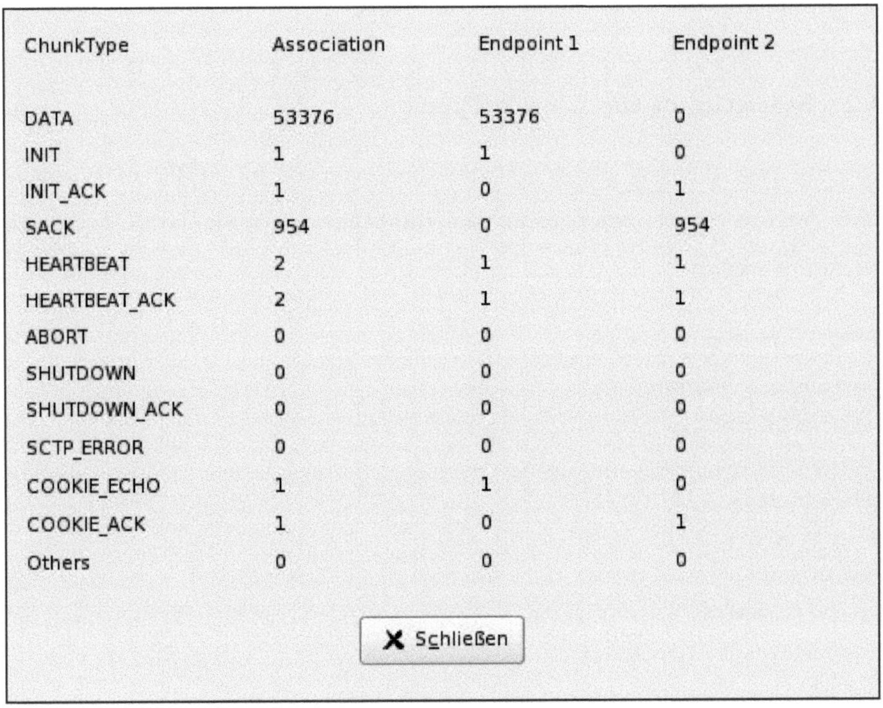

ChunkType	Association	Endpoint 1	Endpoint 2
DATA	53376	53376	0
INIT	1	1	0
INIT_ACK	1	0	1
SACK	954	0	954
HEARTBEAT	2	1	1
HEARTBEAT_ACK	2	1	1
ABORT	0	0	0
SHUTDOWN	0	0	0
SHUTDOWN_ACK	0	0	0
SCTP_ERROR	0	0	0
COOKIE_ECHO	1	1	0
COOKIE_ACK	1	0	1
Others	0	0	0

Figure 4.6: Statistics of the chunk types

For more information, the *Chunk Statistics* button can be clicked to open the window of Figure 4.6. For each important chunk type, its number per endpoint and for the complete association is listed.

4.4.3 Graphical Representation of the Data Transfer

The graphical analysis of the data transfer is performed on a per endpoint basis. Therefore, the user has to select an endpoint via the tabs in Figure 4.5 to open the window in Figure 4.7 and choose the graphical presentation he prefers.

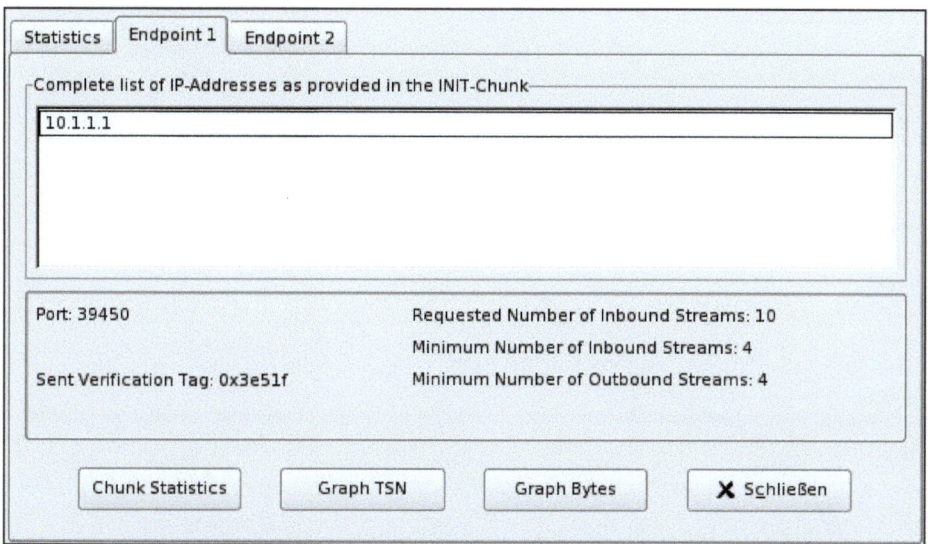

Figure 4.7: Start window for the graphical analysis of the data transfer of an endpoint

4.4.3.1 Analyzing TSNs and SACK chunks

To be able to see the course of the TSNs is very helpful to analyze congestion control issues. Figure 4.8 shows an example. Besides the TSNs, the Cumulative TSN Acks and the TSNs that have been announced in the Gap Ack Blocks are visible, too. To see only the TSNs taken from the DATA chunks or only those from the SACK chunks, the *Show TSNs* or *Show Sacks* button can be clicked. To zoom into the graph a rectangle must be drawn around the area to be magnified (see Figure 4.8). With a click on the *Zoom in* button or into the rectangle, a detailed figure appears like the one in Figure 4.9. A series of Cumulative TSN Acks, gap ack blocks and fast retransmissions are circled in the figure. In this enlarged diagram, the gaps in the course of the TSNs and retransmissions can easily be

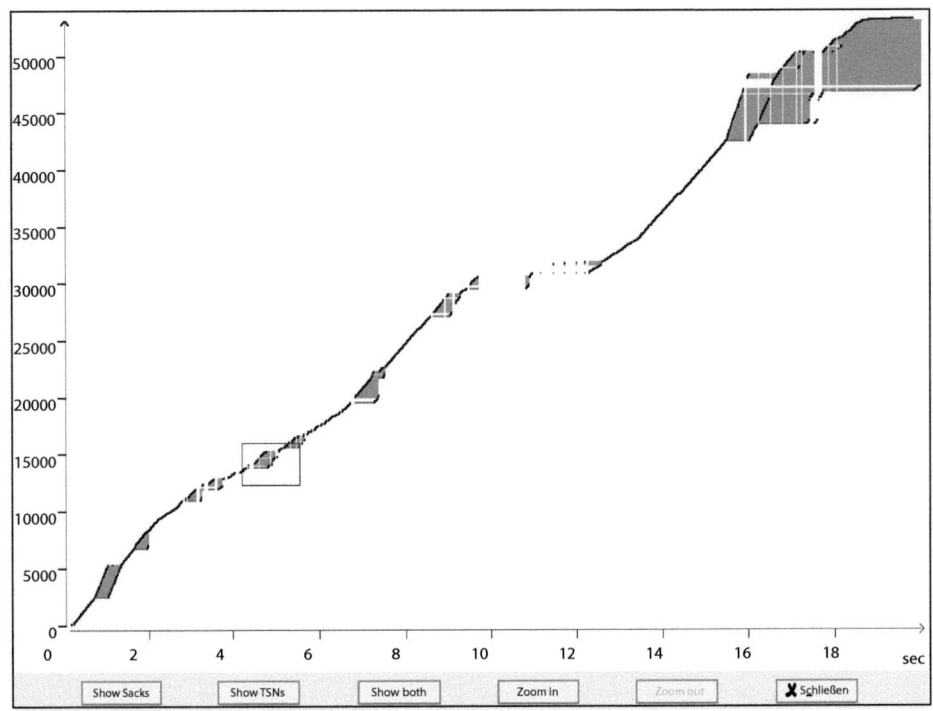

Figure 4.8: TSNs over time

pointed out. In the case of multihomed hosts, timer based retransmissions are not visible, because they are sent on the second path and therefore traced on another interface.

For convenience, the user can pick out one TSN and see its coordinates by clicking on it. A double-click selects the corresponding frame in the main window.

4.4.3.2 Analyzing the Advertised Receiver Window and transmitted Bytes

Another important feature of SCTP besides congestion control is flow control. To analyze flow control scenarios, the size of the advertised receiver window is very important. Choosing the button *Graph Bytes* leads to a window like the one

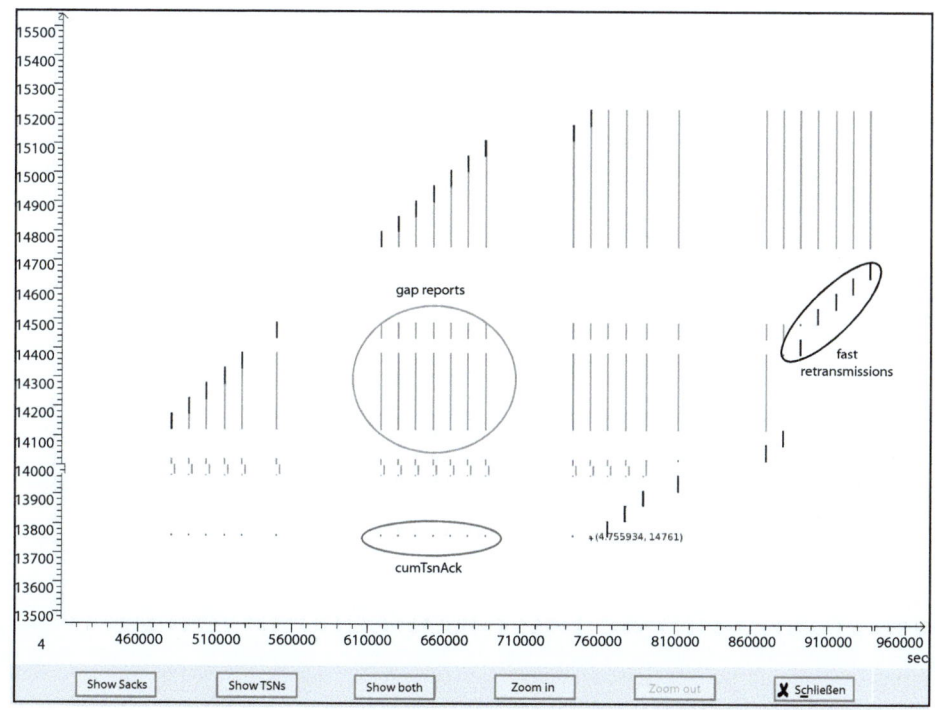

Figure 4.9: Clipping of TSNs over time

in Figure 4.10. The course of the DATA chunks can be observed again, but this time the y-axis shows the accumulated number of bytes instead of the TSNs. The bottom lines represent the arwnd. As this is the representation corresponding to the one in Figure 4.8, the relation between the rise and fall of the arwnd and the data stored at the receiver is well to be seen. The large gap ack blocks in Figure 4.8, starting at about 15 secs, indicate the number of acknowledged TSNs that can not be delivered to the application, because in-order delivery is not possible due to missing TSNs. Therefore, the data has to be cached in the receive queues which reduces the arwnd, as seen in Figure 4.10. The intermediate rise results from the reception of missing TSNs that lead to an increase of the Cumulative TSN Ack parameter.

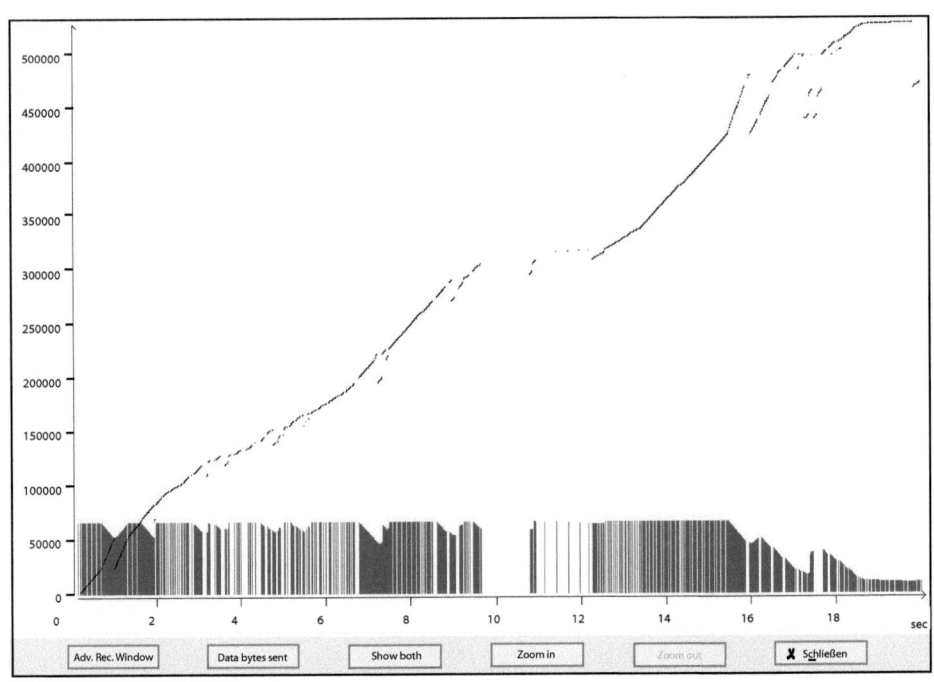

Figure 4.10: Advertised Receiver Window and transmitted Bytes

Chapter 5

Extending the Simulation Framework

As pointed out in Subsections 3.2.3 and 3.2.4, OMNeT++ together with INET offers a variety of tools to facilitate the processing of simulations. However, there were two features missing that were added and will be described in this chapter. The first one is the connection of the simulated to real networks, which can be of great benefit when validating the simulation. The second one is the possibility to distribute the possibly hundreds of runs that a test might add up to, if its reliability should be proved, to several computers without having to change the simulated network itself.

5.1 Connecting the INET Framework with Real Networks

A simulation is an isolated system, in that it can only run in a self-contained environment. Yet, there are situations, where a connection between the simulation and the outside world is desirable.

5.1.1 Simulation - Emulation - Real Network

A problem when dealing with simulations lies in the correct specification of parameters that might have an influence on the performance. Sometimes it is very hard to provide reasonable values for some of them or even model them appropriately. An example is the CPU time needed for handling messages, because it can be influenced by the cache effects of the CPU, or the scheduling of threads. The impact of multiple CPU cores working together is hard to model, too. In general, it is much easier to analyze the generic protocol performance compared to the performance of a specific protocol implementation using a simulation.

When using real implementations for performance analysis, the network between the sender and receiver can be emulated. DUMMYNET (see [75]), a network emulator of the FreeBSD operating system, can be started on one node. Thus, packet loss rates, bandwidth limitations, and delays can be emulated, and with some additional tools also packet duplication and corruption. Similar tools can be obtained for the Linux operating systems, for example NIST Net described in [11]. Going one step further, the network emulation can be replaced by a real network between the nodes. This is done, for example, in a project called PlanetLab [13], where experiments can use an almost global network, which is based on the public Internet. This approach not only provides real endpoint behavior but also incorporates all effects of real network scenarios. However, it is hard to reproduce experiments, because of the various impacts on the network which cannot be controlled. Real systems are also used by Emulab [20]. Here the user first sets up a network scenario by identifying nodes and configuring the connecting links, then this configuration is transferred to real nodes. As these hosts are not arbitrarily distributed, parameters like delay and loss can be controlled.

Having the possibility that nodes within a simulation can interact with nodes in a real IP based network, combines the advantages of these different approaches.

The Network Simulator NS-2 [61] has a limited support for interacting with real nodes, as described in Chapter 46 (Emulation) of the NS-2 manual [22]. An integration of Emulab and NS-2 is outlined in [30], including the usage of this technique for distributed simulation.

5.1.2 Preliminary Considerations

5.1.2.1 Requirements

The device which was called external interface or *ExtInterface* had to fit seamlessly in the INET framework. To achieve this objective, the following requirements had to be met.

- The ExtInterface was supposed to be usable on all platforms that are supported by the INET framework, i.e. most Unix based OSs and a variety of Windows operating system versions.

- The ExtInterface was expected to be easily expandable such that not only SCTP messages, but packets from all IP-based protocols like UDP and TCP, and also OSPF and other protocols could pass from the simulation to a real network and vice versa.

- As multihoming is an important feature, multiple external interfaces had to be supported. Thereby it was to be possible, that these interfaces belonged to one host or were distributed among several network components, such that the simulation was connected by multiple ExtInterfaces to the real network.

- From the simulation's point of view the interface was supposed to look like the already supported interfaces for PPP or Ethernet.

- The following scenarios had to be feasible:

    - Single simulated host connected to a real host or network.
    - A simulated network connected to a real host or network.
    - A simulated network connected via multiple ExtInterfaces to different hosts that communicate with each other through the simulation.

5.1.2.2 Receiving and sending real packets

When an IP packet is received by the host running the simulation for a node being simulated, it must be transformed into an OMNet++ object and injected into the simulated network. The network stack of the host running the simulation should not process these packets. Therefore, the host cannot have the IP addresses of the simulated node configured as addresses of one of its real interfaces. This means that using raw sockets is not an appropriate mechanism for receiving these packets. The packet capture library *libpcap*, however, provides an appropriate way of capturing these packets (see Chapter 4.1).

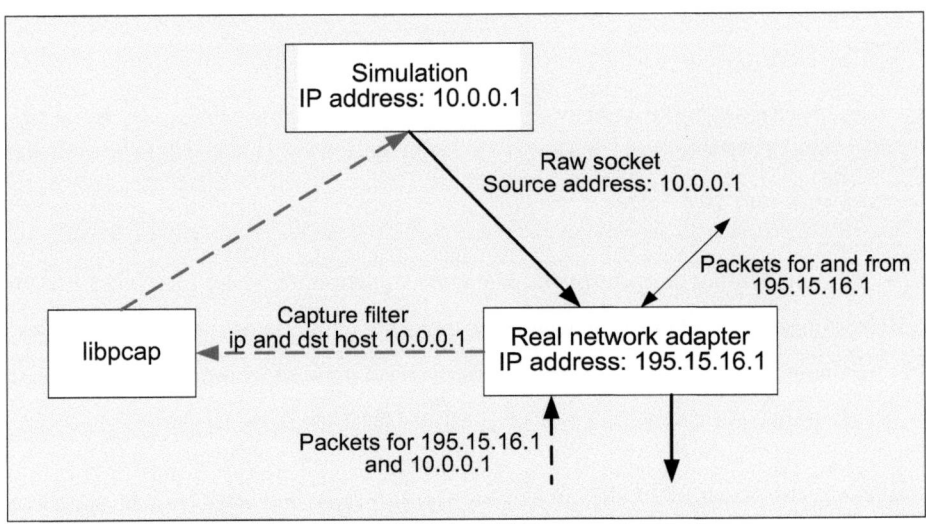

Figure 5.1: Sending and receiving real packets

Figure 5.1 shows the schematic of the sending and receiving process. When packets arrive at the data link of the host, the *libpcap* extracts packets, which are meant for the simulation, by applying a capture filter (here: ip and dst host 10.0.0.1). Thus, it makes sure that only packets which are sent to the simulation are captured and not the ones sent by the simulation. Sending packets from the simulation to nodes in the real network is done by using raw IP sockets (solid lines). Hereby, the host sends packets whose source address is the simulated endpoint's address, i.e they do not belong to the real network adapter. This is not a problem for the Unix based operating systems but may not be supported by all versions of the Windows operating system. In this case the *libpcap* could also be used to send the packets.

The routing in the real network has to be configured such that the host running the simulation acts like a router which provides access to the network being simulated. In the example of Figure 5.1, the real endpoint has to have a route to 10.0.0.1 with the gateway set to 195.15.16.1.

The regular network traffic to and from the host is not influenced by these actions.

For sending packets, a method of transforming the simulation's internal format to the network format has to be implemented for each protocol. This is called a *serializer*. For receiving packets a method called *parser* will transform the packet in network format into the simulation's internal format. The code is structured in a way that these methods are encapsulated on a per protocol basis.

5.1.2.3 Scheduling Events

A discrete event simulation, which also takes interactions with the real external world into account, has to handle two kinds of events: internal events which have their origin in the simulation and external events which stem from the interface to the external world. Also, the simulation time has to be synchronized to the real time. This is possible assuming that there is a speedup in the simulation compared to real-time, i.e. the simulated time runs faster than the real time. As the experiments will show, this is a valid assumption when using state-of-the art computer hardware and networks having a limited total packet rate. Time synchronization is basically done by looking at the time of the next scheduled event. If this time is already in the past, this event is processed. Otherwise external events are processed and the simulation is put to sleep until either the next internal event has to be processed or another external event arrives. It is important to note that internal events have to be given a higher priority.

Due to limitations of the *libpcap* library, the simulation is put to sleep for a fixed small amount of time, if no external event is present. This results also in a time granularity for all internal events. Choosing a small value for this granularity led to good results. It should be noted that operating systems have a systems based timer granularity for putting processes to sleep, hence choosing a smaller value for the simulation granularity than the systems granularity does not provide any benefit.

5.1.3 Realization of the Requirements

To integrate the external interface in the INET framework four new classes were needed: the link layer module ExtInterface, the scheduler, the serializer, and a new message type.

Figure 5.2 illustrates in three parts, how they work together. To initialize the items, the scheduler opens a raw socket. Then the ExtInterface sends a registration request to the scheduler, which opens a pcap device, compiles the filter string, sets the filter, and establishes the connection to the data link.

In the middle part, the message flow leads from the simulation to the real network. The numbers help to follow the process.

1. The network layer sends an IPDatagram to the ExtInterface. The IPDatagram is an INET specific message type on the link layer. It is derived from *cMessage*, the standard OMNeT++ message class.

2. ExtInterface calls the scheduler to serialize the IPDatagram. The message is converted in a network readable format.

3. The serializer returns a buffer with the raw packet and the number of written

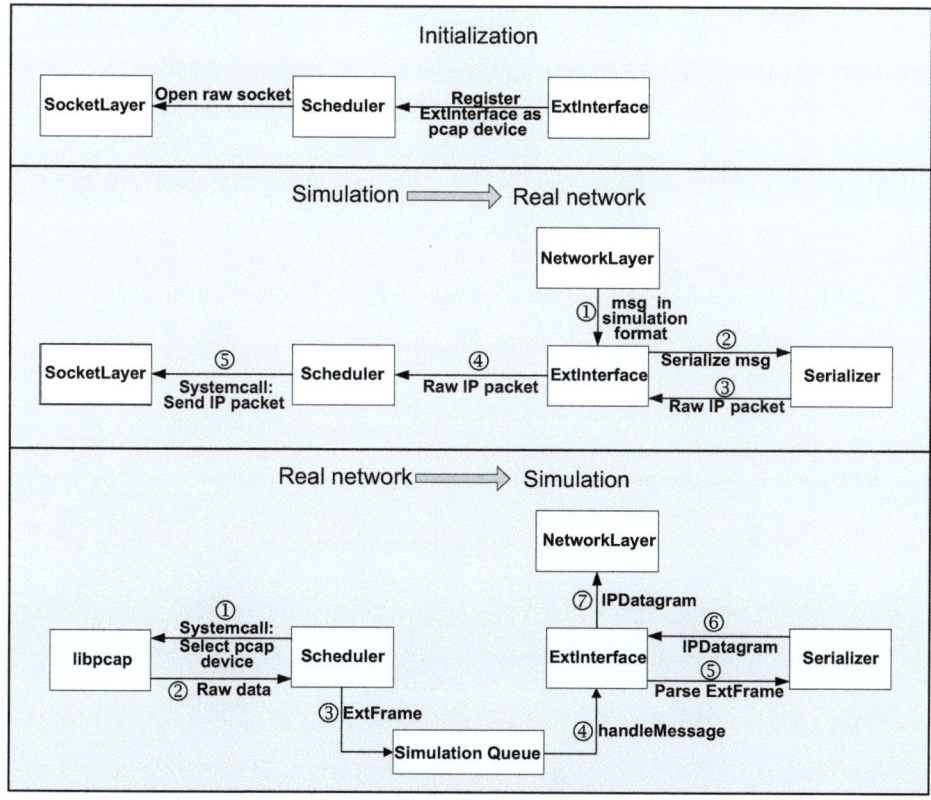

Figure 5.2: Message flow between simulation and real network

bytes.

4. The scheduler is called, and the packet is handed over.

5. The scheduler sends the data via the raw socket to the network.

The opposite direction, from the real network to the simulation, is depicted in the lowest part.

1. The scheduler calls *select()* on the pcap devices.

2. If a device becomes readable, the raw packet is handed to the scheduler.

3. The scheduler encapsulates this packet into an ExtFrame, which is a *cMessage* and thus can be handled by the simulation. After the message's arrival time is calculated, the ExtFrame is inserted into the simulation queue.

4. At the set time, the *handleMessage()* function, which is virtual and present in all modules, is called with the ExtFrame.

5. The ExtInterface orders the parsing of the data. The serializer decapsulates the raw data and converts it in an IPDatagram.

6. The IPDatagram is returned to the ExtInterface.

7. It is sent on to the network layer.

Checking the requirements shows, that they are all met:

- The *libpcap* as a platform independent library guarantees, that the ExtInterface will be operable on all platforms supported by INET.

- There is a serializer for each protocol, that has so far been chosen to use the ExtInterface. The IPSerializer checks the protocol field of the IP header and calls the serializer, which is in charge of the payload protocol. Thus, any IP based protocol can be easily added. To serialize or parse another link layer protocol, a function has to be added to the *ExtInterface.cc*, which makes a decision about the appropriate link layer.

- When the ExtInterface asks the scheduler to be registered, the created pcap device is stored in a list. The select call checks all devices for an incoming message. Thus, several interfaces can be registered and supervised.

- The ExtInterface looks like the other supported interfaces. The Router and the StandardHost modules have been expanded to allow the use of the ExtInterface on a single host and on a router, that forms the border between a simulated network and the real world.

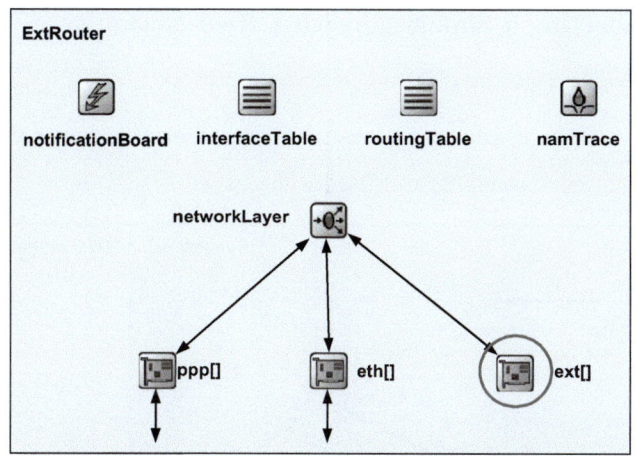

Figure 5.3: The compound module ExtRouter

The compound module ExtRouter is drawn in Figure 5.3. The circled module *ext* on the link layer is organized as a vector, like the other interfaces. Therefore, it is even possible for a router to have several interfaces of different kinds, e.g. two external and three ethernet interfaces. It has to be kept in mind, that each ExtInterface has to correspond to one real network adapter on the host, because the pcap device is bound to a real device it captures packets from.

Some examples for the different required scenarios will be given in the next section. For more scenarios see [96].

5.1.4 Examples to Connect the ExtInterface with Real Networks

The easiest case to use the ExtInterface is to simulate one endpoint of type StandardHost with one ExtInterface, configured to be connected to the outside world. From the simulation's point of view it does not make a difference, whether the real counterpart consists only of one host or a large network. Here, only scenarios where a network is simulated will be discussed.

5.1.4.1 Connecting a Simulated with a Real Network

As an application example for this scenario the *traceroute* command was chosen, which is supported on all common platforms (*tracert* on Windows OS). *traceroute* is a good tool to teach students routing mechanisms.

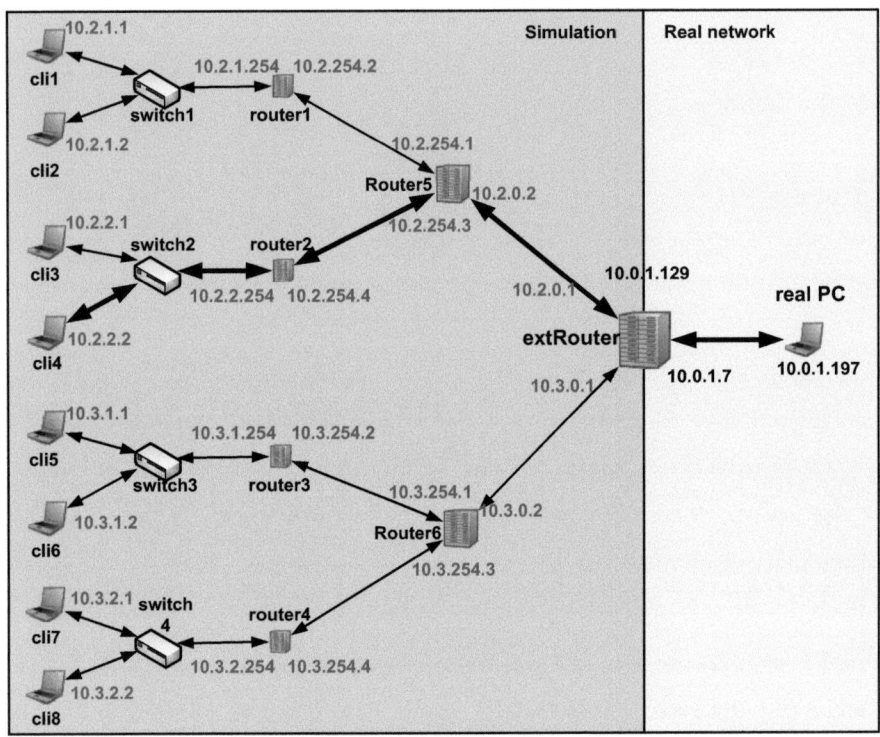

Figure 5.4: Using traceroute to traverse a simulated network

Figure 5.4 shows the layout of the network with the corresponding IP addresses. The part of the network with the dark gray background is simulated, the other part is real. `extRouter` belongs to both worlds by connecting them. Each device, except the switches, needs a routing configuration file to define the addresses and the static routes. For `extRouter` it looks like follows:

```
ifconfig:
```

```
name: ppp0   inet_addr: 10.2.0.1    MTU: 1500    Metric: 1
        POINTTOPOINT MULTICAST
name: ppp1   inet_addr: 10.3.0.1    MTU: 1500    Metric: 1
        POINTTOPOINT MULTICAST
name: ext0   inet_addr: 10.0.1.129  MTU: 1500    Metric: 1
        POINTTOPOINT MULTICAST
ifconfigend.


route:
10.2.0.0     10.2.0.2       255.255.0.0    G  0   ppp0
10.3.0.0     10.3.0.2       255.255.0.0    G  0   ppp1
0.0.0.0      *              0.0.0.0        G  0   ext0
routeend.
```

Two interfaces are configured as PPP interfaces, one is an ExtInterface. The routes are set to the subnets 10.2/16 and 10.3/16 with Router5 and Router6, respectively, as gateways. The default route leads via ext0 to the real network. Note, that the switches in INET are implemented to only use Ethernet as link layer protocol. As a consequence, the adjoining devices (cli1 to cli8 and router1 to router4) have to be configured with one Ethernet interface. The routers also have a PPP adapter. To set up the *libpcap* filters and the scheduler, three lines have to be included in the omnetpp.ini of the example:

```
scheduler-class = "cSocketRTScheduler"


**.ext[0].filterString = "ip and (dst host 10.2
   or dst host 10.3 or dst host 10.0.1.129)"
**.ext[0].device = "eth0"
```

The first one belongs in the [General] section at the beginning of the file. As the default scheduler is the *cSequentialScheduler*, it has to be overwritten with

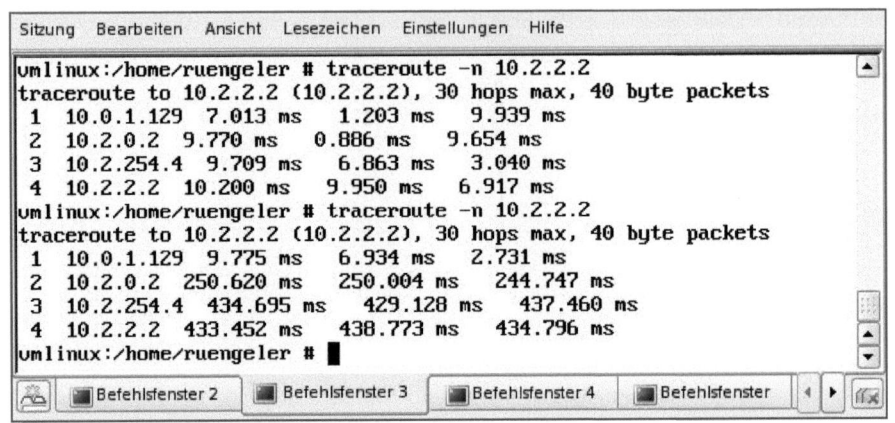

Figure 5.5: Output of the *traceroute* command

cSocketRTScheduler. The next two lines can be placed in the section, where all other interface parameters are configured. By defining the *filterString*, the *libpcap* filter is set to capture all IP traffic destined for the subnets 10.2/16 and 10.3/16 and extRouter itself. Thus, the connection can be tested by pinging extRouter. The *device* has to be set to the name of the real network adapter, which is typically eth0 on Linux and en0 on Mac OS X systems, while the name is driver specific on FreeBSD and on Solaris.

As a last step, a static route has to be added from the source endpoint to the destination via the address of the PC, where the simulation is started from. The command has to be executed with root privileges on the real PC. In this example, the route can be set with

route add -net 10.2.0.0 netmask 255.255.0.0 gw 10.0.1.7

depending on the OS.

The route to trace is the one to cli4, indicated by the thick arrows. Figure 5.5 shows the output. Running the first trace, all links were defined without delay. On the second run, the links between extRouter and router2 were configured with a delay of 100 ms. The delay can be easily observed, as the RTT to 10.2.0.2

is more than 200 ms and to 10.2.254.4 more than 400 ms higher than in the first run. The fourth entry to `cli4` does not add much to the RTT, as the links to the Ethernet interfaces cannot be configured with delay. Of course, this example also works with any other client of the simulation as destination.

5.1.4.2 Capturing on two ExtInterfaces

Multihoming is an important issue in SCTP. Therefore, testing this feature in conjunction with real implementations should be possible. As pointed out in Section 5.1.3, the handles to the pcap devices corresponding to the ExtInterfaces are stored in a vector. By selecting the device that becomes readable, the different interfaces can be distinguished.

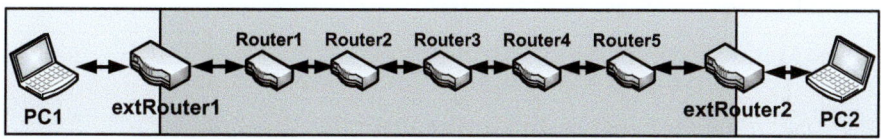

Figure 5.6: Passing through a simulated network connecting real computers

To demonstrate multihoming with a non SCTP protocol, the *ping* example in Figure 5.6 was chosen. There is no host in the simulated network, which only consists of a sequence of routers. The aim is to send a *ping* command from one real computer to another thereby traversing the simulated network, which starts and ends with an ExtInterface. Each of these corresponds to a real network adapter of the PC running the simulation. *filterString* and *device* have to be set for each adapter:

```
**.extRouter1.ext[0].filterString
   = "ip dst host 195.37.125.99"
**.extRouter2.ext[0].filterString
   = "ip dst host 10.0.1.204"
**.extRouter1.ext[0].device = "en0"
```

```
**.extRouter2.ext[0].device = "en1"
```

The host with the IP address 10.0.1.204 needs a route to 195.37.125.99 and the other way around. *en0* has access over a switch to `PC1` (10.0.1.204), while *en1* is directly reachable from `PC2` (195.37.125.99). The sender is an Apple Dual PowerPC G5 2.5 GHz and the receiver an Intel Pentium-4 2.6 GHz.

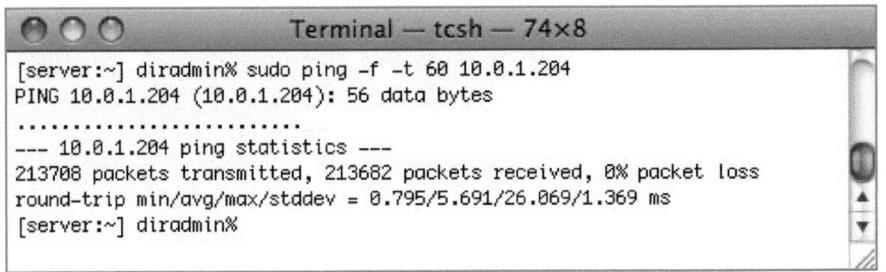

Figure 5.7: Output of the *ping* command

The *ping* command is applied with the `-f` option, which causes the source to send packets as fast as they come back or one hundred times per second, whichever is more. For every reply sent a dot is printed, for every request arriving a backspace. Figure 5.7 shows the output, after the application had run for 60 secs. The dots stand for the replies that did not arrive in time, which means in this case that only 26 out of 213708 replies arrived too late, which results in a packet loss rate of 0.01 %. The average RTT was 5.691 ms, the maximum RTT of 26.069 ms resulted in the late arrival. By letting the simulation run longer than *ping* it was verified that no packets were lost but just arrived too late. The additional packets were still in queues and left the simulation after having been processed.

In this example two ExtRouters with one ExtInterface each were configured. Of course, in another scenario, it is possible to have two ExtInterfaces on one host for 'real' multihoming. In this case *filterString* and *device* would have to be configured for `ext[0]` and `ext[1]`.

5.2 Using Xgrid to Parallelize Simulations

Since the release of OMNeT++ version 4.0 it is possible to iterate over a series of parameters, like configuring runs with user message sizes from 10 to 1450 bytes in 10 byte intervals, and to easily repeat runs with different seeds to confirm the reliability of the results. Thus, hundreds of runs can be set up in just one configuration. Yet, performing these tasks on one machine takes hours or even days. Hence, it is obvious that parallelizing the jobs would improve the situation. In its Eclipse GUI, OMNeT++ offers the feature to use several CPUs, which is not sufficient for the intended purposes. With the parallel discrete event simulation (PDES) [62] included in OMNeT++, the distribution on different hosts or processors is possible, but the partitioning of the simulation model into several logical processes is required, which makes an adaption of the model necessary. The same is true for Akaroa [1], an architecture designed for parallel computation of quantitative stochastic simulations. Each simulation has to be changed to include calls for the communication with Akaroa. Finally the tool-chain [17] based on the Reliable Server Pooling architecture [16] can be used to distribute simulation runs on multiple hosts.

Despite the just described alternatives, it was decided to use Xgrid for the parallelizing of runs, because it is available for Mac OS X and can be controlled with a powerful GUI.

5.2.1 Overview of Xgrid

Xgrid [113] allows the execution of multiple programs on multiple hosts in parallel. There are three main components working together: the *client*, the *controller* and one or more *agents*.

They are shown in Figure 5.8. Although, in the picture, the roles are assigned to separate hosts, they can be combined on one computer. The *client* generates the job and transmits it to the controller, that divides it into tasks. They are

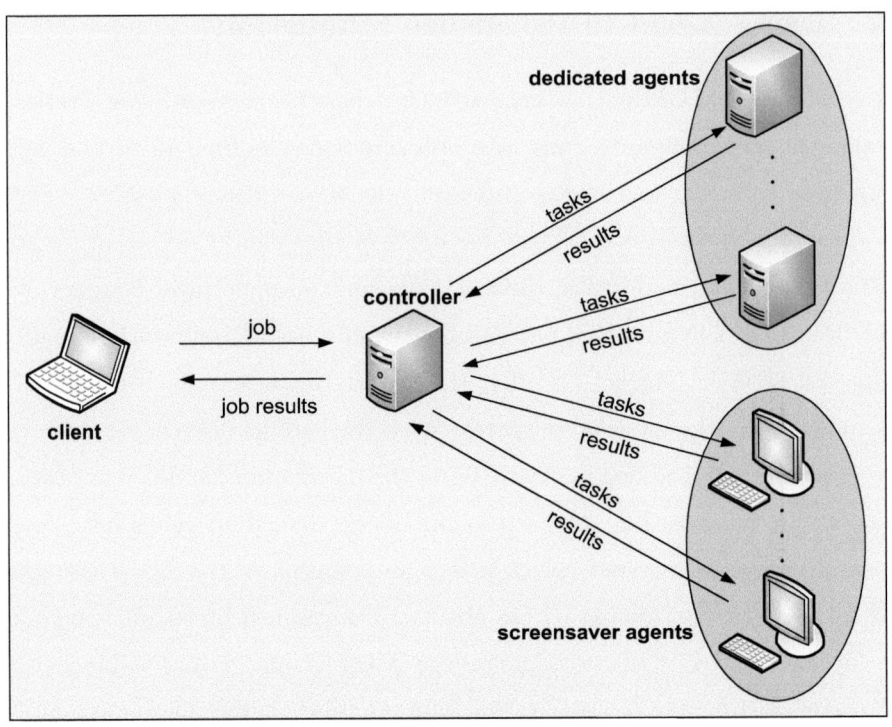

Figure 5.8: The three Xgrid components

distributed among the agents, which can be dedicated, i.e. always available for Xgrid, or so-called screensaver agents, that are only occupied, when idle. Each CPU can handle one task and return the results to the controller, where they can be retrieved by the client.

The progress of submitted jobs can be watched with the administration tool of Figure 5.9. Jobs, that cannot be serviced yet, can still be submitted. Their status is shown and more information is provided by double-clicking on them.

Jobs can be started with one task, or several tasks can be combined in a batch job. All commands are entered via the command line.

To run a simple job, e.g. to print a calendar of March 2009,

```
xgrid -h server -p password run /usr/bin/cal 3 2009
```

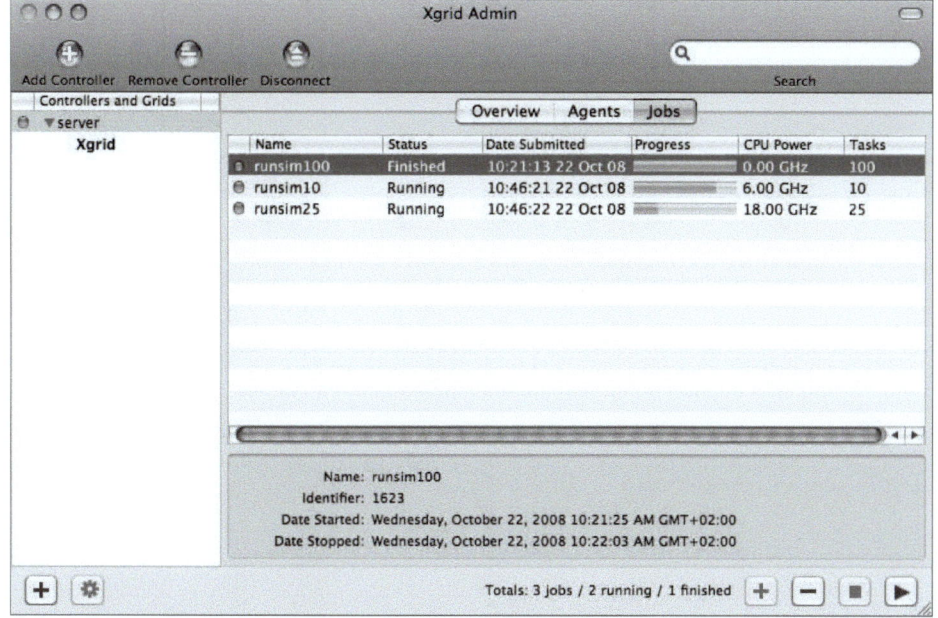

Figure 5.9: The Xgrid administration tool

has to be typed.

5.2.2 Generating Batch Jobs with OMNeT++

Starting an OMNeT++ simulation with just one run in Xgrid can be done without any alterations to OMNeT++. But as simulations normally consist of several runs which correspond to tasks in Xgrid, a batch file is needed to provide the command and the necessary parameters for each task, so that the controller can distribute them. After a job has been started, a job id is returned, that can be used to retrieve the job specification.

`xgrid -job specification -id n`

This batch file is in XML format, and therefore its generation can be automated. A simple batch job has the following structure:

```
jobSpecification =
{
    applicationIdentifier
        = "com.apple.xgrid.cli";
    inputFiles = {};
    name = "/usr/bin/cal";
    taskSpecifications =
    {
        0 =
        {
            arguments = (3, 2009);
            command = "/usr/bin/cal";
        };
    };
}
```

The section *inputFiles* consists of a list of files that are needed by each agent. For OMNeT++ simulations, this is usually the binary, the **ned**-files, the configuration file, routing files and so on. If the agents do not have a shared medium, all input files have to be written in ASCII coded hexadecimal representation in the XML file. The *taskSpecifications* specify the different runs in OMNeT++. All necessary arguments, e.g. the name of the configuration, the number of the run, and the command are listed. Without the integration of the generation of the complete file in OMNeT++, the job specification could be written manually by retrieving the specification file for one run and adding the task specifications for all the others. As this is a very tedious work, when it has to be done for hundreds of runs, the aim is to automate the whole process.

To generate the job specification file automatically, two prerequisites have to be fulfilled:

- It has to be figured out, which files have to be included.
- The possible number of runs has to be known.
- Each file has to be converted letter by letter into the ASCII coded hexadecimal representation.

Looking at small examples in OMNeT++, for instance FIFO, the necessary files are all included in the working directory of the example. But with the growing complexity of the frameworks, the input files can be distributed among different directories. To start, for instance, an example of the INET framework [104], about 170 **ned**-files in 50 different directories are loaded in addition to the example related files. To solve this problem, all directories are searched recursively, and the positions of found files are set relative to a base directory.

Figure 5.10 illustrates the mapping of the original files to the ones in the batch file for the following -n switch

`-n ../..:../../../src`

starting from the working directory
INET/examples/sctp/fair.

The most important task is to map the **ned**-files. The two paths, separated by a colon, refer to the two "base directories" **INET/examples** and **INET/src/**. Each base directory contains a file called **package.ned**, that includes the root package, i.e. the name of the package, from which the hierarchy of all the other **ned**-files below this directory stems. If the files in the ellipses on the left hand side were just copied, the second package file would overwrite the first one, which would result in errors when matching the expected to the package names provided in the **ned**-files. Therefore, each base directory has to be given an individual name, from which the relative paths can start. The directories were just named **temp1** and **temp2**. Thus the hierarchy of the files is kept and can be copied to the agents.

Hence, an entry for one input file has the following layout:

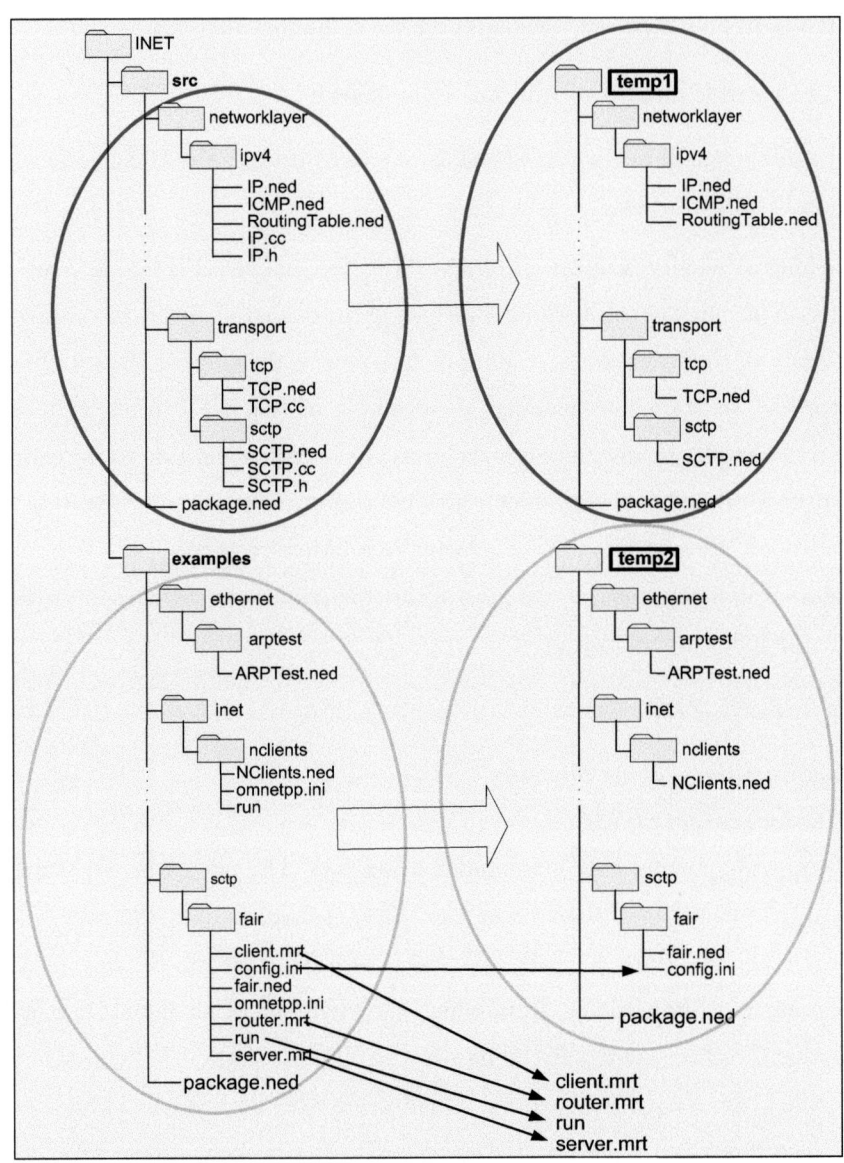

Figure 5.10: Mapping of the original files to the Xgrid hierarchy

```
"temp1/transport/sctp/SCTP.ned"=
{
```

```
        fileData = <7061636b 61676520 696e6574 ....>;
}
```

In addition to the **ned**-files, there are example dependent files, that are needed to run the simulation. In INET, these could be routing files or files to be interpreted by the scenario manager. Assuming, that the necessary files are usually kept in the example's directory where the simulation is started, all files from this directory were included. They are not set relative to `temp2`, but stored in the top directory. It is advisable to provide a subdirectory for the specification files to prevent older files from being included in the actual specification.

The configuration files can be specified with the -f-switch. If no file is defined, `omnetpp.ini` from the working directory is taken by default. In the `ini`-files, the network to use is set and the parameters for the modules the network consists of. As it is expected, that the `ini`-file and the network's `ned`-file reside in the same directory, the location of the `ini`-files must also be transferred to the relative hierarchy of the base directories. An alternative would be to store the `ini`-file in the working directory and provide the complete package path for the network.

The aim was to change as little in OMNeT++ as possible. Therefore, already existing features were taken advantage of, that provided the number of runs, which could be used to write the task specifications. Each task includes the paths for the **ned**-files and the configuration files, that have to be adjusted to the new hierarchy. In this example, one task specification looks as follows:

```
taskSpecifications =
    {
            0 =
            {
                    arguments = (
                        "-n",
                        "temp1:temp2",
```

```
                "-f",
                "temp2/sctp/fair/config.ini",
                "-c",
                "testconfig",
                "-r",
                0
            );
            command = "/home/user/INET/src/inet";
        };
}
```

In the first stage only one new command line switch was added to set the name of the job specification file. The creation of a specification file is started from the example's directory. For a complex framework like INET the command can be as follows:

`../../../src/inet -n ../..:../../../src -u Cmdenv " -f config.ini -c testconfig -s specfile.xml`

In addition to the parameters for the normal run, that is the location of the **ned** and configuration files, the command environment has to be chosen (`-u Cmdenv`), the configuration with the flag `-c` and the name of the specification file. The job can then be started with

`xgrid -h server -p password -job batch specfile.xml`

As mentioned before, also the executable belongs to the input files. This file can easily have a size of several megabytes, which will lead to a very large specification file that has to be transferred to the agents. Xgrid is very inefficient in transferring large files [79], because it repeats the entire file transfer for every task submitted to an agent. To improve the performance, it is advisable to keep the batch file as small as possible. Therefore, usually the executable is left out and stored on a shared medium or copied to the same location on each agent in advance.

Using a shared medium for all the input files can reduce the size of the specification file further. Therefore, the command line switch -t was introduced to give the user the opportunity to decide against a self-contained job and to exclude the input files from the batch file and call them from the shared medium. As a consequence, the job specification is altered to contain only absolute paths to the files of the working directory in the *inputFiles* section and to the **ned** and configuration files in the task specifications.

To take advantage of as many processors as possible, a universal binary for INET is usually generated, that will work for Intel and PowerPC machines alike, and stored on a shared medium. The *omnetpp.ini* file contains a path to a result directory, that can also be accessed by all agents. Thus, it is not necessary to retrieve the results after finishing the job, but they are written continuously to the specified location.

Measurements [79] have shown, that the execution time of a job can be decreased proportional to the number of CPUs provided.

Chapter 6

Integration of SCTP in INET

6.1 Extensions to the INET Framework

In Subsection 3.2.4 the features of the INET framework were outlined with respect to its ability to closely imitate the layers of the OSI reference model.

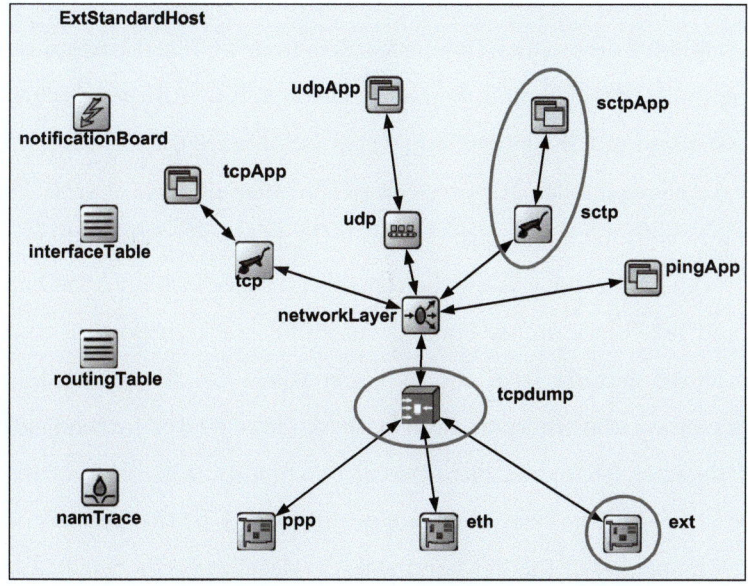

Figure 6.1: Extensions to the StandardHost module

The most interesting module was the *StandardHost*, which already provides a

TCP/IP suite. Therefore, is was obvious to extend this compound module, which then resulted in the structure depicted in Figure 6.1. All circled modules were either added or extended, of which the ExtInterface as an additional interface to connect to real implementations was already described in Section 5.1.3. The simple module *sctp* is the main item of the simulation as it features the complete SCTP protocol. Invaluable information regarding the realization of this module was provided by Andreas Jungmaier's SCTP implementation in the OPNET Modeler [45]. In addition, applications (*sctpApp*) were needed to provide the transport layer with the necessary information and messages using a basic socket API. The dump module (*tcpdump*) helped to test the implementation. These modules will be discussed in the next sections.

6.2 Simulation Architecture

SCTP is a complex protocol combining features from TCP and UDP plus realizing new concepts like streams, multihoming, and bundling. All these characteristics had to be realized in the simple module *sctp* (see Figure 6.1).

Figure 6.2 shows a schematic overview of the different parts of *sctp*. The major blocks that have to be distinguished specify the behavior of the data sender, the reaction of the data receiver, and the control messages including the handshakes to setup and take down an association. As SCTP is a transport protocol, it has interfaces to the network layer and its upper layer. On the right hand side the primitives connect the transport layer with the upper layer by sending notifications, for instance, that data has arrived, or requests, e.g. that an association should be started. The control messages are passed to the network layer and sent on to the peer. On the left hand side the data sender is depicted including the congestion control mechanism and bundling, in the middle the data receiver influenced by flow control.

In the following sections a detailed description of the main parts of the imple-

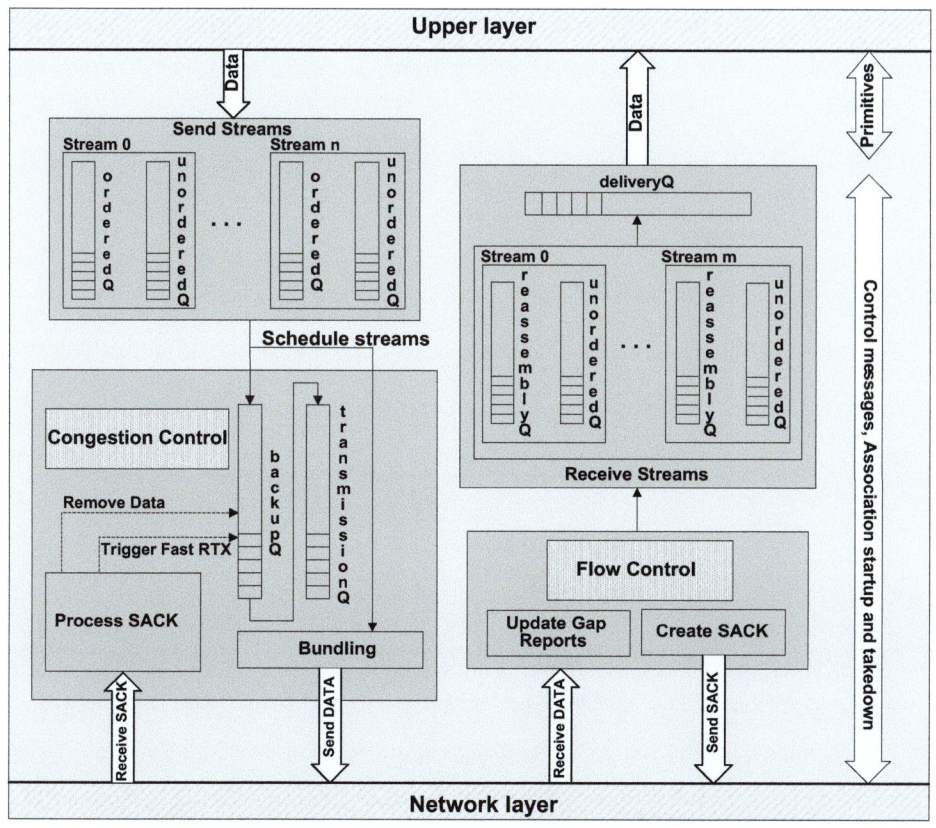

Figure 6.2: Simulation Architecture of the simple module *sctp*

mentation will be given.

6.2.1 Messages

The means of communication in OMNeT++ are messages. For each simple module the virtual function *handleMessage()* should be redefined to handle incoming messages. This function is called from the simulation kernel when the next message in the simulation queue is bound for that module and its scheduled time is up.

OMNeT++ provides two main message classes, *cMessage* and *cPacket* with *cPacket* being derived from *cMessage*. They can be superclasses for customized message classes. In the *cMessage* class attributes and corresponding methods are declared for sending and receiving messages, like the sending and arrival gate, the creation time, and a control info. *cPacket* contains additional attributes, which make this class more suitable for the transmission of protocol data, like the message length, a flag to indicate bit errors, and a method to encapsulate other messages.

To realize the different kinds of communication in Figure 6.2, three main types of messages were needed:

- Messages containing the SCTP packets.

- Commands to send primitives.

- Timers to trigger events.

Figure 6.3 shows the principal hierarchy of the messages that form an SCTP packet. As an example an attribute and a method are added to each class diagram. *SCTPMessage* contains the SCTP message common header and a dynamic array of pointers, one to each chunk. To be able to easily identify the chunk types, the classes for the different chunks are derived from *SCTPChunk*, which contains the chunk type. Some chunk classes just consist of the header like the `COOKIE_ACK` chunk, some contain several parameters which can be mandatory or optional. This is the case for the `INIT` or `INIT_ACK` chunk. Each parameter has to be derived from *SCTPParameter*, consisting of a header with the type and length information and a body containing the value.

The definition of new message classes is specified in a message declaration file (*.msg*). Only the data members are introduced like e.g. in the following declaration of *SCTPMessage*.

```
message SCTPMessage extends cPacket
```

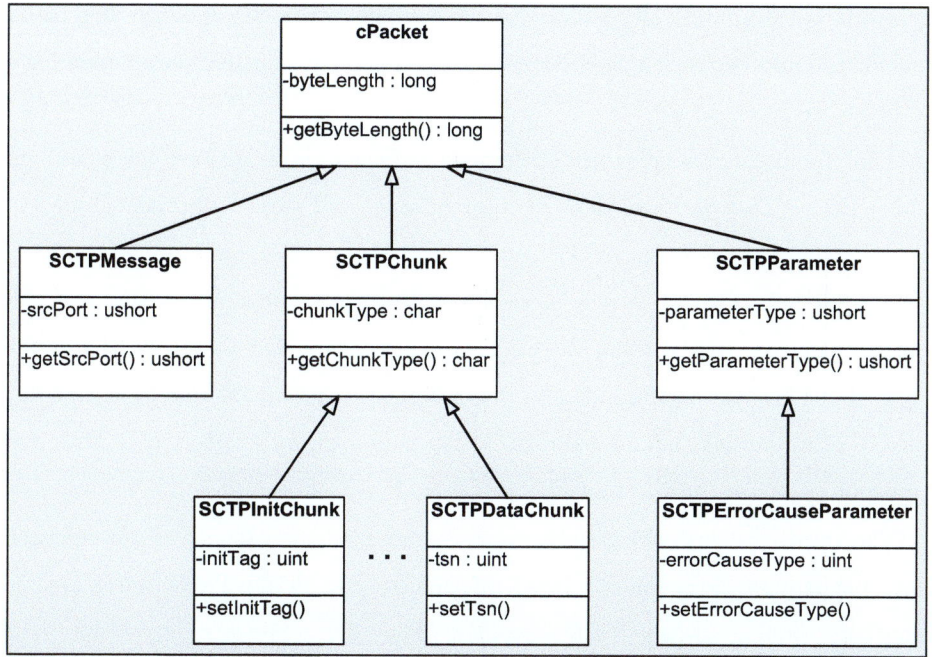

Figure 6.3: Hierarchy of the SCTP messages

```
{
    @customize(true);
    uint16 srcPort;
    uint16 destPort;
    uint32 tag;
    bool checksumOk;
    abstract cPacketPtr chunks[];
}
```

At compile time corresponding *C++* and header files are generated that include the methods to set and get the attributes. In case simple methods to get or set parameters are not sufficient, the @customize property can be set and the methods redefined. This has to be done for *SCTPMessage*, because the handling of dynamic arrays is not automatically supported. If a single parameter message has to be included in another message, encapsulation is used, but multiple parameters have to be stored in an array.

The command messages are exchanged between the transport layer and its upper layer. They are also derived from *cPacket* and carry information specific to the command type. An *SCTPConnectInfo*, for example, contains information that is needed to set up a new association, like the number of streams and the port to bind to. In the other direction indications are sent to inform the upper layer about events. Commands and indications are distinguishable by a number, the *SCTPCommandCode* and the *SCTPStatusIndication*, respectively. They are transported as *controlInfo* in a *cPacket*.

The third category, the timers, are *cMessages*, as their length is not relevant and they do not carry encapsulated information. In OMNeT++ timers are realized by sending so-called *self-messages*. They get a certain arrival time and are inserted in the list of scheduled events. After their expiration time they are handed by the simulation kernel to the *handleMessage()* method. Thus, they are handled like other messages and can even carry information. Timers are very important throughout the simulation to trigger events. Besides the ones mentioned in Figure 6.4, a lot more are needed to trigger the retransmission of **DATA** chunks, to send **SACK** chunks or **HEARTBEAT** chunks.

6.2.2 Association Setup and Take-down

A four way handshake starts an SCTP association (see Figure 2.4). It consists of the control chunks **INIT**, **INIT_ACK**, **COOKIE_ECHO**, and **COOKIE_ACK** chunk and is initiated by sending the primitive SCTP-ASSOCIATE from the upper layer to the transport layer. The receiving side must have sent an SCTP-OPEN-PASSIVE before, so that a listening socket has been created. The handshake is normally started by a client wishing to set up a connection with a server, but a peer-to-peer communication is also possible with both peers opening listening sockets and starting the setup combining their control data to one association. Both alternatives are realized in the simulation and will be referred to in Section 6.4.1.

As OMNeT++ is a discrete event simulation environment, it uses state machines and provides methods to react to occurring events. In Figure 6.4 the different possible states of the simulation are shown with the corresponding events and the necessary actions to transit from one state to another. The upper half of the figure presents the setup, the lower half the take down. `DATA` chunks are only accepted in the states ESTABLISHED and SHUTDOWN-PENDING.

Besides the transition from one state to another, Figure 6.4 depicts events that result in staying in a state, indicated by a circled arrow. These events occur when timers expire before the acknowledgment for a control message has arrived. This is the case, for example, in the COOKIE-WAIT state. When the client sends an `INIT` chunk, it starts an INIT-Timer to expire after the default 3 seconds or another configured time. When the `INIT_ACK` chunk arrives during that time, the timer is stopped, a `COOKIE_ECHO` chunk is sent and the COOKIE-ECHOED state is entered. If the timer expires, the `INIT` chunk has to be retransmitted and the state is not left. The same behavior is true for the COOKIE-ECHOED, the SHUTDOWN-SENT and the SHUTDOWN-ACK-SENT states.

6.2.3 Data Sender

After the upper layer has received the information that an association had been established, it can start sending data (see the events in the ESTABLISHED state of Figure 6.4). SCTP provides the use of several streams for incoming and outgoing connections whose number is negotiated in the setup process. Each stream can carry data messages, which can be either unordered or ordered. As the use of the streams is application dependent, the upper layer has to provide the number of streams and also the information which stream each data message belongs to

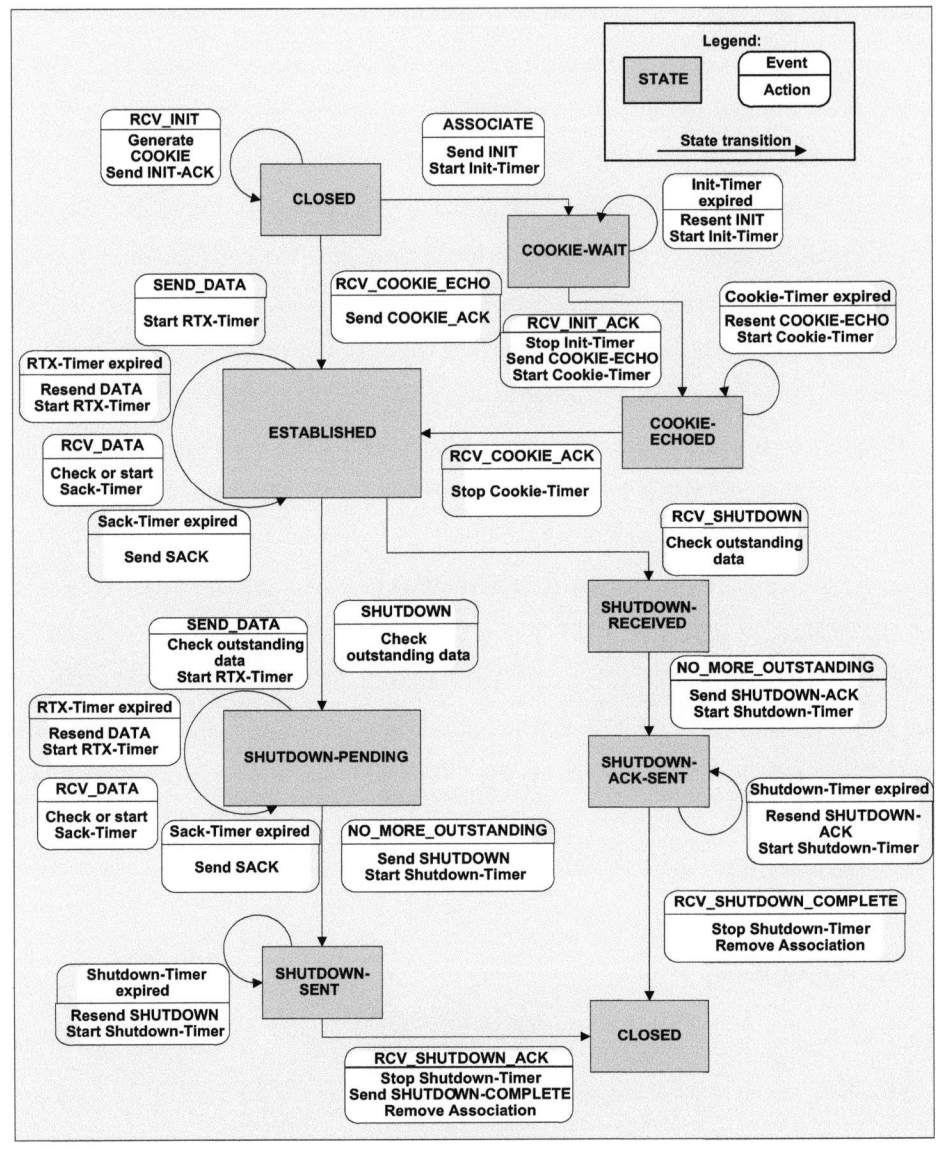

Figure 6.4: Simulation State Machine

and an indication whether it should be delivered ordered or unordered.

The raw data, which can be a message from an upper layer protocol, are stored in an array of characters in an *SCTPSimpleMessage*. The message specific information that the application provides is set in an *SCTPSendCommand*. A *cPacket* is created with the *SCTPSendCommand* as control info. After the *SCTPSimpleMessage* has been encapsulated, *cPacket* is sent to the gate leading to the *sctp* module.

Arriving at the transport layer (see Figure 6.2), the data messages are sorted into the appropriate send stream queues provided by the *SCTPSendCommand*. The overall send queue size can be unlimited or limited with configurable size. This has the advantage that in a bulk transfer not all messages to be sent are scheduled at the beginning of the simulation, but in smaller entities. Thus, the number of messages is not limited by the memory any more. Whenever the limited queue is emptied to half its size, a notification is sent to the upper layer to order more data.

The sequence in which the stream queues are emptied is controlled by the stream scheduler. The scheduling strategy to be used is not specified by the RFC 4960 [85]. At present only the Round Robin queuing strategy is realized, but in a current project (see Section 1.1) different strategies will be implemented and compared.

The amount of data that may be sent is influenced by many factors. It has to be calculated from the number of outstanding bytes, the congestion window, the advertised receiver window and, of course, the amount of data provided in the send streams. This calculation will be discussed in Section 6.2.5. If the user has configured the sender to consider the Nagle algorithm to reduce the number of small packets (see [59] for details) and there are still messages in flight, every packet is bundled with **DATA** chunks up to the (configurable) Nagle point. Before inserting the chunks in the packet, a TSN has to be assigned for each chunk to have a unique means of identification. The data messages that are sent to the peer are stored in the backup queue, until they can be finally removed. A second queue, the transmission queue, is provided for the temporary storage of messages that have to be retransmitted. The information on which path retransmissions occurred, their number, whether the data has been acknowledged or counts as outstanding, and many more attributes characterize a data message and have to be stored with the data. When assembling a packet, the messages scheduled for retransmission have to be considered first and only the remaining space can be filled with new data.

An arriving `SACK` chunk influences the transmission of data as it announces the Cumulative TSN Ack (CumTSNAck). All TSNs up to this number can be finally removed from the backup queue, i.e. they can not be revoked any more (see 6.2.6). Present gap reports lead to an increase in the gap report count of the missing TSNs if a TSN higher than the highest in the last `SACK` chunk has been acknowledged. If the user defined gap report limit has been exceeded, the chunk is copied from the backup queue to the transmission queue to be fast retransmitted as soon as possible.

6.2.4 Data Receiver

The data receiver is featured on the right hand side of Figure 6.2. The reception of the data messages is influenced by the flow control mechanism that will be discussed in Section 6.2.6. As the TSNs have to be in sequence, the missing ones are announced in the gap reports that are sent back to the sender for information. The acknowledged data messages are stored in the receive streams. Again each stream consists of two queues, one for unordered and one for ordered data. The order is provided by the SSNs that are maintained for each stream. If data with the appropriate SSN is found, it is stored in the delivery queue, and an SCTP-DATA-ARRIVED-NOTIFICATION is sent to the upper layer, that in turn asks to deliver the data.

The `SACK` chunk summarizes the results of the TSN analysis and reports the actual CumTSNAck and the information about the gap reports and possible duplicate TSNs back to the data sender. Only the first and the last TSN in a gap acknowledgment block is included. In contrast to RFC 4960, the *sendSack()* routine in the simulation includes the absolute values of the start and end TSNs in the gap acknowledgment blocks. Thus, they have to be transformed to their value relative to the CumTSNAck if a connection to a real network is established.

In addition, the size of the updated advertised receiver window (see Section 6.2.6) is added to the `SACK` chunk.

6.2.5 Congestion Control

The congestion control mechanism that SCTP uses is in most parts derived from TCP. Yet some important differences are due to special SCTP features.

As SCTP allows a host to be multihomed, the congestion control mechanism has to be applied to each path separately. This means that a path has its own congestion window, slow-start threshold (ssthresh), counter of outstanding bytes, and retransmission timeout calculation.

As mentioned before, congestion control influences the amount of data to be sent separately for each path in that not more than the difference between cwnd and the number of outstanding bytes may be transmitted, if permitted by the receiver's arwnd.

Figure 6.5 shows a flowchart for the calculation of the congestion window for each path. The event that has the greatest influence on updating the cwnd is the arrival of a `SACK` chunk. An increase is only allowed if acknowledged data has led to an advance of the CumTSNAck (ctsnaAdvanced) and the cwnd is fully utilized (osb $\geq$ cwnd). When in slow start, the only additional requirement is that fast recovery must not be active. This status is entered, when a fast retransmission has occured, and left again, when the cumTSNAck has reached the TSN that has been the highest at the time, when fast recovery has started. During that time no cwnd update will be performed. The behavior in congestion avoidance differs from the one in slow start in that the updates are not as frequent. The variable *partialBytesAcked* counts the number of acknowledged bytes, and only if they reach the size of cwnd, may an MTU be added.

All other cases lead to a decrease of cwnd. When a fast retransmission is necessary, the window is halved or set to $4 \cdot MTU$, in case of a timer based retransmission it is even left at one MTU. The cwnd timer expires if the cwnd has not been updated for a set time indicating that the path has been idle. Therefore, the condition of the path is not known, and the cwnd is decreased to the value at initialization time. The cwnd may not grow beyond the number of outstanding bytes plus *maxBurst* times the MTU. *maxBurst* is set to 4 by default and limits the number of packets that may be sent at once.

While TCP is bytes stream oriented, SCTP is message based, and thus, the overhead of many chunks bundled in one packet can lead to a discrepancy between the transmitted bytes and the sent user data, which can have an impact on the fairness on the link. This topic will be further investigated in Section 8.3.

6.2.6 Flow Control

Flow control, as adopted from TCP, shall protect a receiver from a fast sender. Therefore, the receiver announces the maximum size of the arwnd in the `INIT` or `INIT_ACK` chunk and the amount of empty space in the receive buffer by sending the arwnd attribute in the `SACK` chunks. The simulation follows this approach by reducing the arwnd with every arriving data chunk and increasing it when data is delivered to the upper layer. If the window is reduced to zero, the data sender may only send one chunk to probe the window. Only if a suitable TSN arrives, i.e. one that fills a gap or advances the CumTSNAck, it is accepted. All others are dropped. As the window is full at that time, room has to be made for the new TSN. Therefore, the highest TSN accepted so far is deleted from the receive queue

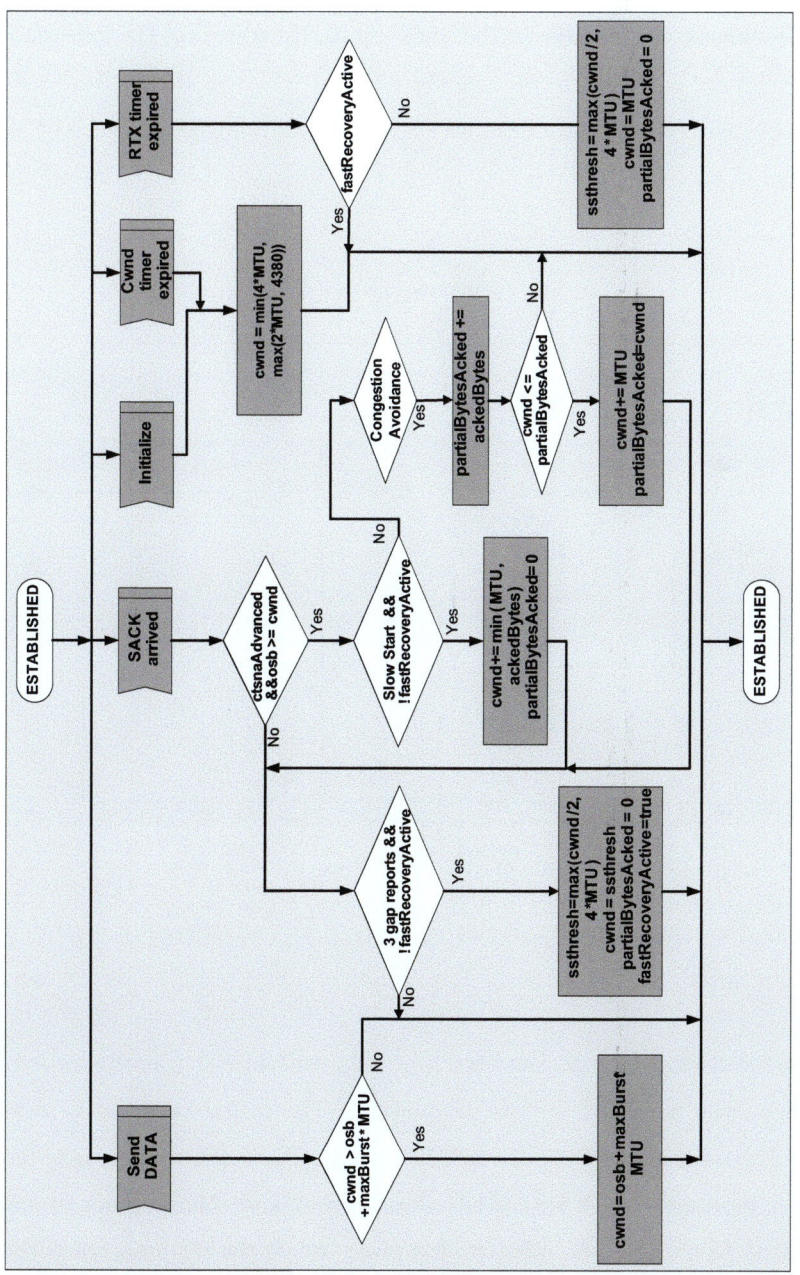

Figure 6.5: Flowchart for the calculation of the congestion window

and the new TSN is inserted instead. Thus the former TSN is unacknowledged again. Announcing this change in the SACK chunk by adjusting the gap reports leads to a change in the attributes of the affected TSNs in the backup queue. Therefore, even TSNs that have been accepted and acknowledged have to be kept in the queue in case they are revoked and have to be marked as unacknowledged again.

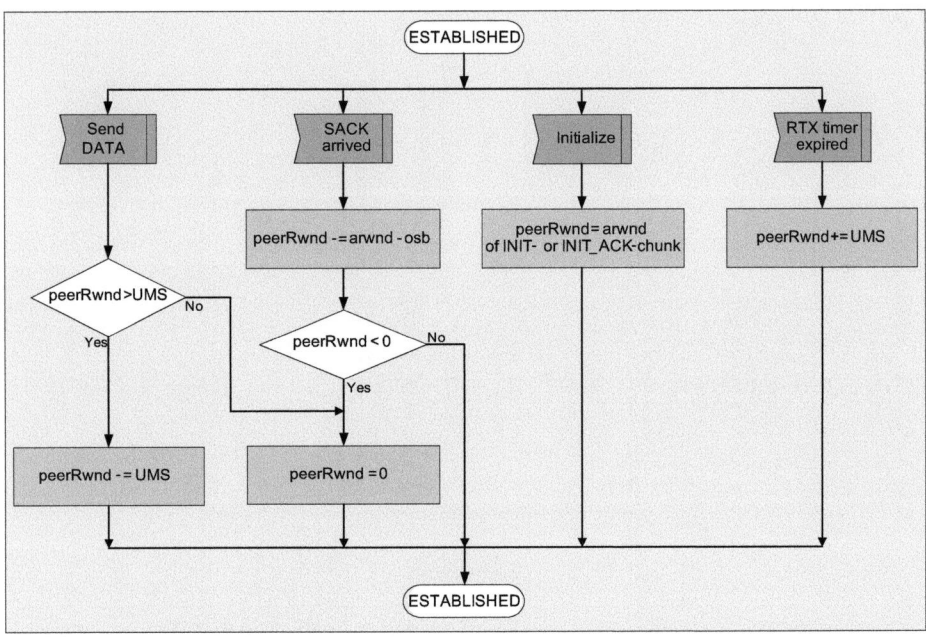

Figure 6.6: Flowchart for the calculation of the peer's advertised receiver window

The sender always tries to keep track of its peer's arwnd (peerRwnd). Figure 6.6 shows the flowchart for the calculation. The initial value is the arwnd that was advertised in the INIT or INIT_ACK chunk. Then the window is reduced by the user message size (UMS), when data is sent and there is enough space left. A reason to increase the peerRwnd is given, when the retransmission timer expires. Then it is assumed that the DATA chunk has not reached the peer, and thus, its arwnd has not been reduced. The TSN does not count as outstanding any more, and the peerRwnd can be increased by the UMS of the lost **DATA** chunk. Even before the peer announces an arwnd of zero, the sender predicts this value and starts sending zero window probes to prevent the receiver from being overloaded. As the calculation is not accurate and just an estimation of the peer's behavior, the peerRwnd is updated each time a **SACK** chunk arrives. It is set to the arwnd minus the data in flight which the peer could not include in its calculation, yet. Further information about the flow control mechanism in message based in contrast to bytes stream oriented protocols is given in Section 8.2.

6.2.7 Simulation Structure

As OMNeT++ and INET are written in C++, the structure of the *sctp* module must be object-oriented. Figure 6.7 shows an overview of the most important classes. The hierarchy of the message types has already been introduced in Subsection 6.2.1 and is left out here, as well as the various container classes like maps, vectors, and lists.

All arriving messages, whether from the lower or from the upper layer, or whether they are self-messges, are handled by the *SCTP* class. Here, the creation of a new *SCTPAssociation* is initiated, when the upper layer sends an SCTP-ASSOCIATE or an SCTP-PASSIVE-OPEN command. To keep track of the associations, the IDs and important information are organized in maps.

SCTPAssociation with all its implemented methods is a very important class. Sending and receiving SCTP messages, the expiration of timers and the realization of the congestion and flow control are handled in this class. To store the numerous flags, counters, chunks for retransmission, and other parameters that change over time, an instance of the *SCTPStateVariables* is needed. Each path has its own characteristics, like IP address, cwnd, path MTU, RTO and so on. *SCTPAssociation* manages them in a map, containing the IP address and an instance

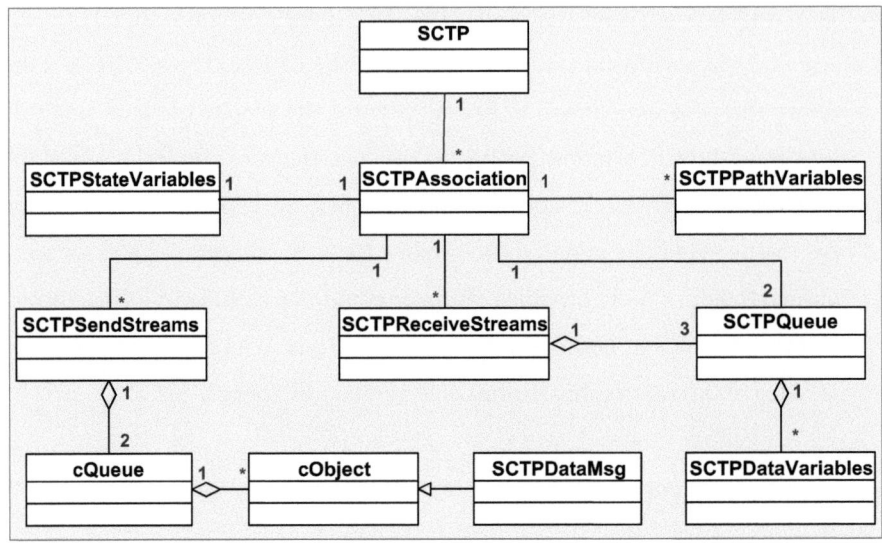

Figure 6.7: Class diagram of the simulation

of the *SCTPPathVariables* class.

As already shown in Figure 6.2, send and receive streams are needed to organize the queueing of messages. The data coming directly from the upper layer are converted into *SCTPDataMsg* objects and inserted in the ordered or unordered send queues. They are realized as *cQueues* in an object of type *SCTPSendStreams*. The backup and the transmission queue are *SCTPQueues*, which can contain *SCTPDataVariables*. This is the class whose attributes represent the properties of a DATA chunk, like its TSN, the stream identifier and sequence number, its destination, number of retransmissions, and flags to indicate whether it has been acknowledged or counts as outstanding. The same queuing type is used for the delivery of data to the upper layer in the unordered and ordered queue of each receive stream of type *SCTPReceiveStream*.

6.3 Implemented Protocol Extensions

All the extensions that are described in Section 2.3 are also implemented in the simulation.

6.3.1 Partial Reliability (PR-SCTP)

Partial Reliability is initiated by the upper layer. The *SCTPSendCommand* has a variable *prMethod* that is set to a value greater than zero if PR-SCTP should be applied. The two methods "timed reliability" and "limiting the number of retransmissions", introduced in RFC 3758 [84], were realized. The *lifetime* parameter of the *SCTPCommand* is used to carry the information about the lifetime or the number of retransmissions for this specific message, depending on the method defined. Instead of a Forward_TSN_Supported parameter just a flag was added to the `INIT` and `INIT_ACK` chunk to indicate that the host supports PR-SCTP. In the case of the lifetime method, an expiration time is set in the *SCTPDataVariables* and checked against the simulation time. Whenever a message is sent, it is checked first whether it has to be abandoned. Is this true, the upper layer is informed and a `Forward_TSN` chunk is sent with the peer's CumTSNAck set to the new value. As a consequence, the receiver has to adjust its own CumTSNAck and consider all TSNs up to this point as received. The second method is handled in the same way, only the requirements to abandon a TSN are changed to the number of retransmissions already performed.

6.3.2 Stream Reset

To simulate the Stream Reset behavior, the peer has to be informed that Stream Reset is supported. This is done during the handshake. For testing purposes the user can configure a timer to start one of the three Stream Reset request types *Outgoing SSN Reset Request*, *Incoming SSN Reset Request* or *SSN/TSN Reset*

Request. It is also possible to request the reset of the incoming and outgoing streams at the same time. Of course, a new *SCTPChunk* type and *SCTPParameters* for the request, as well as for the response, had to be added. Furthermore, new primitives had to be defined to inform the user about the outcome of the request.

6.3.3 Dynamic Address Reconfiguration (Add-IP)

Whereas PR-SCTP and Stream Reset are features initialized by the application, ADD-IP is initiated by the transport layer. To add an address, the ADD-IP type (SET_PRIMARY_ADDRESS, ADD_IP_ADDRESS, DELETE_IP_ADDRESS), the time, and the affected address have to be configured in the *omnetpp.ini* file of the example. At the designated time an ASCONF chunk is sent with the appropriate parameter. After the arrival of the ASCONF_ACK chunk, the new address can be used, or, if it was deleted, not used any more.

This extension will be needed for the realization of the SCTP NAT in Chapter 9.

6.3.4 Authenticating Chunks (AUTH)

Authenticating chunks in a simulation is not really worthwhile, as the messages do not go over the wire and there is no buffer to apply the encryption algorithm on. But with the implementation of the ExtInterface and the testing against real networks, AUTH had to be implemented to meet the requirements for ADD-IP [92]. With every new feature also the serializer and the parser had to be adjusted and the new chunk types and parameters added. Flags in the INIT chunk had to be transformed into complete parameters and added to the chunks. To realize AUTH meant to create real keys, serialize all chunks first, compute the Hash Message Authentication Code (HMAC) and insert it in the AUTH chunk. On the way back, the actions had to be performed in the reverse order, before the chunks could be converted in the simulation format.

As AUTH always has to be applied if an `ASCONF` or `ASCONF_ACK` chunk is sent, this feature is also needed in SCTP NATs (Chapter 9).

6.3.5 Packet Drop Reporting (PKTDROP)

PKTDROP, too, is an extension concerning the transport layer. Except for the flag to switch PKTDROP on or off, no additional parameters have to be configured. As the usual behavior of an IP stack is to drop packets that have a bit error, this is also the case in INET. Therefore, all packets on the link layer, whether they have a bit error or not, have to be sent up to the network layer. If the transport protocol is SCTP, the packet is delivered further, while all others are deleted. Thus, SCTP can handle packets, even if they have an error, and report them in a `PKTDROP` chunk.

6.4 Additional Modules

6.4.1 SCTP Applications

The SCTP module (Figure 3.5) has interfaces to the network layer and the application layer. The interoperability between the transport and its upper layer is realized by sending notifications and primitives (Figure 6.2) as specified in RFC 4960 [85]. In the simulation both a callback and a socket API are realized to provide the upper layer with calls to *bind()*, *listen()*, *connect()*, *send()* or *receive()*. Thus, the application layer takes the initiative to start an association. SCTP answers by either sending notifications, indicating for instance that the ESTABLISHED state (Figure 6.4) has been entered, the peer has closed the connection, or data are waiting in the receive queue to be picked up.

sctpapp represents the highest layer in the *ExtStandardHost* module in Figure 6.1. The easiest way to write an application is a simple module, that acts as a client or server. To test more complex applications, like complete protocols or a layer to adjust messages between different protocol stacks, *sctpapp* must be realized as a compound module. As examples for simple modules, the simulation provides three different applications which work as traffic generators and/or collectors. One is a client with a callback API, one a server with a socket API and the third is a peer that combines both client and server functionality.

The client as a sender can be either configured to send a predefined number of data chunks of a certain length or to start at a certain time and stop at a set time independent from the number of packets. If the packets shall not be sent as fast as possible, a sending interval can be defined. When sending a very large number of messages, the client uses limited send queues, as described in Subsection 6.2.3. To allow for a very large number of messages, a send queue size can be configured to fill the send queue in smaller portions instead of scheduling all required messages at once. The client can also work as a receiver being able to discard or echo the messages.

The server can send or receive data. As it is implemented as a combined server, incoming packets can be discarded or echoed. But the server can also generate data, just like the client, representing a peer-to-peer network. The server keeps a record of the amounts of all the sent or received data for each association, thus providing statistical data for further use.

To support multihoming, the function *sctp_bindx()* is realized. The user can either set the IP addresses that should be bound explicitly or just leave the default value (empty string) if all available addresses should be used. The bound addresses are included in the `INIT` or `INIT_ACK` chunk.

When the peer is initialized, it starts by calling *bind()* and *listen()*, thus being configured as a server. When a certain start time is set, the peer sends a request to SCTP to associate. The peer application is useful, when testing the so-called initialization collisions i.e. when both parties try to set up an association at the same time.

More applications for special purposes are implemented. One is adjusted for performing the rendezvous of the Network Address Translation (NAT) feature, which will be explained in Chapter 9.

6.4.2 Dump Module

Although the GUI of OMNeT++ helps to observe the flow of data, it did not provide a satisfying overview of the packets that were sent to and from the hosts. A dump module for TCP with one input and one output gate already existed, which could have been placed between the network and the transport layer. As it was important to distinguish between the interfaces the message passes through, the layout of the module was changed to support a vector of gates. Therefore, the dump module was placed between the link layer and the network layer (Figure 3.5). To be able to analyze the traffic, methods were included to examine all chunks and their important parameters.

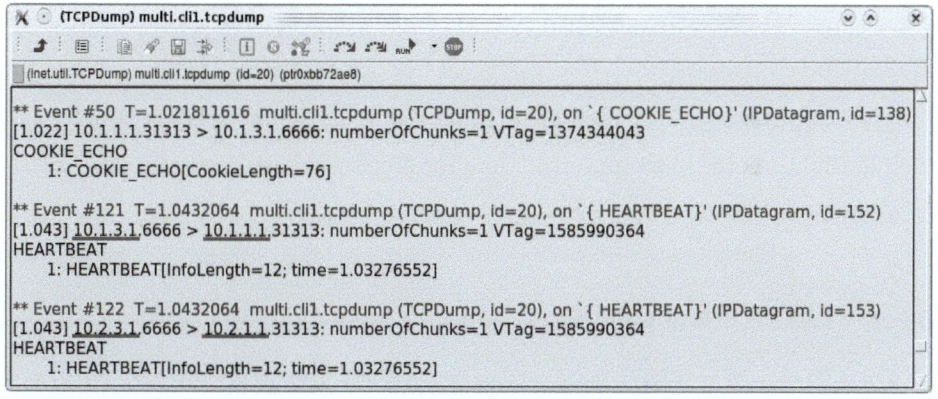

Figure 6.8: Output of the dump module

The incoming packets are examined by decapsulating the messages and analyzing their contents. Afterwards they are transferred unchanged to the next layer. Figure 6.8 shows part of the four way handshake and two HEARTBEAT chunks to different destinations on the client side of the communication. The different IP addresses of the client, to which the `HEARTBEAT` chunks are sent, and the corresponding source addresses of the server are underlined.

The dump module has one drawback, in that it can only be used in *Run* or *Fast* mode. When the simulation runs take longer, this is very inefficient. After the realization of the ExtInterface (see Section 5.1), the dump module can be also used to trace the traffic at any speed and save the result in a *pcap* file. When a name for a dump file is given in the *omnetpp.ini*, this file is opened and writing is started with the pcap file header. When passing through the module, each packet is handed to the serializer, where it is converted to the external format, and together with the pcap packet header written to the file, which can then be analyzed with Wireshark.

6.5 Validating the Simulation

As a simulation is self-contained, the question arises how it can be tested to evaluate its correctness.

The obvious way is to configure scenarios, test them and see whether the results are plausible. As the most important and most complicated features in SCTP are congestion and flow control, they were validated first.

6.5.1 Testing Flow Control

To test the implementation of the flow control algorithm, the bandwidth-delay product was inspected. It states that the maximum amount of data in flight is limited by the achievable link bandwidth BW multiplied by the RTT. This limit is given by the advertised receiver window W.

$$BW \cdot RTT = W \tag{6.1}$$

Taking W and replacing RTT by the twofold of the link delay LD leads to an equation for the throughput:

$$Throughput = \frac{W}{2 \cdot LD} \qquad (6.2)$$

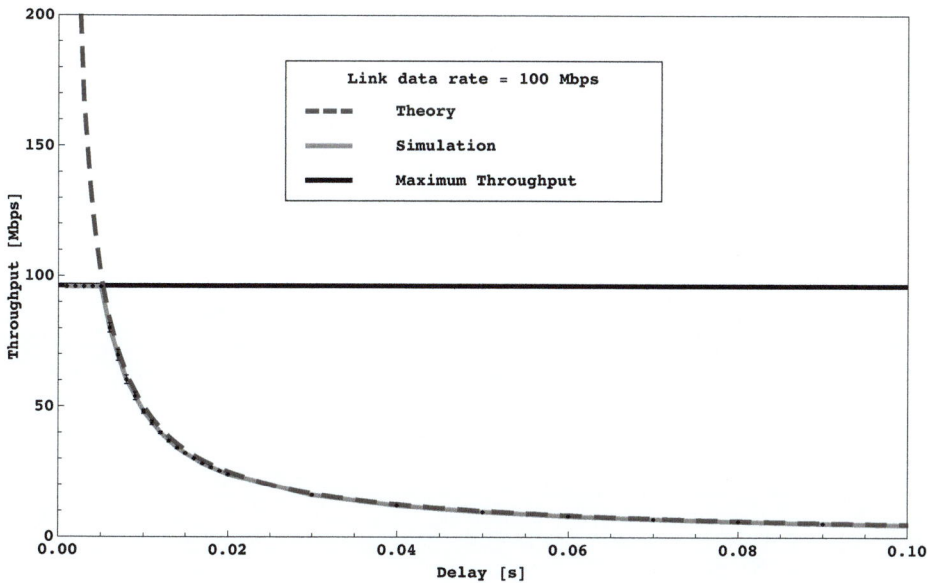

Figure 6.9: Verifying the bandwidth-delay product

In Figure 6.9 the maximum theoretical throughput according to the above equation is plotted. The straight black horizontal line gives the maximum theoretical throughput for the given link with a data rate of 100 Mbps, an MTU of 1500 bytes, and messages of 1452 bytes length. The simulation runs have been repeated 10 times. The outcome is shown in the light solid line. The 95% confidence intervals are so small that they are only recognizable as black dots. For small values for the delay the throughput is limited by the arwnd, for higher values it follows the course of the theoretical result.

6.5.2 Testing Congestion Control

6.5.2.1 SCTP fairness

One indication for the correctness of the congestion control algorithm is the verification that different SCTP clients are fair towards each other, meaning that they share the bandwidth evenly independent from their start times.

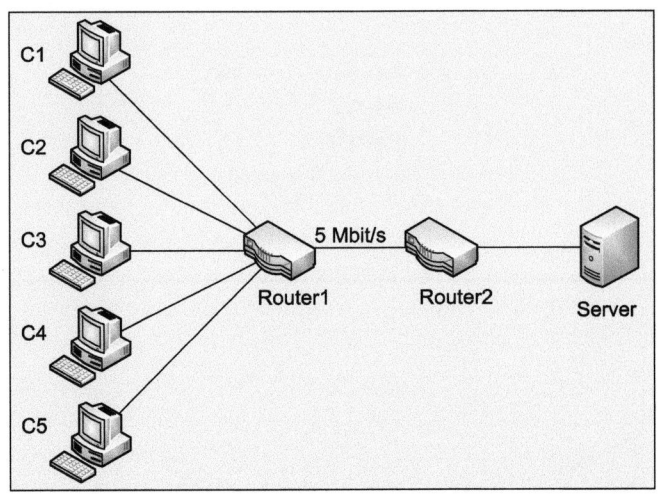

Figure 6.10: Network with five clients sharing a limited link

Figure 6.10 shows a scenario, where five clients are connected with the same server over a bottleneck link with a data rate of 5 Mbps. Their start and stop times were configured so that every 60 seconds an event occurred, meaning that either a new client joined or one stopped transmitting.

Figure 6.11 shows the throughput of the first client, that sends data starting at 1 s and stopping at 360 s. The start and stop times of the other clients are marked in the graph. Up to now, the throughput of an association was always obtained by dividing the total number of received bytes by the time it took to receive the data. In this example the goal was to measure the throughput over time and show that it is decreased, when the link has to be shared and increased again if another

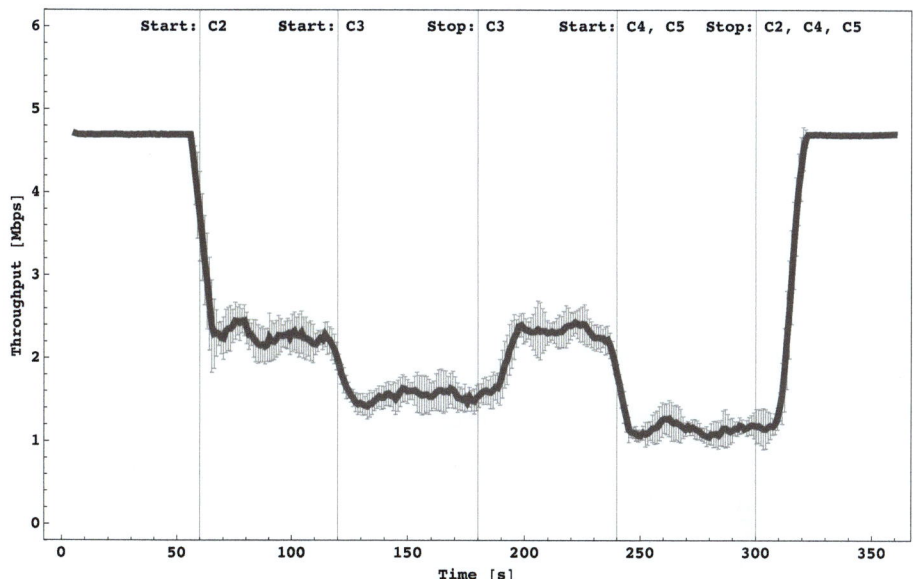

Figure 6.11: Five clients sharing a limited link

host stopped sending. To achieve this, the accumulated number of received bytes was counted for C1 every time, a message arrived at the server. Before calculating the moving median of the difference quotient of consecutive values, the amount of measuring points was reduced to one per second. The average of five runs leads to the graph, which depicts the expected results. The light bars represent the 95% confidence interval. The delayed adjustment of the graph, after a client stopped transmitting, is due to the shutdown process of an association. When the application requests a shutdown from SCTP, all remaining messages have to be processed and acknowledged, before the association can finally be removed.

6.5.2.2 Testing Congestion Control on Lossy Links

Packet loss has a significant impact on the congestion control, as fast retransmissions and timer based retransmissions lead to a decrease of the congestion window. If packet loss does not only result from exhausted router queues but error-prone links, the throughput is affected.

In Chapter 7 a formula for the throughput of SCTP associations will be derived, when error rates and delays influence the quality of the link. To get a further indication for the correctness of the congestion control algorithm of the simulation, it was tested against Equations 7.10 and 7.12. The results are described in Section 7.4.5.

6.5.3 Analyzing Trace Files

Testing a program is not a straight forward process but requires many iterations as bugs are suspected and finally found and eliminated. The dump module (see Subsection 6.4.2) and the graphical analysis of trace files in Wireshark, which were discussed in detail in Section 4.4, turned out to be of great benefit. The first tool helped to find errors that were due to the wrong choice of parameters or a misunderstanding of the protocol features. The latter assisted in detecting suspicious variations in the message flow, especially those that were related to congestion or flow control, which then could be localized and corrected.

6.5.4 Validating the Simulation by Using External Sources

A more systematic approach for the validation is the use of testcases. After the implementation of the external interface, it was possible to connect to an external computer. An SCTP testtool and the corresponding ETSI (European Telecommunications Standards Institute) conformance tests are provided in [93]. The testtool ran on the external computer and used the simulation as an SUT (System under test). After the simulation had passed the tests it was proved that the most important features of the protocol were implemented correctly.

But still the RFCs leave the possibility to interpret some specifications in different ways. Therefore, interoperability events bring developers of various implementations together to test their products against each other. In 2006, the

8th SCTP InterOp in Vancouver, Canada, and in 2007, the 9th SCTP InterOp in Kyoto, Japan, were attended. Each time bugs were found and corrected, which would not have been found just by testing the simulation itself. Thus, the simulation could be improved, its correctness and robustness increased.

6.5.5 Measuring the Throughput against Real Implementations

One aspect that always matters is the performance of an implementation. Of course, a simulation cannot be as efficient as a real implementation, because a lot of additional information is stored, other data structures are used, and performance is normally not the most important issue when designing a simulation model.

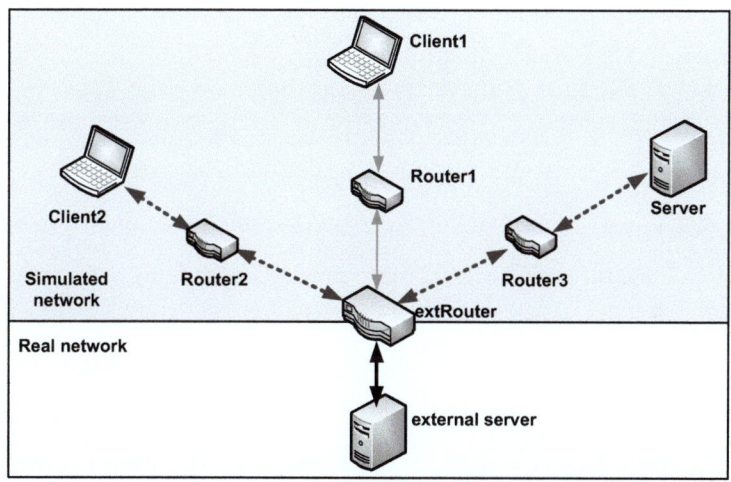

Figure 6.12: **Client1** sends data via **extRouter** to a real PC while internal traffic from **Client2** to **Server1** is passing through **extRouter**

Nevertheless, to show the limits of the simulation, it was tested against a real implementation. Figure 6.12 shows the setup, where the simulated parts are marked by a gray background. The external interface can be considered as part of both worlds. Here **Client1** is linked via a router with the external interface,

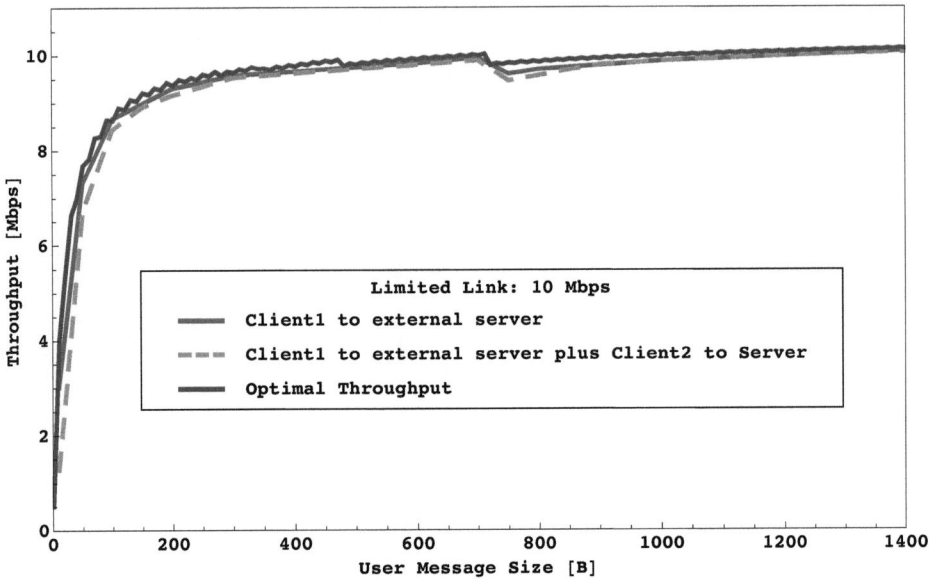

Figure 6.13: Throughput of the SCTP association between `Client1` and a real PC

which is connected to a real server. The channel between the client and the router is limited to a data rate of 10 Mbps. First 200,000 data chunks of increasing sizes between 10 and 1400 bytes were sent and the throughput was measured. In Figure 6.13 the red graph in the middle shows the result. As a comparison, the maximum theoretical throughput according to Equation 7.5 is represented by the darker red graph. The zigzagging of the graph and the pronounced steps are typical for SCTP and will be explained in Section 7.3. The figure shows that the simulation is able to fully utilize a link of 10 Mbps.

A second series of measurements was performed to find out whether additional traffic passing through the router has an impact on the throughput, meaning that the processing of the events from the external router could not keep up with the packets arriving. Therefore, `Client2` was to start earlier than `Client1` and had to run longer than the external association. The route, the traffic took, led from

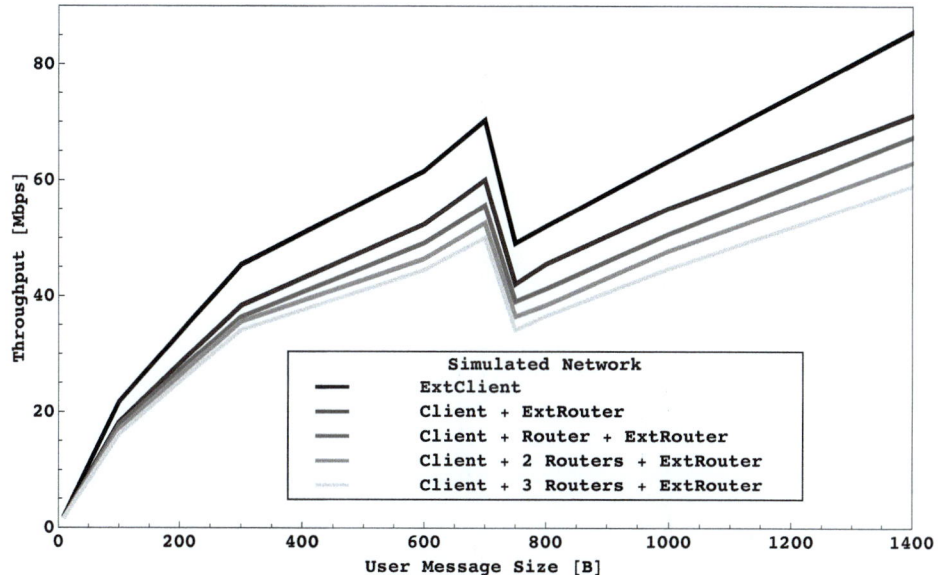

Figure 6.14: Throughput of the SCTP association between Client1 and a real PC with varying number of routers

Client2 over extRouter to the Server. It is marked by the dashed arrows in Figure 6.12. The throughput is shown by the lowest dashed graph in Figure 6.13. It is obvious that the internal traffic has no significant influence on the external traffic.

Another point of interest was the time it takes for a router to process a packet. Therefore, the throughput was measured without internal traffic but with 0, 1, 2, and 3 routers between the client and the external router. The data rate was not limited. From Figure 6.14, the conclusion can be drawn that the time a router needs to handle the packets is nearly constant. Subtracting the measured times for the particular user message sizes from one router to another and dividing the difference by the number of packets that passed through the routers, an average process time of about 11 μs per packet can be assumed.

Chapter 7

Calculating the Theoretical Throughput of SCTP Associations

7.1 Term Definitions

The performance of a network is a measure for its quality. However, it is not always clear, what the term comprises. In this thesis the terms bandwidth, throughput, and goodput are used as measures for the performance of an association. In the following these terms will be defined and distinguished from each other.

Bandwidth is the theoretical data-carrying capacity of a network or data transmission link. When used in formulae to compare simulation results, it is the data rate that can be set for a channel in a simulation. In real network scenarios, it is the minimum speed of all the network adapters which are involved in the transmission of the data.

The term *throughput* has to be differentiated from *goodput*. The throughput specifies, how much actual data can be sent per unit of time across a network, channel or interface. The throughput is limited by the bandwidth.

The *goodput* is the throughput on the application level. Throughput is the more general term. It depends on the protocol layer where the calculation is performed. Looking at the transport layer, which is the main focus of interest, the throughput includes all the data transmitted, including retransmissions. If the network adapter does not drop packets with incorrect checksums, even they would be included. However, measuring the goodput only regards the data that arrive at the application.

Throughout this thesis the more common term *throughput* will be used, even though generally the application throughput is measured. Only in situations, when both have to be distinguished, they will be used in the sense described here.

7.2 Message Orientation versus Byte Stream Orientation

As just mentioned, the calculation of the throughput leads to different results depending on the layer. Looking at TCP, apart from retransmissions, the maximum throughput on the transport and the application layer only differ by about 2.7 % if full packets are assumed. An Ethernet frame has a maximum payload of 1500 bytes. It includes the headers of the network and the transport layer[1]. This leads to a maximum user message size of 1460 bytes if no IP or TCP options are included.

With SCTP as a message oriented protocol, the situation is different. Each chunk has its own header, which is 16 bytes in the case of a `DATA` chunk. When full size packets with a payload of 1452 bytes are sent[2], the calculation of the throughput for SCTP and TCP are alike. But when smaller user message sizes are needed, the throughput depends to a great extent on the payload size, because each chunk adds 16 bytes to the overhead.

As this results in a different maximum throughput for the message oriented protocol SCTP, two formulae will be developed, one under ideal conditions and one taking error rates and round trip times into account.

---

[1]IP header $H_{IP} = 20\ bytes$, TCP header $H_{TCP} = 20\ bytes$
[2]With SCTP header $H_{SCTP} = 12\ bytes$ and `DATA` chunk header $H_{Chunk} = 16\ bytes$.
The maximum SCTP user message size is $1500\ bytes - H_{IP} - H_{SCTP} - H_{Chunk} = 1452\ bytes$

7.3 Calculating the Maximum Throughput under Ideal Conditions

To be able to compare and validate the simulation results, a formula is needed for the maximum throughput. Assuming ideal conditions, no error rate or delay is considered.

The theoretical throughput for SCTP is calculated as follows

$$Throughput = CPP \cdot UMS \cdot PPS \tag{7.1}$$

with the average user message size per packet UMS, the number of packets per second PPS, and the number of chunks per packet CPP, which is again calculated as

$$CPP = \left\lfloor \frac{MTU - H_{IP} - H_{SCTP}}{Size_{Chunk}} \right\rfloor \tag{7.2}$$

with the IP header length H_{IP}, the SCTP common header length H_{SCTP} and the chunk size $Size_{Chunk}$ adding up to

$$Size_{Chunk} = UMS + P_{UMS} + H_{Chunk} \tag{7.3}$$

where H_{Chunk} denotes the length of the DATA chunk header, and P_{UMS} is the number of padding bytes.

The number of packets per second PPS can be computed as

$$PPS = \frac{bandwidth}{H_{IP} + H_{SCTP} + CPP \cdot Size_{Chunk}} \tag{7.4}$$

Using equation (7.2), (7.3), and (7.4) results in

$$Throughput = \left\lfloor \frac{MTU - H_{IP} - H_{SCTP}}{UMS + P_{UMS} + H_{Chunk}} \right\rfloor \cdot UMS$$

$$\cdot \frac{bandwidth}{H_{IP} + H_{SCTP} + \left\lfloor \frac{MTU - H_{IP} - H_{SCTP}}{Size_{Chunk}} \right\rfloor \cdot (UMS + P_{UMS} + H_{Chunk})} \tag{7.5}$$

Figure 7.1 shows the maximum throughput according to Equation 7.5 for SCTP associations for channel data rates of 50 Mbps and 100 Mbps, considering an MTU

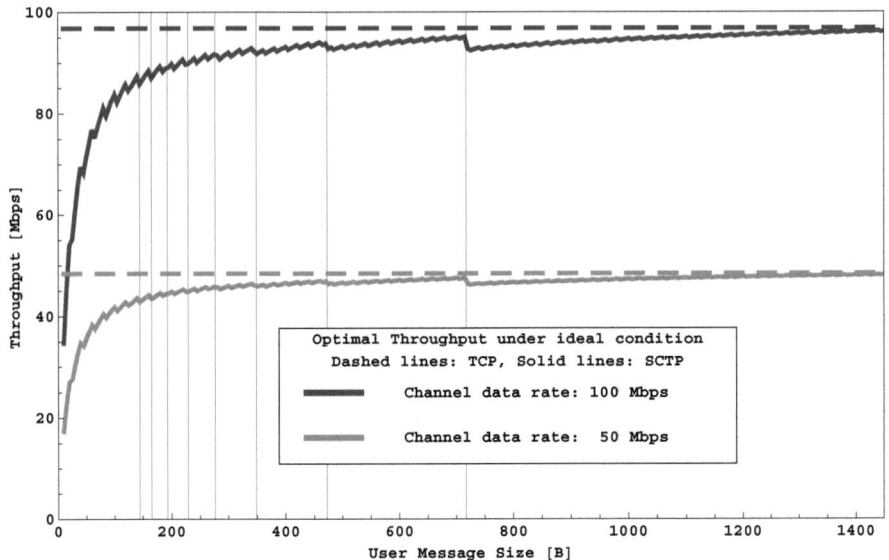

Figure 7.1: Maximum throughput for two different data rates

of 1500 bytes, 7 bytes for the PPP header, and 1 byte interframe gap, which are the values used in the simulation. The user message size ranges from 10 to 1450 bytes in 10 byte intervals. As a comparison the throughput for TCP connections is drawn. It is well to be seen, that the throughput for SCTP messages with smaller payload sizes is much less than the throughput that can be achieved with full packets, which is equal to the TCP throughput. Noticeable is also the zigzagging of the graphs, which is caused by the padding bytes, that have to be added to get the UMS 32 bit aligned. The pronounced steps are caused by the bundling boundaries, meaning that k DATA chunks with a UMS of N bytes can be assembled into one packet but only $k-1$ or less of size $N+1$ bytes. This leads to a reduction of the cumulated payload of the packet of $N-k+1$ bytes. The vertical lines show these bundling boundaries. The rightmost line indicates the step from two chunks to only one fitting into one packet.

7.4 A Rule of Thumb for the Calculation of the Throughput

The link that connects the communicating hosts is supposed to provide a certain rate. In the case of ideal conditions, when the link is free of errors and the delay is insignificant, the link can almost be fully utilized by one connection, provided the network adapter and the CPU can handle the data. However, the available bandwidth, i.e. the throughput, is influenced by the error rate and the delay of the channel. Therefore, it is of interest to find out which throughput can be expected in a specific scenario.

As the throughput is the amount of data delivered from one node to another in a certain time, it is important to look at the mechanism that influences the data transfer. The amount of data released from the sender depends to a great extent on the congestion control algorithm (see Subsection 2.2.5).

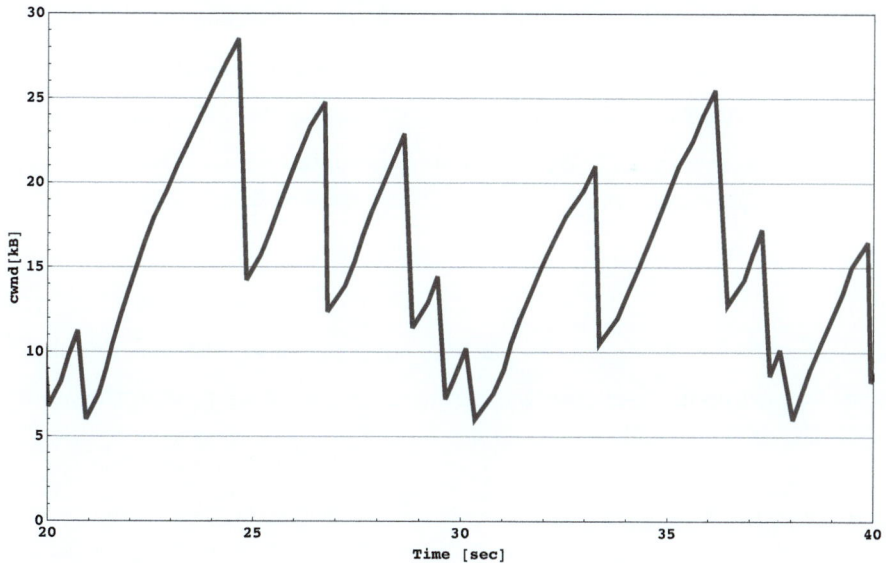

Figure 7.2: Evolution of the congestion window during a simulation

Figure 7.2 illustrates the evolution of the congestion window (cwnd) in congestion avoidance during a simulation over time. First the congestion window rises for a few seconds. Then an event occurs that causes the window to be halved, before it can rise again. This event is a packet loss, that might be caused by a bit error or a full router queue and results in a retransmission.

7.4.1 Mathis' Formula to Calculate the Throughput for TCP

In [53] Mathis generalized the behavior of the congestion window evolution and introduced a model to predict the throughput of a TCP connection when the packet loss rate P_P and the round trip time RTT were given.

$$Throughput = \frac{MSS \cdot C}{RTT \cdot \sqrt{P_P}} \qquad (7.6)$$

The parameter C is the constant of proportionality, that combines several terms that are typically constant for a given TCP implementation. As TCP is byte stream oriented, all data are transmitted in packets of the maximum segment size (*MSS*), which is the MTU reduced by the headers preceding the TCP payload. SCTP is message oriented, and therefore, the packet size depends on the message length. For payload sizes which fill up the packets, Equation (7.6) can be used for SCTP, too (see Section 7.2). But for smaller user message sizes, Mathis' model is not applicable. Another important difference to TCP is, that small messages can be bundled in SCTP. Each `DATA` chunk consists of its header of 16 bytes and the user message. Especially for small user message sizes, where the overhead takes a great proportion of the packet, the difference between *MSS* and the payload cannot be neglected. Therefore, Mathis' model must be adapted to the needs of SCTP.

7.4.2 Model Assumptions

The model that is used for the following calculations can be characterized as follows. One client is connected to one server, which runs as a discard server. The throughput is not limited by the bandwidth of the link, i.e. there is no bottleneck link. The server's receiver window is sufficiently big to read all incoming data, hence flow control is not a limiting factor. The connection is already established and the state of congestion avoidance is reached. All errors can be corrected by sending fast retransmissions. Thus no timer based retransmissions will cause the connection to leave congestion avoidance and go into slow start again.

In Subsection 2.2.5 it was pointed out that the congestion window controls the amount of data in flight. Looking at TCP, where congestion control was first introduced, the data in flight are the user messages without the headers. In SCTP, where the messages can be bundled and thus the headers can use a great proportion of the transferred data, the question arises whether the data in flight should be calculated with or without taking the headers into account. RFC 4960 defining SCTP does not specify whether the message specific headers have to be considered when updating the parameters for congestion control. Therefore, in the following subsection, a formula will be derived for the throughput without taking the headers into account, and in Subsection 7.4.4 the headers will be included and the differences to the first formula will be pointed out.

7.4.3 Calculating the Throughput without Considering the Headers

Figure 7.3 shows the evolution of the SCTP congestion window in the status of congestion avoidance. In contrast to Mathis' model, cwnd is measured in bytes instead of packets. The maximum cwnd is assumed to be X bytes. For each arriving SACK chunk the window grows by $1 MTU$. Thus in $\frac{X}{2 \cdot MTU}$ roundtrip times half the window is filled. The growth of the congestion window is stopped when a fast retransmission is triggered by the arrival of three successive SACK chunks announcing a gap in the list of TSNs.

During this time

$$\frac{X}{2} \cdot \frac{X}{2 \cdot MTU} + \frac{X}{2} \cdot \frac{X}{2 \cdot MTU} \cdot \frac{1}{2} = \frac{3 \cdot X^2}{8 \cdot MTU} \qquad (7.7)$$

bytes, which is equivalent to the area below the dotted polygon, are transmit-

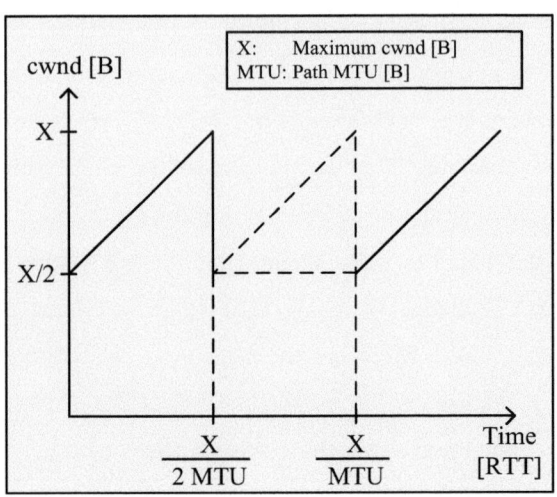

Figure 7.3: Evolution of a window cycle

ted.

Assuming a packet loss rate of P_P, $\frac{1}{P_P}$ packets will be transmitted, before an error occurs. As bytes and not packets are important here, the probability for a byte error can be calculated to be

$$P_B \simeq \frac{P_P}{D} \qquad (7.8)$$

with D corresponding to the payload of the packet.

Hence the number of error-free transmitted bytes in one cycle is $\frac{D}{P_P}$. Equating (7.7) and $\frac{D}{P_P}$ and solving for $\frac{X}{2}$ leads to

$$\frac{X}{2} = \sqrt{\frac{2 \cdot D \cdot MTU}{3 \cdot P_P}} \qquad (7.9)$$

The throughput is calculated as the ratio of the data per cycle to the time per cycle. The data comprises the actual payload without counting the headers, the time per cycle equals $RTT \cdot \frac{X}{2 \cdot MTU}$.

$$\begin{aligned}
Throughput &= \frac{data\ per\ cycle}{time\ per\ cycle} \\
&= \frac{D \cdot \frac{1}{P_P}}{RTT \cdot \frac{X}{2 \cdot MTU}} \\
&= \frac{D \cdot \frac{1}{P_P}}{RTT \cdot \frac{1}{MTU} \cdot \sqrt{\frac{2 \cdot D \cdot MTU}{3 \cdot P_P}}} \\
&= \frac{\sqrt{D \cdot MTU} \cdot \sqrt{\frac{3}{2}}}{RTT \cdot \sqrt{P_P}}
\end{aligned} \qquad (7.10)$$

7.4.4 Including the Headers in the Calculation of the Data in Flight

In congestion avoidance the congestion window increases linearly by one MSS in the case of TCP, which corresponds to one MTU for SCTP. This amount is independent from the user message size. Therefore, the cwnd in Figure 7.4 is the same as in Figure 7.3. The amount of data transferred in one RTT is dependent on the size of the headers, which results in the factor H. H is the ratio of the user message size plus the chunk header to the user message size.

$$H = 1 + \frac{H_{Chunk}}{UMS} \qquad (7.11)$$

with H_{Chunk} meaning the size of the **DATA** chunk header and UMS the average payload of a **DATA** chunk in a packet.

Following the same conclusions as in Subsection 7.4.3 results in Equation (7.12)

$$Throughput = \frac{\sqrt{D \cdot MTU} \cdot \sqrt{\frac{3}{2}}}{RTT \cdot \sqrt{P_P \cdot H}} \qquad (7.12)$$

Figure 7.5 shows a detailed comparison between Equation 7.10 and Equation 7.12 for a packet loss rate of 1 % and a link delay of 200 ms. For message sizes less than 300 bytes the throughput drops by 38 % for 10 bytes, 13 % for 50 bytes and 7 % for 100 bytes, when the headers are taken into account.

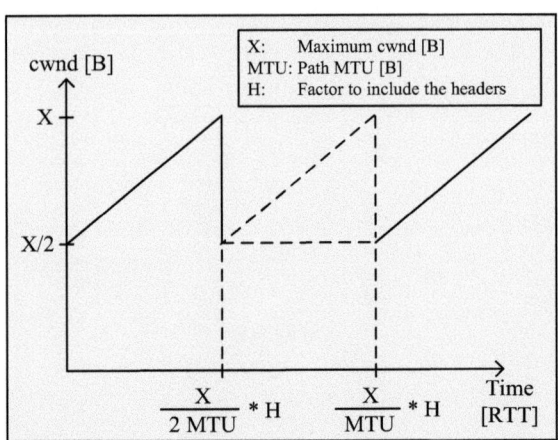

Figure 7.4: Evolution of a window cycle, when the headers are taken into account

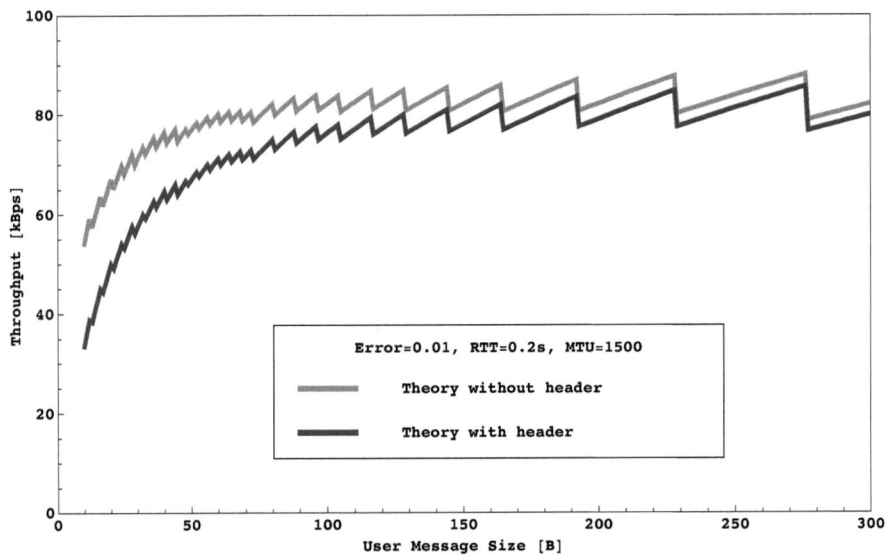

Figure 7.5: Comparison between Equation 7.10 with Equation 7.12

7.4.5 Verifying the Rule of Thumb for the Calculation of the Throughput

The rule of thumb of Equation 7.10 was verified by comparing it to the simulation. Figure 7.6 shows four different tests, each consisting of two graphs representing the

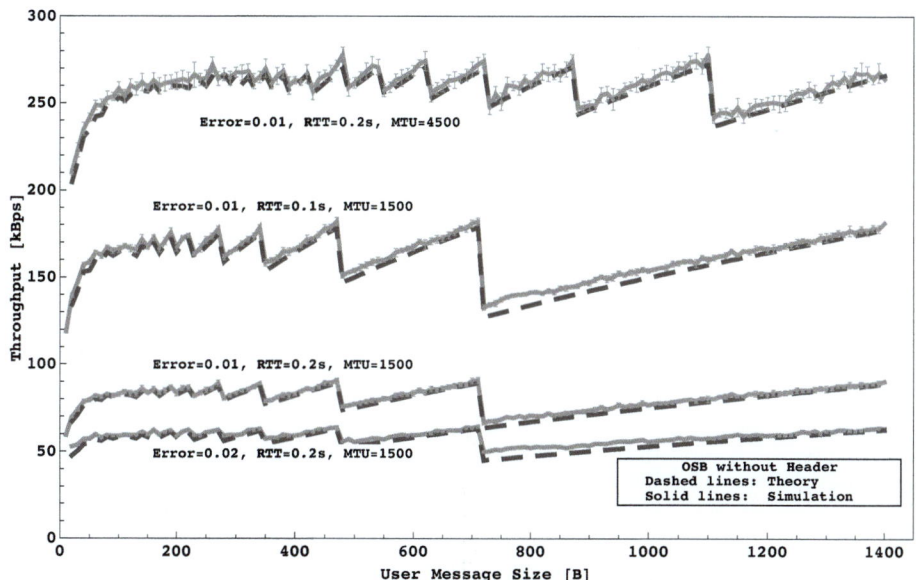

Figure 7.6: Comparison between simulation and theory for varying parameters

theoretical (dashed lines) and the simulated values (solid lines). As the throughput is dependent on the payload, user message sizes from 10 to 1450 bytes in steps of 10 bytes were chosen, and each run was performed 10 times. The figure shows the mean of these runs and the corresponding 95 % confidence intervals. The second lowest graph with an *MTU* of 1500 bytes, an *RTT* of 200 ms and a packet loss rate of 1% can be looked upon as the base run. The configuration of the others differ in just one parameter. It is well to be seen, that the simulated curves follow the theoretical ones almost exactly.

The same correspondence was obtained, when the results were compared and thereby the headers taken into account.

Chapter 8

Validating and Improving the Protocol

In the last chapters all the necessary tools were introduced, that were designed and implemented as a prerequisite to validate the behavior of SCTP, the influence of parameters and the impact of new features. In the next sections protocol specific properties will be examined and solutions will be presented for improving the protocol behavior. Thereby, the choice of subjects to investigate was for the most part motivated by observing the real implementations and their characteristics.

8.1 Comparing Kernel Implementations

8.1.1 The Test Scenario

Comparing different implementations can only lead to significant results, when the measurements are not dependent on the hardware. Therefore, six identical PCs were used with Intel Pentium-4 2.6 GHz CPU, 1 GB RAM and 2 additional Intel Pro/1000 MT Server Adapters and one PC to function as a router. Figure 8.1 shows the outline of the test scenario.

The onboard network adapters connect the PCs via a Catalyst 2950 with the rest of the lab network and then via a gateway with the internet. With the help of the two extra cards two subnetworks are established. In one they are all directly connected over a Cisco Catalyst 2970 switch. In the other they are separated by virtual Local Area Networks (VLANs). Each VLAN consists of one of these six

PCs and the router, which can be configured to run Dummynet [75] to emulate the data rate, the delay, or the packet drop rate.

As test application a discard server and a corresponding client were programmed, that can send messages of given sizes to the server. Either the number of messages has to be specified or the time, that the association should exist, before it is gracefully closed. Furthermore, parameters can be set to switch the Nagle algorithm off, define the IP address to bind to, which is always done in a multihomed scenario, configure the send and receive buffer size, and many more. Batch files help to organize a series of runs.

8.1.2 Measuring the Throughput

The first interest was directed towards the throughput. The test application writes the results of the runs to the command line, which can be redirected to a file. One entry consists of the message size, the number of messages, start and stop time, the lifetime, and the throughput.

In Figures 8.2 to 8.4 the same measurements are presented which were made over a period of three years, starting in spring 2006 with the graphs in Figure 8.2. For each curve the message size varied from 10 to 1450 bytes, a run took 60 seconds. In the lower right hand corner sender and receiver run the same operating system, but on different hosts, whereas in the other diagrams the sender stays the same and the receiver changes.

In Figure 8.2 the poor performance of the Linux implementation is striking. Especially when FreeBSD is the sender and Linux the receiver, the throughput only rises for messages greater than 1050 bytes. When Linux is the sender, the graphs do not exceed 40 MBps, whereas the values for Solaris to Linux are in most parts double as high. The Solaris implementation is very unstable, the worst oscillations occur for Solaris to Solaris.

After these measurements had been interpreted, the persons who are respon-

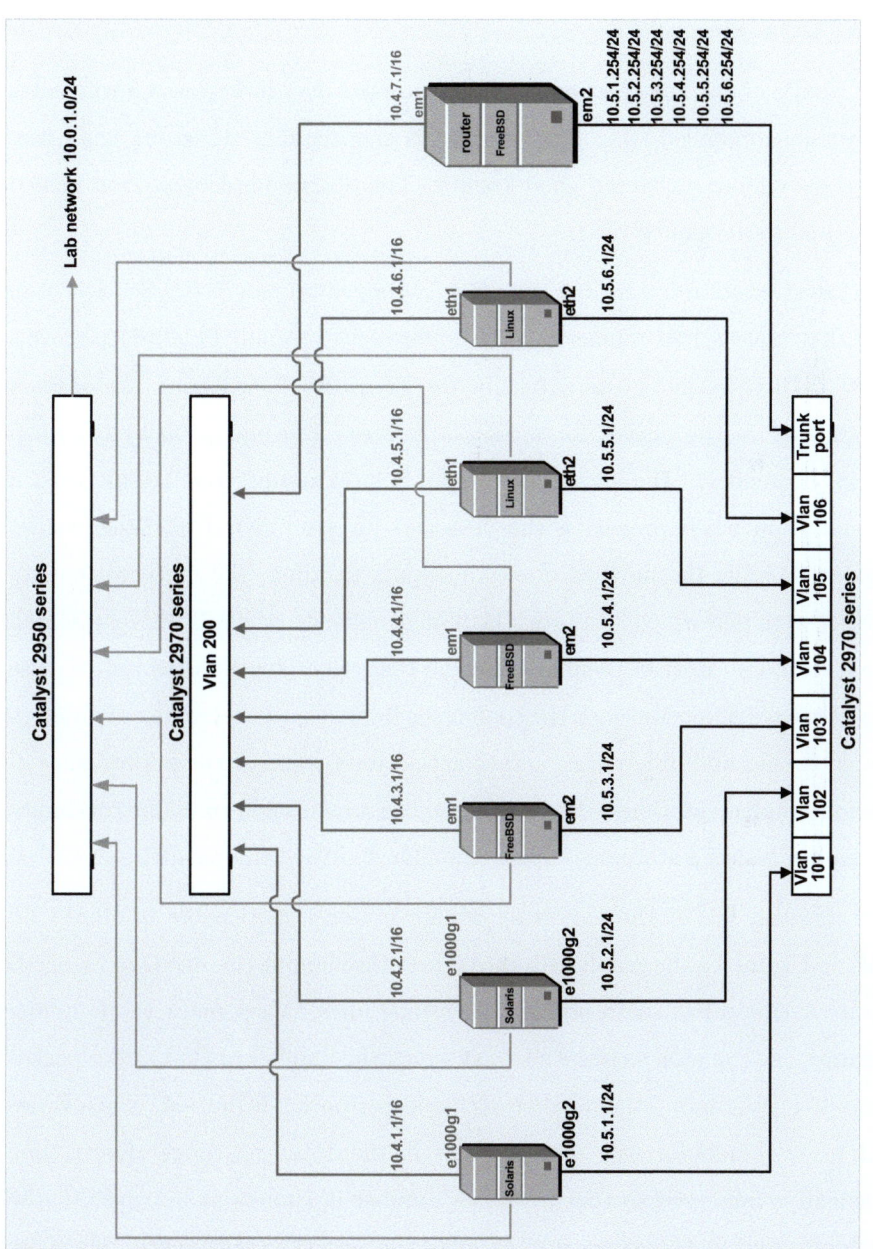

Figure 8.1: Outline of the test scenario

sible for the implementation were informed about the speculation concerning the reasons for the behavior.

The results of the next performance tests are the ones in Figure 8.3 with later kernel versions installed. The improvement is considerable. Even for small user message sizes Linux delivered good results. The Solaris implementation gained stability and performance.

The latest tests are seen in Figure 8.4. Meanwhile, new features have been added, that have a bad impact on the performance. Again FreeBSD performs the best. There seems to be a bug in the Linux implementation that causes the slight rise in the curves for messages between 700 and 1100 bytes, when Linux is the sender. The zigzagging of the Solaris graphs could result from a CPU limitation when preparing the messages for sending. The higher values are achieved, when the payload does not require padding. All measurements of Figure 8.4 were performed 10 times, the 95% confidence intervals are represented by the black bars. Most of them are so small that only a black dot is visible. The graphs of the older versions lack the confidence intervals, as they were only used to detect anomalies and differences, and to get an impression of the performance of the various implementations. But as one graph represents 145 runs, the continuity of the curves makes a statement about the plausibility of the results.

The rise and fall of the curves at certain points is noticeable in almost all graphs. In Figure 8.5 the graph with the highest throughput (FreeBSD to FreeBSD in Figure 8.4) is drawn with additional vertical lines. They mark the bundling boundaries, i.e. the user message sizes, at which the number of chunks per packet is reduced. Furthermore, the number of chunks per packet is plotted, which varies from 1 to 52 chunks for user message sizes in the displayed range. Every time the payload is increased so that a smaller number of chunks fit in a packet, the throughput drops and slowly rises again until the next change happens. The most pronounced decrease is the one from 716 to 717 bytes. Whereas a full packet holds

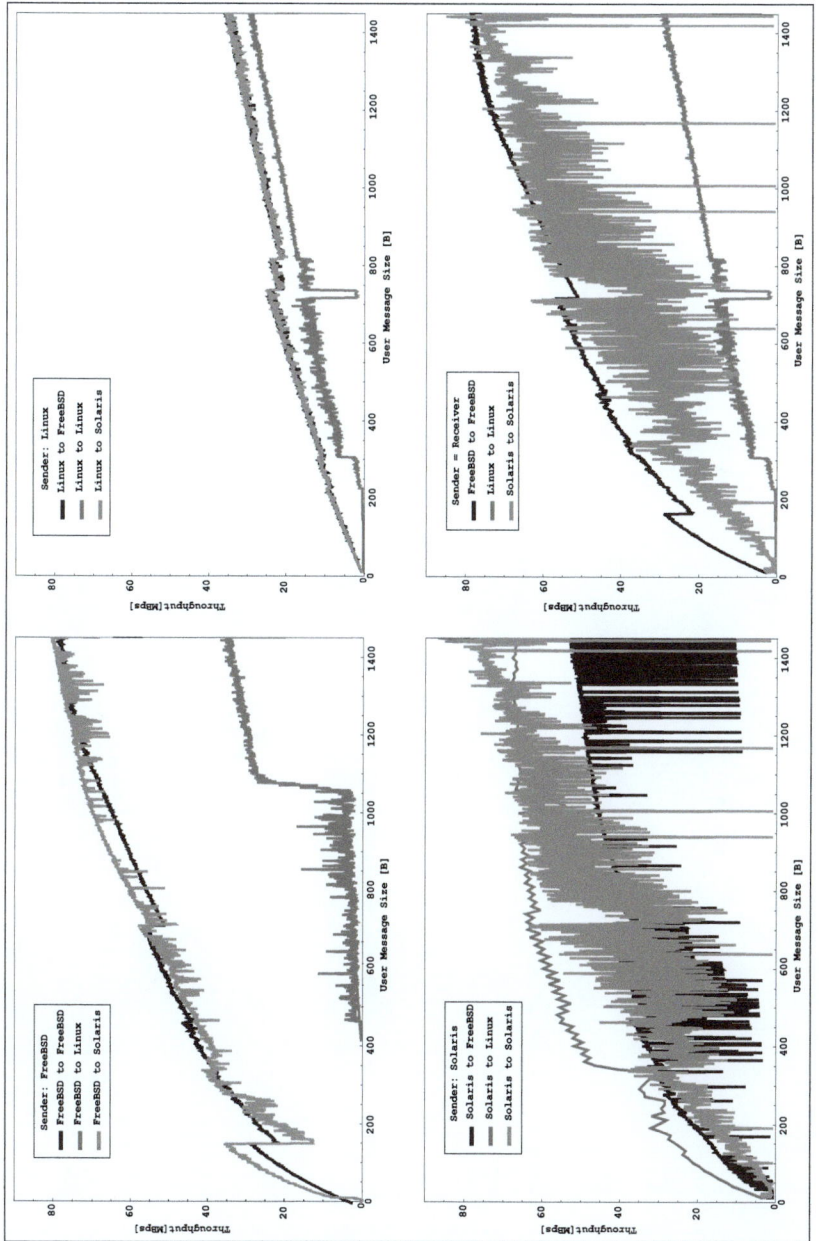

Figure 8.2: Throughput measurements version 1

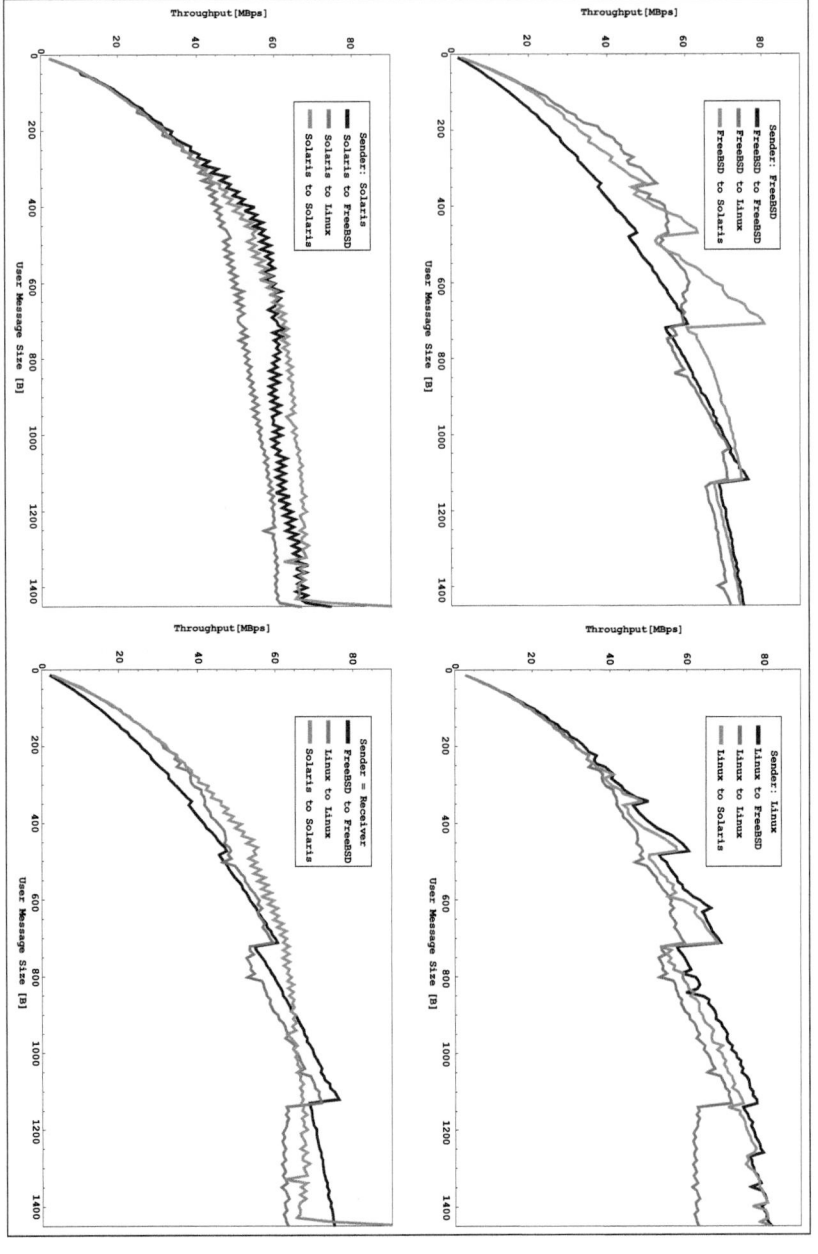

Figure 8.3: Throughput measurements version 2

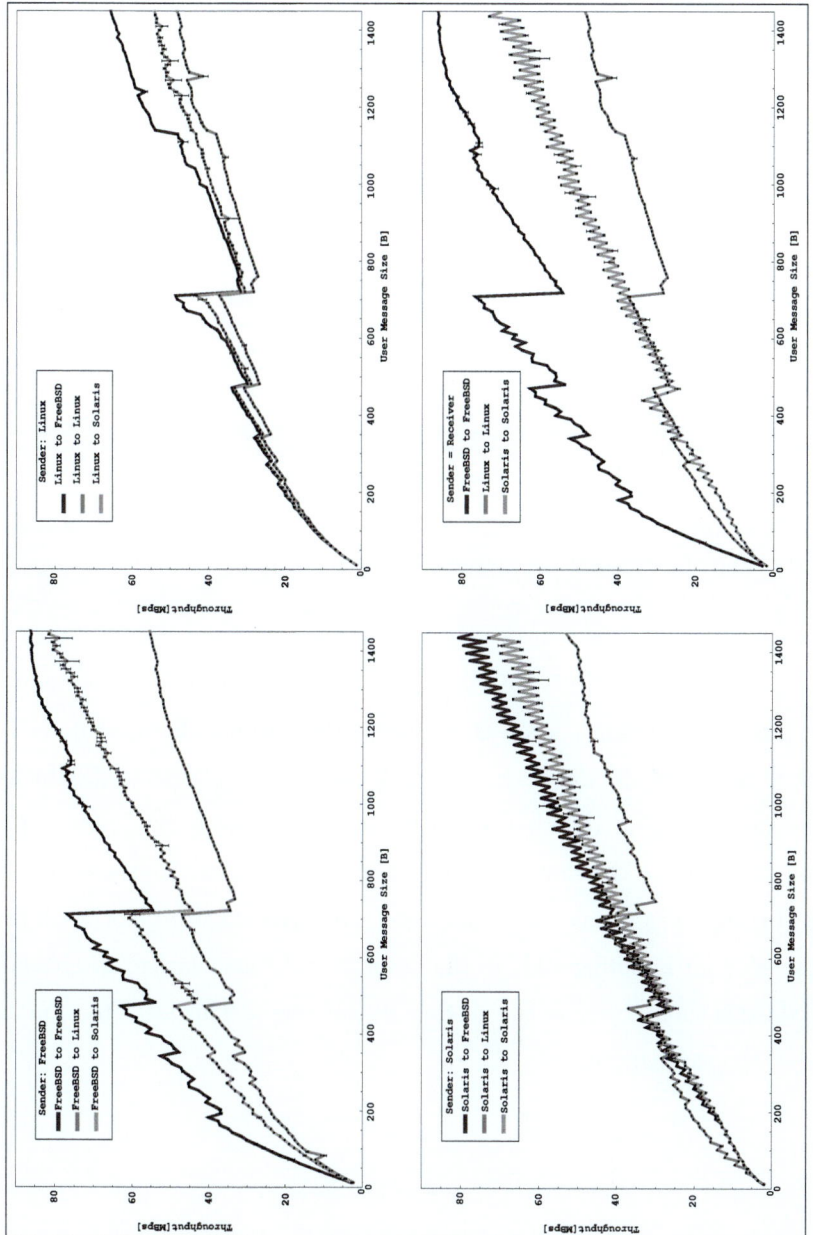

Figure 8.4: Throughput measurements version 3

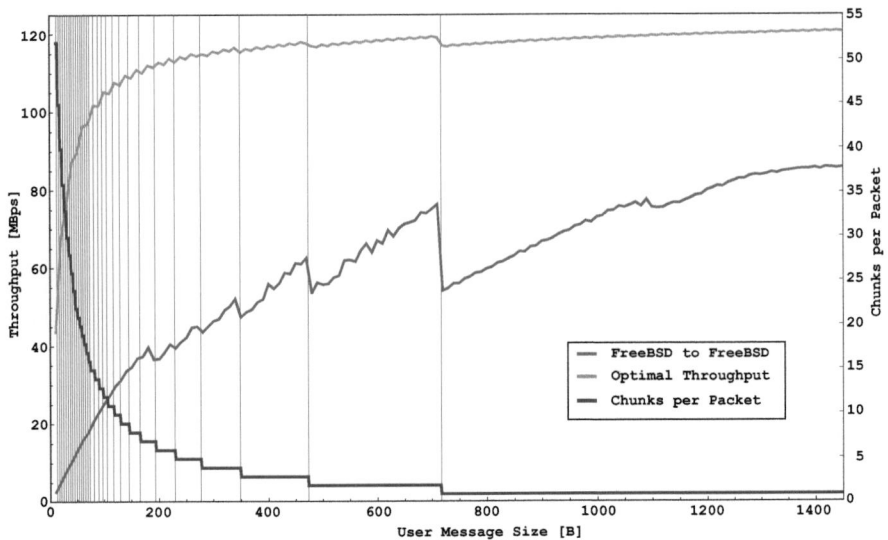

Figure 8.5: Comparison between the performance of the real implementation and the optimal throughput

1496 bytes with 1432 bytes of user messages in the first case, the 717 bytes result in packets with a total size of 768 bytes in the second case. This reduces the throughput considerably. As a comparison, the optimal throughput for a 1 Gbps link is added to the diagram. The link cannot be fully utilized, which is due to the small MTU of 1500 bytes and the low CPU speed. But more important is the difference in the slope for small user message sizes. It shows that the bundling of many DATA chunks into one packet overloads the processor, such that the time needed for bundling adds to the lifetime of the association, whereas the actual payload is small, because the headers do not count. This leads to a further reduction of the throughput.

8.1.3 Identifying Path Failures

As pointed out in Section 2.2 multihoming is a very important feature of SCTP. In RFC 4960 one path is marked as primary, while the second and all other paths are used for redundancy or for timer-based retransmissions. To make sure that the paths can be used when needed, each endpoint supervises their reachability. If an endpoint has recently sent a message successfully on a path the state is `Active`, in the other case `Inactive`.

If a path has not been used recently for user message transfer, it is called an idle path. Idle paths are supervised by sending SCTP messages containing `HEARTBEAT` chunks. The time between sending these SCTP messages is the retransmission timeout (RTO) plus the heartbeat interval ($HB_{Interval}$) which is usually 30 seconds. If no SCTP message containing a `HEARTBEAT_ACK` chunk is received within RTO, a path specific error counter $RTX^{(P)}$ is incremented. It is cleared whenever a `HEARTBEAT` chunk is answered by a `HEARTBEAT_ACK` chunk. The SCTP specification [85] states in one place, that a path is considered `Inactive`, if $RTX^{(P)} >= RTX^{(P)}_{Max}$, and in another one, that this happens if $RTX^{(P)} > RTX^{(P)}_{Max}$, where $RTX^{(P)}_{Max}$ is the maximum number of retransmissions per path with the default value of 5. The difference is one additional testing with a `HEARTBEAT` chunk. In the following the case will be considered where the path becomes `Inactive`, when $RTX^{(P)}$ exceeds $RTX^{(P)}_{Max}$ because this is what [85] intends and which has in the meantime been clarified by Errata 1440 [95].

Taking exponential backoff into account the time $T^{(P)}_{failure}$ between a failure of an `Active` path and the path becoming `Inactive` can be computed as

$$T^{(P)}_{failure} = RTX^{(P)}_{Max} \cdot HB_{Interval} + \sum_{i=0}^{RTX^{(P)}_{Max}} RTO_i \tag{8.1}$$

with

$$RTO_{i+1} = \min(RTO_{Max}, 2 \cdot RTO_i) \tag{8.2}$$

for $i \geq 0$ and

$$RTO_0 = RTO_{Min} \tag{8.3}$$

if a round trip time measurement has been performed and resulted in a value smaller or equal to RTO_{Min} or

$$RTO_0 = RTO_{Initial} \tag{8.4}$$

if no measurement has been performed.

It should be mentioned that RFC 4960 requires the replacement of RTO_i by $C_i \cdot RTO_i$ with a randomly chosen $0.5 \leq C_i \leq 1.5$ to avoid synchronization effects. C_i is not regarded in the above formulae.

Therefore, the parameters RTO_{Min}, RTO_{Max}, $HB_{Interval}$ and $RTX_{Max}^{(P)}$ determine $T_{failure}^{(P)}$. In SS7 networks requirements for $T_{failure}^{P}$ exist and are used in network dimensioning to find values for the parameters to be used. All of these parameters can be configured via the SCTP socket API defined in [88] by setting fields named `srto_min`, `srto_max`, `spp_hbinterval` and `spp_pathmaxrxt` in C-structures.

For the measurements the test scenario of Figure 8.1 was used and the path supervision of Solaris, Linux and FreeBSD compared. The test application was altered not to send data, so that only the association had to be set up and the paths supervised. For all test runs the parameter `spp_hbinterval` was set to 1000 ms, `srto_min` to 20 ms, `srto_max` to 200 ms and `spp_pathmaxrxt` to 5. The tests revealed that the three kernel implementations not only differ in the way they measure the heartbeat intervals, but also in the algorithm they use to detect the failure.

The first difference lies in the calculation of the $HB_{Interval}$. When a value for `spp_hbinterval` is set in the socket API of FreeBSD, $HB_{Interval}$ is the product of the number of paths and the given value. All other values could be set as expected. When using a dual-homed setup, the $HB_{Interval}$ is twice as large as would be expected.

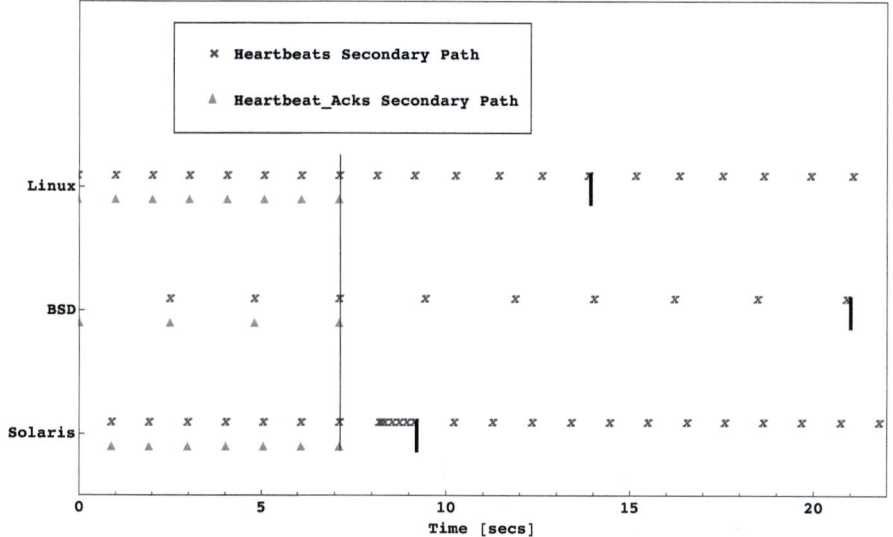

Figure 8.6: Path failure detection on FreeBSD, Linux and Solaris

To measure the time to detect a path failure the network connections for the second path at the receiver side were interrupted. Figure 8.6 shows the behavior of the three operating systems. For a better comparison the times were normalized, so that the first HEARTBEAT chunk was sent at the same time in all test runs. The interruption happened some time between the reception of the last HEARTBEAT_ACK chunk and the next HEARTBEAT chunk that was not acknowledged any more, indicated by the long vertical line. The short black bars indicate the time when the kernel informed the upper layer that the peer was not reachable any more on that path.

The Linux implementation behaved as expected and the path became Inactive after 5.7 seconds, which is what $T^P_{failure}$ gives for the considered parameters.

FreeBSD takes much longer. One reason is that $HB_{Interval}$ is 2000 ms. Another reason is that it does not add a jitter to RTO of ±50%, but always adds a random delay of 0 ms to 255 ms. So this could be described as

$$T^{(P)}_{failure,FreeBSD} = RTX^{(P)}_{Max} \cdot N \cdot HB_{Interval} + \sum_{i=0}^{RTX^{(P)}_{Max}} (RTO_i + 128) \tag{8.5}$$

where N is the number of paths. FreeBSD took 11.2 seconds, whereas the formula adds up to 11.5 seconds, which is reasonably close since random numbers are involved.

The shortest time is needed by Solaris. After the first timeout, the retransmissions are performed every RTO_i. This can be described by

$$T^{(P)}_{failure,Solaris} = HB_{Interval} + \sum_{i=0}^{RTX^{(P)}_{MAX}} RTO_i \tag{8.6}$$

which leads to a much faster detection of a path failure than in the case of the other OSs. This formula yields 1.95 seconds, whereas the measurement resulted in 2 seconds. It should be noted that Solaris uses an $RTO_{Initial}$ of 50 ms instead of a measured RTT.

As a result it is clear that the path supervision and thus the detection of path failure is to a high degree implementation dependent. Especially in the case of FreeBSD in a multihomed environment the user has to know exactly which heartbeat interval times to set in order to prevent the application from a delayed failure detection.

8.1.4 Detecting Association Failures

In addition to a path specific error counter $RTX^{(P)}$ there is also an association specific error counter $RTX^{(A)}$ which is incremented whenever a path specific one is incremented. An association fails, when $RTX^{(A)}$ exceeds an association limit $RTX^{(A)}_{Max}$ which has a default of 10.

In [85] it is recommended that the value for $RTX^{(A)}$ should not exceed the summation of $RTX^{(P)}_{Max}$ of all the destination addresses for the remote endpoint.

If this condition is not met, it can happen that all paths become `Inactive`, but the association has not failed. Then this association is called to be in a dormant state.

As the default value for $RTX_{Max}^{(A)}$ is 10 and for $RTX_{Max}^{(P)}$ 5 this is not the case in a single homed scenario, using the default values of the parameters.

The behavior of the three implementations was tested by sending data and then causing a path failure on the only path. Solaris continued sending retransmissions until the $RTX_{Max}^{(P)}$ was exceeded and the transport layer had announced the loss of the communication.

Before the association was finally aborted, FreeBSD continued sending packets containing `DATA` chunks or `HEARTBEAT` chunks, but waited until the error count for $RTX_{Max}^{(A)}$ was exceeded.

The behavior of Linux could not be judged meaningfully because a bug in the used kernel release led to unexpected retransmission behavior.

As a conclusion it is important to set the value for the $RTX_{Max}^{(A)}$ according to RFC 4960 to avoid unpredictable behavior.

8.1.5 Handling Flow Control

As flow control is a major feature of SCTP, it is supported in all available implementations. The advertised receiver window corresponds to the important resource receiver window, but the sizes are not necessarily the same. Upon arrival of a packet, the kernel has to provide memory for the storage of each chunk. Besides the actual user message, information has to be stored, like the stream sequence number, the TSN and so on. The amount of memory needed depends on the operating system.

To examine the change of the advertised receiver window in the test scenario of Subsection 8.1.1, a slow receiver was needed, that did not read arriving data immediately. Two scenarios were distinguished to see whether the implementations behaved in a different way, when gaps were reported or not.

1. The application at the receiver was completely precluded from reading.

2. The first TSN was left out. Thus a gap was created preventing SCTP from pushing data to the upper layer.

The experiment was performed by using the SCTP testtool [93] to generate SCTP packets. Test scripts were programmed with the Guile scheme implementation [29] to create the desired message flow on the sending side.

FreeBSD behaved differently in the two scenarios. In the first one, the arwnd was reduced by the payload size plus an overhead of 256 bytes, which is equal to the memory that the kernel allocates for a chunk. In the second case the arwnd was only decremented by the payload size. For small message sizes a limit of the maximum number of chunks that were accepted was observed. When this limit of 3200 chunks was reached, the arwnd was not reduced any more, and newly arrived packets were dropped. This limit is a means for the kernel to protect resources. It can be configured by the network administrator, if necessary. Hence, the number of chunks accepted by FreeBSD can be computed by

$$n = \max(3200, \left\lceil \frac{arwnd}{256 + UMS} \right\rceil) \tag{8.7}$$

In Figure 8.7 the reduction of the arwnd is illustrated for user message sizes of 10 and 30 bytes. As the maximum chunk limit is not reached for 30 bytes chunks, the window is reduced further. It is worthwhile noting that the graph "30 bytes, if a gap report is present" drops short to 1 once the arwnd falls below 3000 bytes. This is an indication that silly window syndrome avoidance is realized.

Linux showed the same behavior in both scenarios. The arwnd is always reduced by the user message size. For messages smaller than 176 bytes, only

$$n = \left\lceil \frac{arwnd \cdot 2}{176 + UMS} \right\rceil \tag{8.8}$$

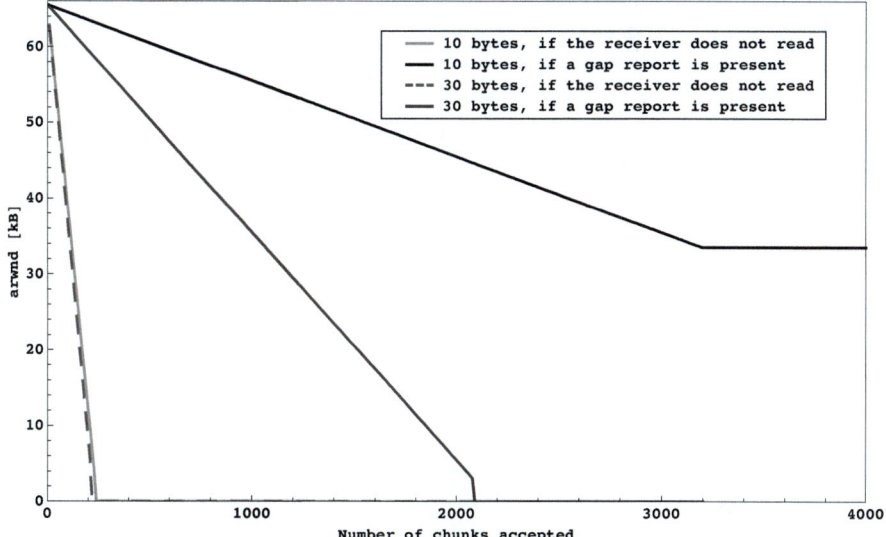

Figure 8.7: FreeBSD: Reduction of the advertised receiver window with and without real memory utilization

chunks are accepted. Then the arwnd is not reduced any more.

Solaris decrements the arwnd by the UMS until the next message does not fit any more. Thus the window is reduced to a value smaller than UMS and the number of accepted messages equals

$$n = \left\lfloor \frac{arwnd}{UMS} \right\rfloor \qquad (8.9)$$

Neither in the Linux nor in the Solaris SCTP kernel the silly window syndrome avoidance principle is implemented.

Figure 8.8 shows the number of chunks that are accepted by the transport layer for the three operating systems. For Linux the 176 bytes limit is well to be seen. It results in a very low number of accepted chunks below this value. For bigger sizes the graph of Solaris is joined. For FreeBSD the two different scenarios are shown. The limit of the number of accepted chunks is clearly recognizable. When the user message size increases, so that less than 3200 chunks fill the complete arwnd,

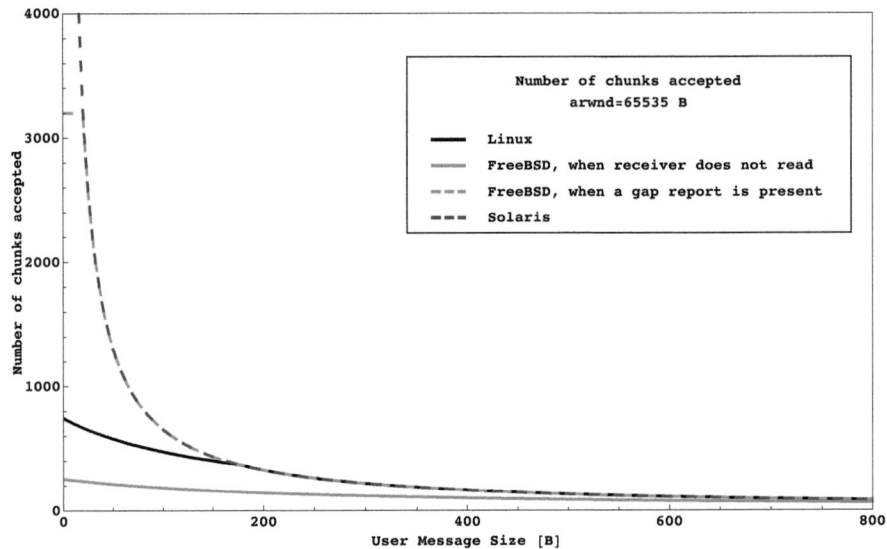

Figure 8.8: Number of chunks accepted for a given arwnd

the graph follows the one from Solaris. When FreeBSD reduces the window by the amount of bytes that it really needs for one chunk, the arwnd is exhausted very fast.

The tests reveal that in all three cases the requirements of the protocol are not met if packets with small user message sizes are sent and flow control has to be applied. Either the receiver window exhausts before the arwnd reaches zero, or a chunk number limit is reached, which is the same from the sender's point of view: Via the **SACK** chunk, the sender receives the information that the receiver is still willing to accept data, while in reality, all arriving packages are dropped.

In the next section the behavior of the implementation will be simulated to find a solution to the observed problem.

8.2 Reducing the Network Load by Adjusting the Advertised Receiver Window

8.2.1 Simulating the Behavior of the Implementations

The behavior of the implementations, especially Linux, can lead to undesirable reactions on the side of the sender. As the receiver stops acknowledging data and does not set its receiver window to zero, the sender will keep on sending data. It will supervise the path by sending HEARTBEAT chunks, that will be answered with a HEARTBEAT_ACK chunk, thus indicating that the path is active.

Keeping in mind that all implementations need extra memory to store the received user data, and that the arwnd is coupled with the receiver window, it was obvious to examine the effects of the different implementation dependent algorithms and their impact on interoperability. Therefore, the simulation was extended by a parameter for the additional memory needed per incoming chunk. The peer, trying to follow the receiver's arwnd, can apply another new parameter for the number of bytes it assumes the receiver needs for the data. A third parameter was added that was to limit the number of accepted chunks, but this concept was not further followed, because it only applied to FreeBSD.

The interoperability of the peers was tested in a simple scenario with just a client and a server that were connected via an unlimited link.

8.2.2 Simulation Results

As seen in Linux and partly in FreeBSD, the receiver reduces its receiver window by the UMS plus the additional memory, but announces an arwnd, that is only decremented by the UMS. The sender, not knowing that the arwnd does not report the true value, tries to keep track of its peer's window and adjusts the value every time a SACK chunk arrives.

To simulate this behavior and examine its impact on the network load, a slow

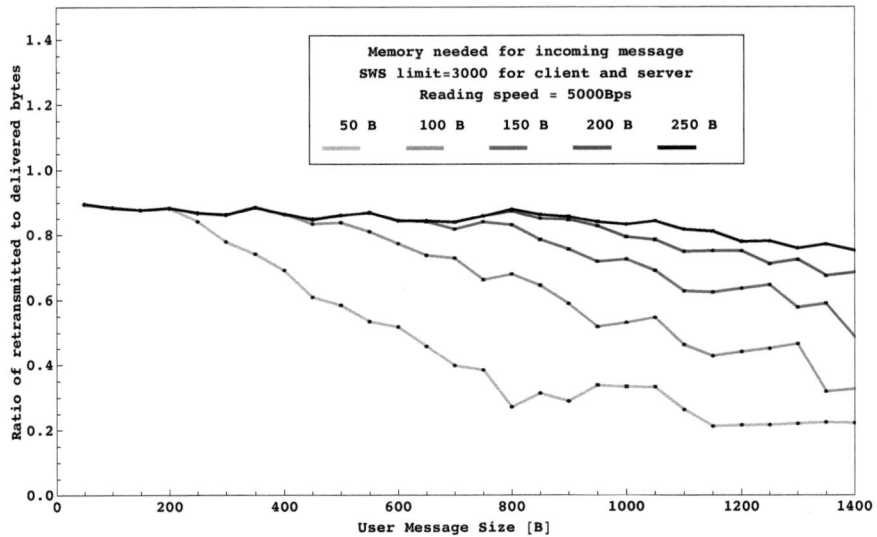

Figure 8.9: Ratio of retransmitted to delivered bytes for a varying amount of additional memory

receiver was configured by distributing the reading intervals exponentially with a mean of $\frac{UMS}{5000}$ s. After each interval, one message was read, so that approximately 5000 bytes were read per second independent from the UMS. Figure 8.9 shows the results for 50 to 250 bytes for the additional memory. Here and in the next simulations, each run was repeated 10 times. The black dots represent the 95% confidence intervals. To visualize the amount of retransmissions, the ratio of the retransmitted bytes to the data that reached the upper layer was calculated. For an overhead of 250 bytes, which is even less than the memory needed by FreeBSD, almost every chunk is retransmitted. The other graphs show that the number of retransmissions is less for larger message sizes. Nevertheless, the ideal ratio of 0 is never reached. Noteworthy is also the slight inclination of the lowest graph for larger message sizes. This can be explained as follows. When an arwnd of 0 is announced, the sender is allowed to send zero window probes in the absence of outstanding data. Zero window probes consist of one DATA chunk. The method that was chosen to simulate a slow receiver implies that the reading intervals are much smaller for small message sizes than for bigger ones. Thus the probability that data has been pushed and a new chunk can be accepted is higher for smaller messages. As a consequence the larger messages are more likely to be dropped.

Another difference between the operating systems is the implementation of the silly window syndrome avoidance algorithm. Of the three operating systems only FreeBSD has integrated this feature. In the following, the impact of its availability will be examined.

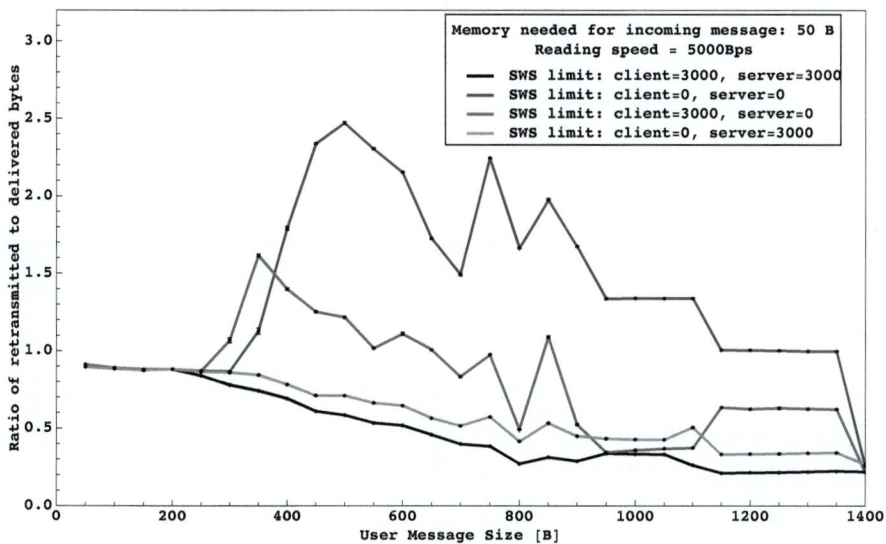

Figure 8.10: Ratio of retransmitted to delivered bytes in the absence or presence of the SWS avoidance algorithm

The presence of SWS avoidance for receiver and sender was varied by setting the SWS limit to 0 if the algorithm was not implemented, and to 3000 if it was, assuming that the endpoint acted according to the algorithm if the arwnd fell short of the threshold. Again, the ratio of retransmitted to delivered bytes was plotted. An additional memory of 50 bytes was chosen, because the graphs representing the measurements with the more realistic memory size of 250 bytes were so close together, that a graphical judgment was almost impossible. Figure 8.10 shows the results for this scenario. As the measurements of Figure 8.9 were taken with SWS enabled for sender and receiver, the lowest graph of Figure 8.10 is equal to the 50 bytes graph of Figure 8.9. It is well to be seen, that the complete absence of the SWS avoidance algorithm can lead to more than two retransmissions per chunk. The two graphs in the middle show that the implementation of the SWS avoidance algorithm on the receiving side is more important than on the sending side.

Although the confidence intervals reveal that the measured values are not far apart the graphs show an unsteady course. The following Figure 8.11 should clarify the reason for the run of the curves. The darker graph shows the same simulation results as the top graph of Figure 8.10. This time the UMS varied in 10 byte intervals. The lighter graph shows the number of packets that can still fit in the arwnd that is the last to be announced when the receiver starts dropping packets. If for example the receiver announces an arwnd of 5000 bytes although it is actually 0, the sender will send data nonetheless.

The lower graph is calculated according to Equation 8.10. $arwnd_{initial}$ is the arwnd that is announced in the INIT or INIT_ACK chunk, CPP the number of chunks per packet as in Equation 7.2, and M the additional memory needed by the receiver. The numerator calculates the number of chunks that are left by reducing the number of announced chunks by the ones that really fit in the arwnd.

$$Number\ of\ packets = \left\lfloor \frac{\left\lceil \frac{arwnd_{initial}}{UMS} \right\rceil - \left\lceil \frac{arwnd_{initial}}{UMS+M} \right\rceil}{CPP} \right\rfloor \quad (8.10)$$

It is well to be seen that for values higher than 450 bytes the two graphs rise and fall synchronously. For smaller values than 400 bytes the amount of data to be sent is bound by the congestion window, which normally rises in these scenarios not higher than 7000 bytes. So, although the arwnd might be more than 10000 bytes, the sender may send at most 7000 bytes.

As the payload to header ratio is even worse for small messages if they are

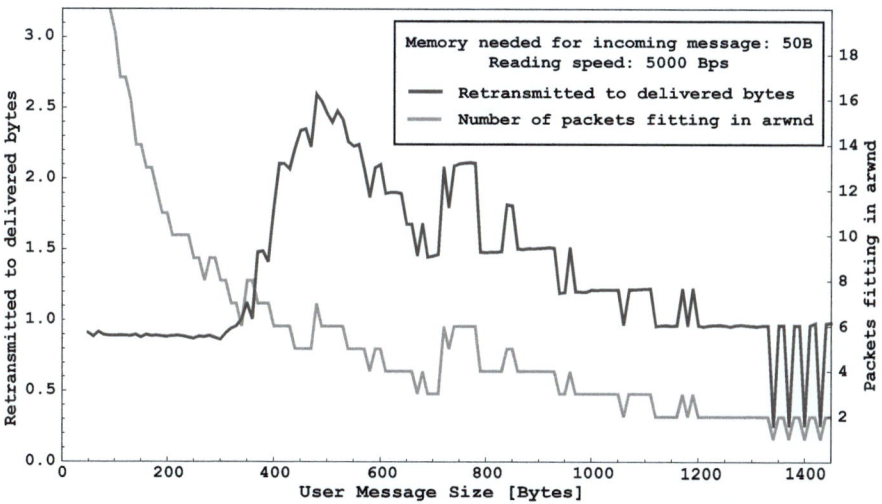

Figure 8.11: Comparison of the course of the ratio of retransmitted to delivered bytes to the number of packets fitting in the arwnd

sent individually, bundling achieves better results. The Nagle algorithm [59] is a feature, first introduced in TCP by John Nagle, to improve the efficiency of IP based networks by preventing the sending of small packets if there are still data in flight. For SCTP this means that chunks have to be bundled, until the next chunk does not fit in the packet any more, unless there are no bytes outstanding. Applying this algorithm can lead to delaying the sending of data. To examine the impact of the Nagle algorithm on the network load, the same runs as in Figure 8.10 were carried out and the execution of the Nagle algorithm was disabled. The results showed that the application of the Nagle algorithm had no influence on the retransmission behavior. Further studies showed that the Nagle algorithm has no impact on the network load if the sender is sending constantly, thus being always able to fill a complete packet. In Subsection 8.4.2 a scenario will be discussed where the use of the Nagle algorithm has a negative impact.

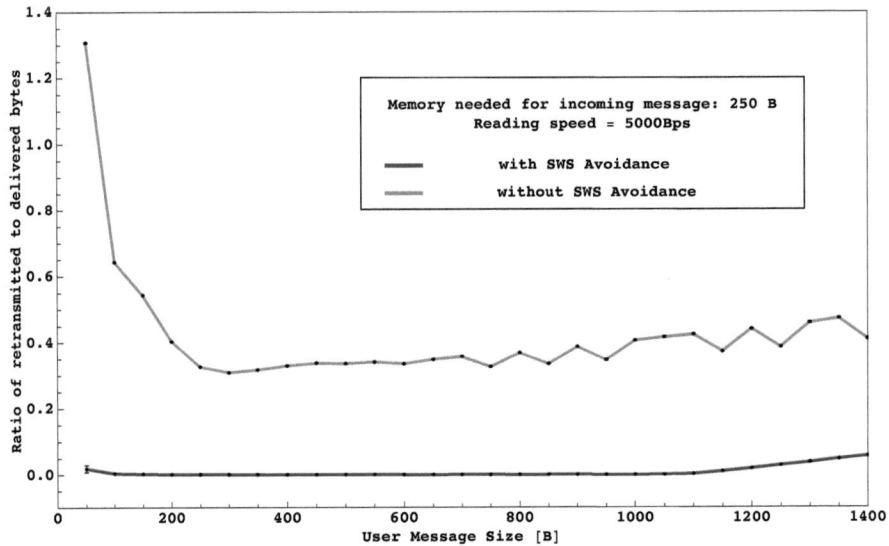

Figure 8.12: Ratio of retransmitted to delivered bytes, if the size of the real receiver window is announced

8.2.3 Solutions

The first idea to solve the problem of undesirable retransmissions was to notify the sender about the amount of additional memory needed. Thus, the sender was to be able to predict the reduction of the arwnd more exactly. However, simulation runs with this feature did not lead to significantly better results.

The best outcomes were achieved by "telling the truth". Just like in FreeBSD, when the receiver did not read, the arwnd was reduced by the payload and the additional memory. Even if the sender cannot follow the peer window closely, the regular updates are enough to guide the sender.

Figure 8.12 shows the retransmitted to delivered bytes ratio for an additional memory of 250 bytes when SWS avoidance is present on both sender and receiver or on none. It is well to be seen that there are almost no retransmissions needed, if SWS avoidance is applied. Even for the worst case that SWS avoidance is not present the results are much better. The reason for the increase of the graph for larger user message sizes has been explained in the last subsection.

As a consequence, the strategy for implementors to avoid retransmissions in case of flow control is to set the size of the advertised receiver window to the size of the real receiver window. Thus, it is not possible that the receiver window runs out of memory before the arwnd reaches zero.

RFC 4960 [85] states that the receiver decrements the arwnd by the number of bytes received and buffered. As this is not a MUST, the implementations can be altered in accordance with the RFC.

8.3 The Influence of Byte-Counting on the Network Load

8.3.1 Counting Outstanding Bytes

In Subsection 7.4.4 it was pointed out that for message oriented protocols the throughput can depend on the way the outstanding bytes are calculated. Especially for small UMS the share of the DATA chunk headers in the complete message cannot be neglected. Therefore, the way the outstanding bytes that limit cwnd are counted should be examined.

Looking at an SCTP packet containing several DATA chunks, the sum of user data in a packet can vary significantly with the size of the individual payloads assuming the same packet length.

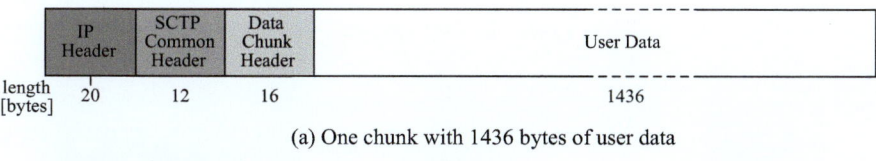

Figure 8.13: IP Datagrams containing SCTP DATA chunks

In Figure 8.13(b) the packet contains 33 `DATA` chunks with 28 bytes of user data each, adding up to 924 bytes of user data compared to 1436 bytes in the packet in Figure 8.13(a). Both packets have an overall size of 1484 bytes. Whereas the overhead is just 3% in (a) the headers add up to 37% in (b) and can be more than 60% for even smaller user message sizes.

Therefore, it has to be distinguished between the amount of data that is injected into the network and the user data that arrive at the application layer. Whereas the first has a direct impact on the network load, the second results in the goodput. Both depend on the number of packets (8.11), that are allowed by the cwnd.

$$NoOfPackets = \left\lceil \frac{cwnd - OSB}{CPP \cdot Size_{Chunk}} \right\rceil \quad (8.11)$$

The number of the chunks per packet (CPP) is calculated (see also (7.2) and (7.3)) as

$$CPP = \left\lfloor \frac{MTU - H_{IP} - H_{SCTP}}{UMS + P_{UMS} + H_{Chunk}} \right\rfloor \quad (8.12)$$

The average user message size (UMS) per packet and the corresponding padding bytes (P_{UMS}) feature the variable parts of the packets.

The outstanding bytes (OSB) depend on the number of outstanding chunks (OC) and the average UMS with or without including the headers.

$$OSB^+ = OC \cdot Size^+_{Chunk} \quad (8.13)$$

$$OSB^- = OC \cdot Size^-_{Chunk} \quad (8.14)$$

The size of the bundled chunks can be calculated with header

$$Size^+_{Chunk} = UMS + P_{UMS} + H_{Chunk} \quad (8.15)$$

and without header.

$$Size^-_{Chunk} = UMS \quad (8.16)$$

Calculating the size of a packet ($Size_P$), the headers for IP (H_{IP}) and SCTP (H_{SCTP}) and the size of the DATA chunks ($Size^+_{Chunk}$) including the overhead have to be considered.

$$Size_P = H_{IP} + H_{SCTP} + CPP \cdot Size^+_{Chunk} \tag{8.17}$$

To compute the number of bytes that are induced into the network and which arrive at the receiver, four different cases are possible:

- Network load taking the header into account

$$Bytes^+_{SCTP} = \left\lceil \frac{cwnd - OSB^+}{CPP \cdot Size^+_{Chunk}} \right\rceil \cdot Size_P \tag{8.18}$$

- Bytes at the application layer if the header had been taken into account

$$Bytes^+_{App} = \left\lceil \frac{cwnd - OSB^+}{CPP \cdot Size^+_{Chunk}} \right\rceil \cdot CPP \cdot Size^-_{Chunk} \tag{8.19}$$

- Network load without taking the header into account

$$Bytes^-_{SCTP} = \left\lceil \frac{cwnd - OSB^-}{CPP \cdot Size^-_{Chunk}} \right\rceil \cdot Size_P \tag{8.20}$$

- Bytes at the application layer if the header had not been taken into account

$$Bytes^-_{App} = \left\lceil \frac{cwnd - OSB^-}{CPP \cdot Size^-_{Chunk}} \right\rceil \cdot CPP \cdot Size^-_{Chunk} \tag{8.21}$$

The following example should illustrate the significance of the different ways of calculating the amount of data to be sent. Assuming a cwnd of 20,000 bytes and 8 packets to be outstanding, Table 8.1 shows the different values for the byte counting on the transport and the application layer for user message sizes of 30 and 60 bytes.

The difference between the scenarios with and without header is significant. For the same cwnd and a user message size of 30 bytes the amount of data on the link is increased by 150%, if the header is not taken into account. For 60 bytes

	UMS=30 bytes		UMS=60 bytes	
	+	-	+	-
SCTP	8832	22080	8856	14760
APP	5400	13500	6840	11400

Table 8.1: Amount of bytes on the transport and application layer, when calculating the outstanding bytes with and without header for user message sizes of 30 and 60 bytes

the increase is still 67%. As cwnd grows, even more data may be transmitted if the header is not taken into account.

As one property of fairness is the evenly distribution of the link bandwidth, the behavior of associations with and without header inclusion will be examined in more detail.

8.3.2 TCP-friendliness

When SCTP was designed, one of the major goals was to guarantee TCP-friendliness. In RFC 2309 [8] a *TCP-friendly* or *TCP-compatible* flow is defined as follows:

> A TCP-compatible flow is responsive to congestion notification, and in steady state it uses no more bandwidth than a conforming TCP running under comparable conditions.

Since TCP is a byte stream oriented protocol, all packets are filled with enough user data to result in full sized link layer frames if sufficient data are provided in the send queue. The overhead consists of the IP header and the TCP header, which is independent from the user message size.

Although SCTP and TCP implementations, which were inspected for the differences in the handling of header bytes, are readily available, the solutions will be based on simulation results. Since some implementations have bugs that substantially influence the measurement results, it was decided to use a simulation for the measurements instead of waiting for the bugfixes to be included in the implementations.

8.3.3 Simulation Scenario

Although TCP is integrated in the INET framework [104], not all optional TCP features that are common nowadays, like Appropriate Byte Counting (ABC) [2] or delayed acknowledgments [3], are implemented. However, some of these features are mandatory for SCTP and are, therefore, implemented in the INET SCTP model. Hence, a meaningful comparison between SCTP and TCP is not possible with INET. Nevertheless, TCP-friendliness for flows with and without counting the header bytes should be examined. Therefore, an SCTP association transporting user data messages of 1452 bytes length was used to mimic the behavior of a state-of-the-art TCP connection. From a congestion control perspective, such an SCTP association behaves identical to a TCP connection. When talking about including or excluding the header, the DATA chunk header of 16 bytes is always referred to.

Figure 8.14 shows the scenario for the simulation. The SCTP client sends data with configurable user message sizes from 12 to 204 bytes to the SCTP server. As the impact of the header bytes is only significant for small message sizes, longer messages are not regarded. To exclude effects resulting from padding, i.e. a zigzagging of the graph, multiples of 4 were chosen as UMS. The TCP-like client only sends full packets with a payload of 1452 bytes, the headers are not included. Including them does not change the result, since the difference is neglectable for large user messages. The connections have to share a bottleneck link with a data rate of 1 Mbps. The router queues behave according to the Random Early Detection (RED) queuing discipline. This strategy, which drops packets randomly, was recommended by Floyd and Jacobson [25] to mitigate 'phase effects', which can result in the discrimination of one connection.

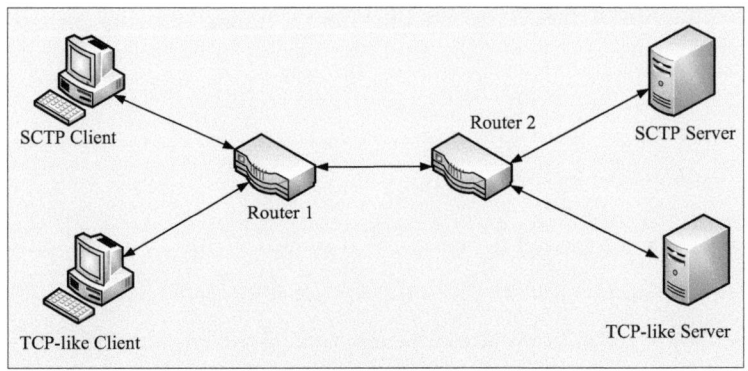

Figure 8.14: Testbed

To test the behavior with and without counting the header bytes, the SCTP simulation has been extended by two parameters, *osbWithHeader* and *padding*. They are boolean variables that can be set to true, if the header and the padding bytes should be taken into account for the congestion control calculations. Tests showed that the influence of the padding bytes is not significant. Therefore, all described simulations were run with either both variables true or false.

8.3.4 Fairness on the Transport Layer

The SCTP association and the "TCP-like" association have to share the bandwidth equally. This means that all bytes that have been sent over the network have to be counted, including the retransmitted bytes. To assure that the same time interval is chosen and the associations have reached a steady state, a start and stop time can be configured for counting the bytes that have arrived at the server. The timers were set for the measurement to start after 50 s and continue for 400 s. As the ratio of additional header bytes to the user message size is only significant for small payload sizes, user messages from 12 to 204 bytes length in 12 byte intervals were chosen. Each simulation run was repeated 100 times with different seeds for the random numbers to ensure validity. Figure 8.15 shows the throughput on the transport layer. The short vertical bars represent the 95% con-

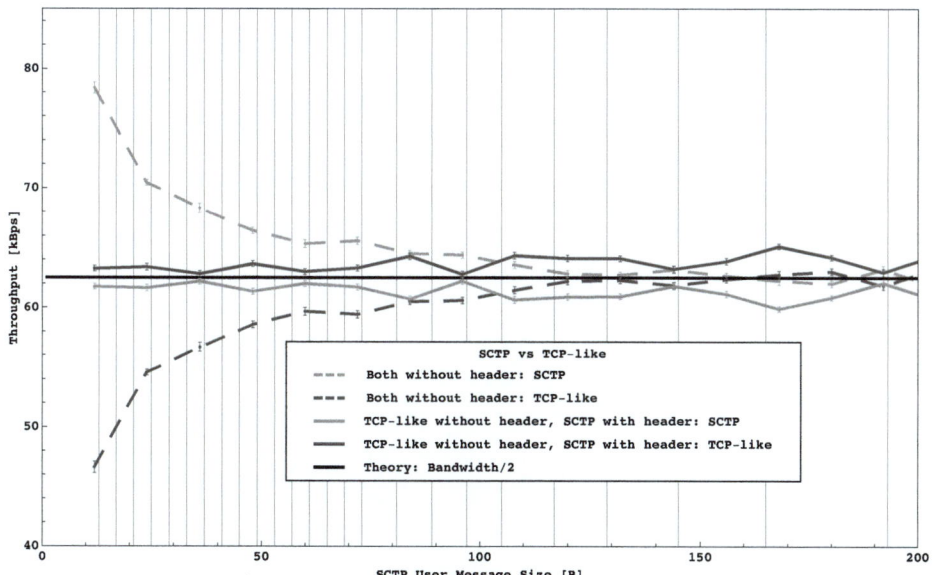

Figure 8.15: Throughput on the transport layer

fidence intervals. The graphs are symmetrical to the theoretical bandwidth, which implies that together they fully utilize the link. It is obvious that the associations that calculate the outstanding bytes with header share the link, symbolized by the straight black line, equally. Yet, it is noticeable that the graphs perform an axis-symmetric wave movement. The reason are the bundling boundaries, mentioned in 7.3, that result in a temporary decrease of the throughput. As the TCP-like client only sends full packets it is not affected by bundling. Hence, whenever the throughput of the SCTP client is decreased due to passing a bundling boundary, the TCP-like client takes over the link bandwidth and thus increases its throughput.

The outer pair of graphs show the throughput, if the header is not taken into account. The SCTP client is not fair towards the TCP-like client. It utilizes the link much more intensively than the TCP-like client, thus taking bandwidth from the other connection.

8.3.5 Fairness on the Application Layer

The behavior on the transport layer has an influence on the throughput on the application layer (goodput). Therefore, the same setup as in the last section was chosen and the bytes were counted that arrived at the user level of the servers during a predefined time period. Figure 8.16 shows the graphs when the header is

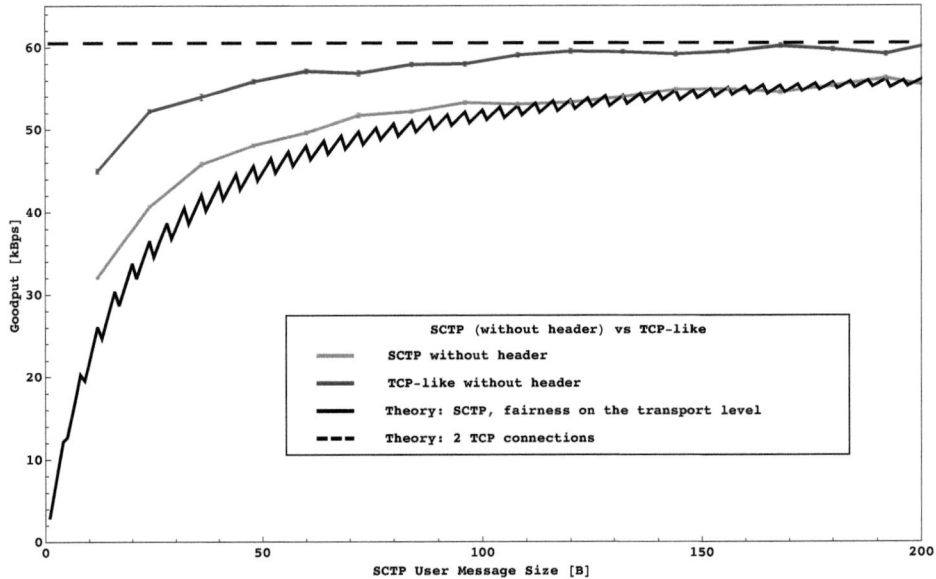

Figure 8.16: Goodput, if the header is not taken into account

not taken into account. Although the TCP-like client achieves a higher goodput than the SCTP client using the different message sizes, the goodput is much lower than it should be. As Figure 8.15 indicated, the SCTP client takes over so much bandwidth that the TCP goodput is considerably reduced. The two theoretical graphs show the ideal case, where the SCTP client (lowest graph) and the TCP-like client (top graph) share the link equally.

The graphs in Figure 8.17 illustrate the results if the header is taken into account. Now the curves show the desired behavior and fit the theoretical graphs.

As a result it can be postulated that all implementations of message oriented

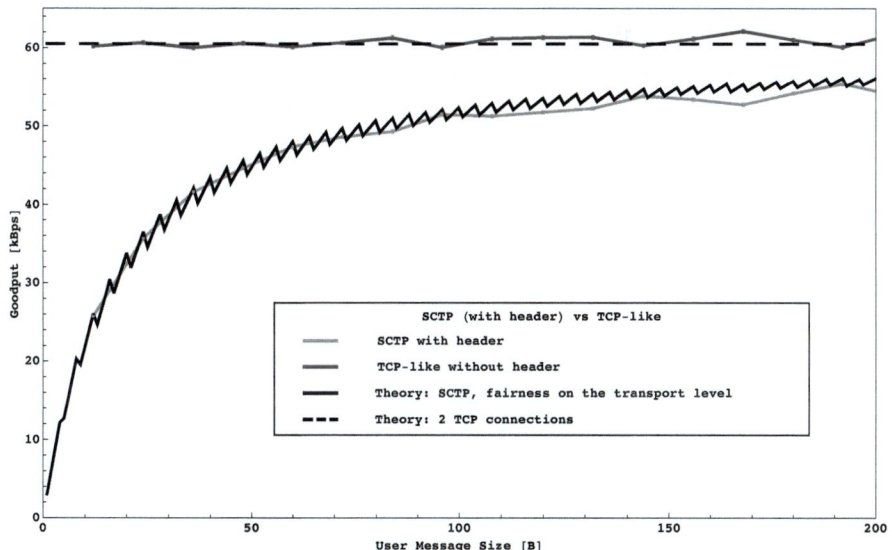

Figure 8.17: Goodput, if the header is taken into account

protocols with bundling should take the headers into account, when calculating the outstanding bytes, in order to be TCP-compliant.

8.4 Improving the Handling of Acknowledgments

In Section 2.2 it was mentioned that only after every second packet a SACK chunk is sent to acknowledge the data. To increase efficiency, it is recommended in the RFCs 1122 and 2581 [3, 9], that acknowledgments should be sent for every second full-sized segment within 500 ms of the arrival of the first unacknowledged packet. This feature has been introduced in RFC 813 [14] and is known as "delayed ACK". It is integrated in all TCP implementations. The time to delay the acknowledgments can be tuned by changing a kernel parameter.

This concept has been adopted by SCTP, too, but not in all cases it is beneficial to send SACK chunks only after every second packet. Therefore, SCTP does not delay the acknowledgment for the first received packet containing a DATA chunk, and in cases where gap ack blocks or duplicate TSNs are present, or the receiver has initiated the shutdown of the association. It is important to note, that all these exceptions are defined for the receiver of the `DATA` chunks.

However, there is no way a sender can signal the receiver that it needs the reception of a `SACK` chunk as soon as possible. Therefore, a flag was introduced in the `DATA` chunk to indicate, that this chunk has to be acknowledged right away at arrival. This extension was called SACK-IMMEDIATELY and the corresponding flag I-Bit [97]. The sender of a `DATA` chunk sets a bit in the flags field of the `DATA` chunk header with the intension that the receiver of this chunk does not delay the sending of the corresponding `SACK` chunk.

In the following sections, it will be pointed out how applications can benefit from this extension and describe several scenarios and the impact, the use of the I-Bit can have on throughput and resources. It will be distinguished between scenarios where the kernel triggers the use of the I-Bit and those where the application is solely responsible.

8.4.1 Kernel Initiates the Use of the I-Bit

8.4.1.1 Fairness Considerations

To show the influence of the delayed ack timer on the throughput on the application layer, the simulation network in Figure 8.18 was set up.

`Client 1` is connected to `Server 1` and `Client 2` to `Server 2`. Both clients send full packets with a payload of 1452 bytes. `Client 1` is configured to send delayed `SACK` chunks for every second packet, but the timer is varied from 0 to 500 ms in 10 ms intervals. `Client 2` sends selective acknowledgments for each packet, so no delayed ack timer is set. The connections share a bottleneck link with a data rate of 100 Mbps. No delay or bit error rates are configured.

The solid graphs of Figure 8.19 show the performance results of the runs. Each run was repeated 100 times. The vertical bars show the 95% confidence intervals.

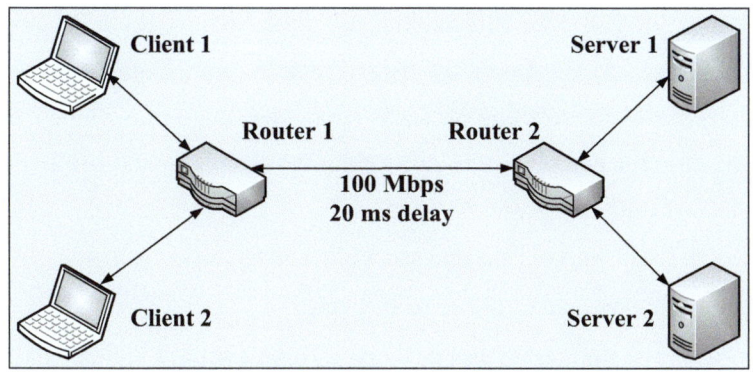

Figure 8.18: Scenario with bottleneck link

It is obvious that the associations without delayed SACK chunks have a 10% higher

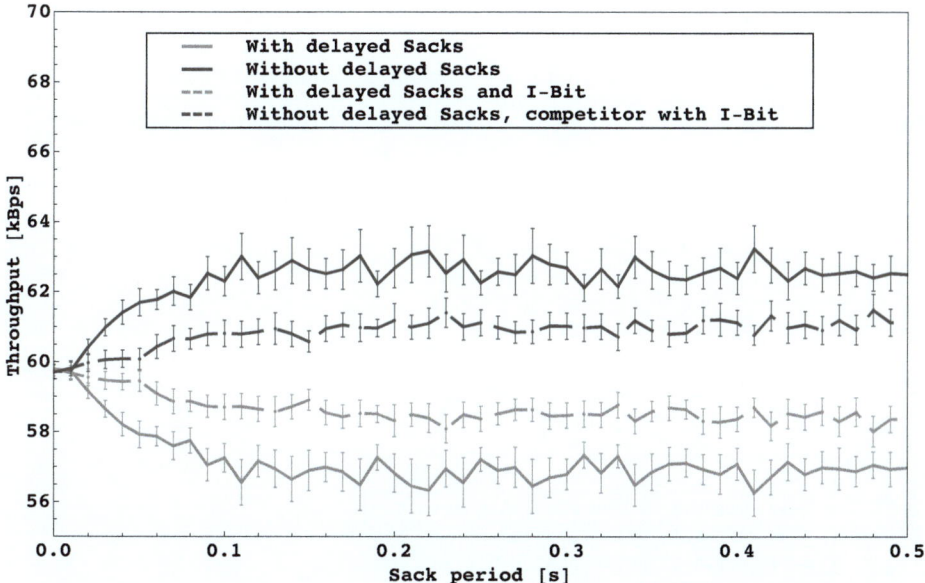

Figure 8.19: Delayed SACKs with and without SACK-IMMEDIATELY option

throughput than the ones without delayed SACK chunks. From 100 ms on there is no increase any more. Associations, which are configured with the default delay time of 200 ms, fall in this category.

To find out the reason for this difference in performance, the RTT of the `DATA` chunks was measured. Whenever the delayed SACK-timer expired, meaning that in the last, e.g. 200 ms only one packet arrived, the congestion window suddenly dropped, leaving the competitor the possibility to send more data. Further investigation showed that the reason for the delay was a lost packet that was the last in a flight of at least two packets that were allowed by cwnd. A loss of consecutive packets led to an even longer phase to recover.

For the tests the simulation was changed to send the `DATA` chunk, that was the last in the group of packets before cwnd was exhausted, with the I-Bit set.

The results are reflected by the dashed pair of graphs in Figure 8.19. The difference in throughput between the connections with and without delayed SACKs has decreased to 4%.

This strategy to set the I-Bit for the last `DATA` chunk before the cwnd forbids the sending of more data, can also be beneficially used on error-prone links.

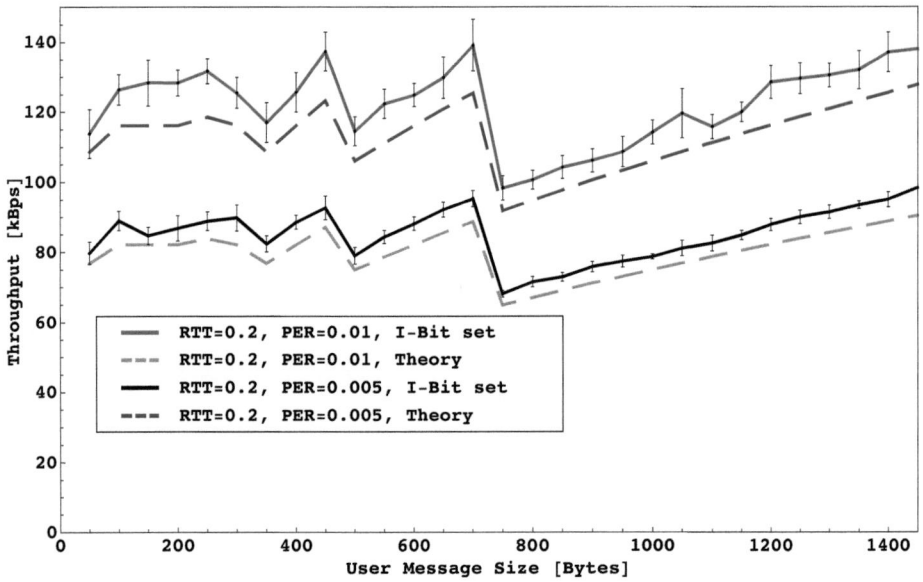

Figure 8.20: Delayed SACKs with and without I-Bit on error-prone link

Figure 8.20 compares the results for links with a packet error rate of 1% and 0.5%. The gain in throughput is up to 10%, if the I-Bit is set in the last packet, before the cwnd is exhausted.

8.4.1.2 The sender has reduced its RTO

As mentioned in Section 2.2, SCTP was designed as transport protocol for signaling networks. These networks have a high demand concerning availability and fault tolerance. A packet should not need more than 800 ms to reach the receiver including necessary retransmissions [38]. Therefore, RTO and the heartbeat timer have to be configured according to the measurement results in [48], for instance 10 ms for RTO_{Min} and 1 s for the Heartbeat Interval Timer. As a consequence, timer based retransmissions will be sent already after 10 ms if the sender has not received an acknowledgment for the message. If the sender has no influence on the configuration of the parameters on the receiver side, the fact that the delayed acknowledgment timer is still set to the default value of 200 ms can lead to the graph in Figure 8.21.

Every 400 ms a **DATA** chunk is sent. After RTO milliseconds the timer expires and a timer based retransmission is initiated on the second path. If the sender has no influence on the configuration of the parameters on the receiver side and the receiver has not changed the default values, timer based retransmissions will be initiated on the second path after 10 ms. On the reception of the second packet, a **SACK** chunk will be sent immediately. The value for RTO is doubled, until the next **HEARTBEAT** chunk is sent and acknowledged to prove the activity of the path, which results in the resetting of the path failure counter and the value for RTO.

A solution for this unnecessary sending of timer based retransmissions is the setting of the I-Bit in the **DATA** chunk to prompt the receiver to send a **SACK** chunk without delay. Every time the sender has reduced its RTO to a value less than the default delay acknowledgment time, the I-Bit should be set.

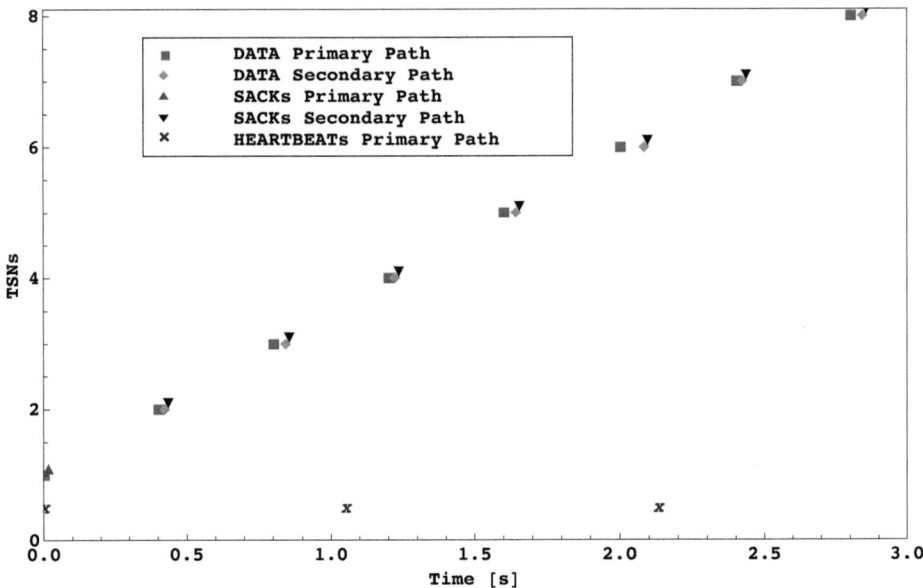

Figure 8.21: Retransmission behavior when parameters on sender and receiver do not match

8.4.1.3 Short-term associations

Another issue that can force an association to be delayed is the shutting down of an association. When the application hands its last message down to the transport layer, the SCTP status changes to SHUTDOWN-PENDING. Then SCTP waits until all messages are sent and acknowledged, until a `SHUTDOWN` chunk is sent. This time it might be the acknowledgment of the last chunk that can cause the delay.

Thinking of short-term associations that occur, for instance, when DNS requests are sent over SCTP, a delay of 200 ms would allocate resources much longer than necessary. Assuming that a server has to answer DNS requests with a rate of λ, then, according to Little's Law, the long-term average number of requests in the system is

$$E[N] = E[V] * \lambda \qquad (8.22)$$

where $E[V]$ is the average time a job stays in the system. When this time can be reduced by 200 ms, then either the number of requests are reduced, too, and the resources are saved, or the arrival rate can be increased. As an association without delayed acknowledgment lasts only 1 or 2 ms, the benefit would be significant.

8.4.2 Application Initiates the Use of the I-Bit

8.4.2.1 Sending is prevented due to the Nagle algorithm

Sending small messages in packets of their own increases the network load because of the transmission of unnecessary header bytes. The Nagle algorithm [59] forbids the sending of packets that could be filled with more messages if there are still data in flight. This situation can occur, when the sender has to deliver a message that fills more than one packet, but not quite two, and has to wait for an acknowledgment before issuing more data, or the send queue is exhausted. Then the Nagle algorithm does not allow the sending of the second part of the message, because it does not fill a complete packet and there are still unacknowledged data, i.e. the first part of the message.

An example is the handshake of the Datagram Transport Layer Security (DTLS) protocol (see [72, 99]), which is outlined in Figure 8.22. The handshake messages are handled like normal `DATA` chunks, i.e. the Nagle algorithm might prevent the sending of successive data, even if they belong to one flight. On the other hand, `SACK` chunks are only sent immediately after the first `DATA` chunk or if the `SACK` chunk can be bundled with a `DATA` chunk. In all other cases delayed acknowledgments are sent after 200 ms. As shown in the example, two `SACK` chunks are delayed due to the Nagle algorithm, which amounts to a delay of 400 ms.

The other delays are caused by DRY events, which will be discussed in the next subsection.

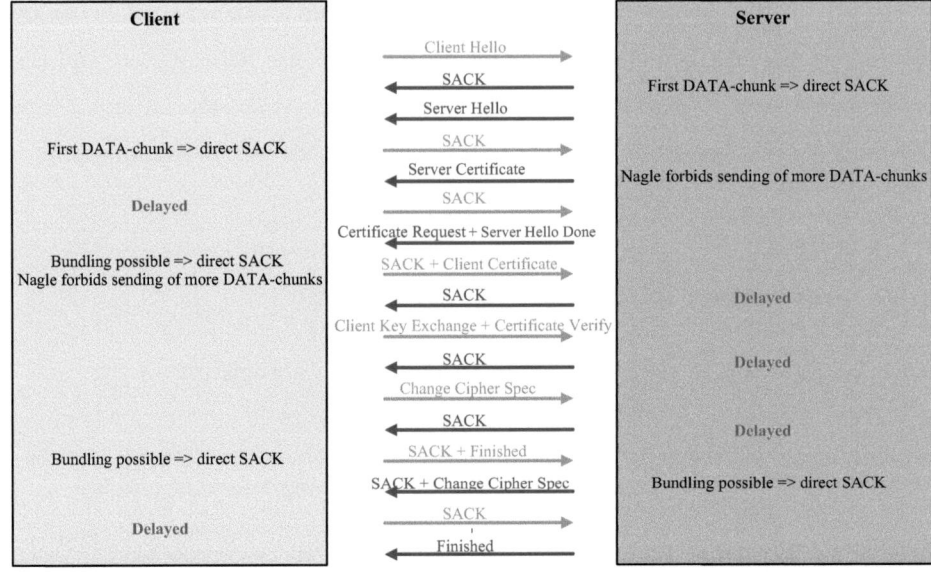

Figure 8.22: DTLS handshake

8.4.2.2 Sending is prevented due to DRY events

The SCTP socket API provides a DRY event which is issued when all outstanding user data have been acknowledged by the peer. If protocols on top of SCTP wait for such an event, delaying the SACK chunk limits the throughput. In the DTLS handshake (Figure 8.22) the DRY event is needed to synchronize all streams, i.e. the sender has to wait for the acknowledgment of all data in all streams, before the next message of the handshake may be sent. This event occurs three times during a DTLS handshake. Together with the two cases, where the Nagle algorithm prevents the sending of the next message, the application of the I-Bit reduces the duration of a typical handshake by 1 second.

8.4.2.3 API and Implementation Considerations

The scenarios for the I-Bit in the last subsections show, that the use of this bit has to be either triggered by the user application or the kernel.

To enable the application programmer to set the I-Bit, the SCTP socket API specified in [88] has to be extended by introducing a new flag which is called SCTP_SACK_IMMEDIATELY. The programmer can then set the bit in the *sendmsg*() call to indicate that the corresponding DATA chunks should have the I-Bit set. This use of the I-Bit is application dependent, and it can be set on a per message basis.

In the kernel on the sending side, the handling of the shutdown procedure and the inclusion of the I-Bit in the last DATA chunk before the congestion window is exhausted has to be implemented. The receiving side only has to interpret the I-Bit correctly.

With the exception of the supervision of the congestion window, this feature is already implemented in the FreeBSD 8.0 Version i.e. the application programmer can set the I-Bit and the last DATA chunk before the SHUTDOWN chunk is sent will be acknowledged immediately.

8.5 Benefitting from Packet Drop Reporting on Lossy Links

In Section 2.3 the PKTDROP feature was introduced, that is implemented in the FreeBSD kernel. A problem when trying to handle link errors on the transport layer lies in the fact that corrupt packets that are discovered because of their false IP checksum are in most cases dropped by the network adapter. Therefore, there is normally no chance for the transport layer to react according to that event. Ongoing research projects [107, 108] show that there is a great demand for passing erroneous packets from the link layer to the transport layer, where measurements can be taken according to the protocol and the application needs. In the next subsections simulation results will be shown that demonstrate that the negative impact of the lossy link on the goodput can be fully compensated by applying the PKTDROP feature. In order to interpret packet drop reports properly, it is necessary that the host receiving them is able to retrieve the information, which TSN has to be retransmitted.

8.5.1 One Association over a Lossy Link

In Figure 8.23 a simple scenario was tested with one client and one server connected over a lossy link with a packet error rate of 1% and an RTT of 20 ms. The throughput of an association with packet drop reporting is compared to one without it. The lower dashed graph shows the theoretical throughput according

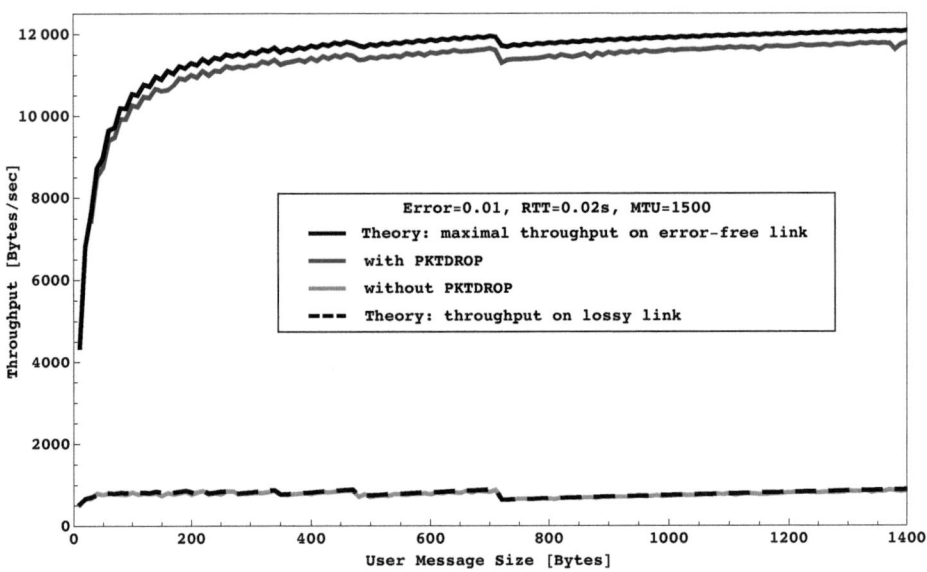

Figure 8.23: Comparison of an association with and without packet drop reporting

to Equation 7.10. As before the simulated results match the theoretical ones. The graph with packet drop reporting is compared to the highest theoretical throughput on an error-free and delay-free link according to Equation 7.5.

It is obvious, that by using packet drop reporting, the negative effect of packet loss caused by corrupted packets can be almost fully compensated.

8.5.2 Applying PKTDROP in a fairness scenario

For the next simulations the network of Figure 8.18 is used. This time the bottleneck link between Router 1 and Router2 is configured with a packet error rate of 1% and a delay of 20 ms.

In the first case no endpoints are configured to use packet drop reporting. The results are shown in the second lowest lines of Figure 8.24. Both associations achieve the same throughput, which is also equal to the theoretical results according to Equation 7.10 of Chapter 7.

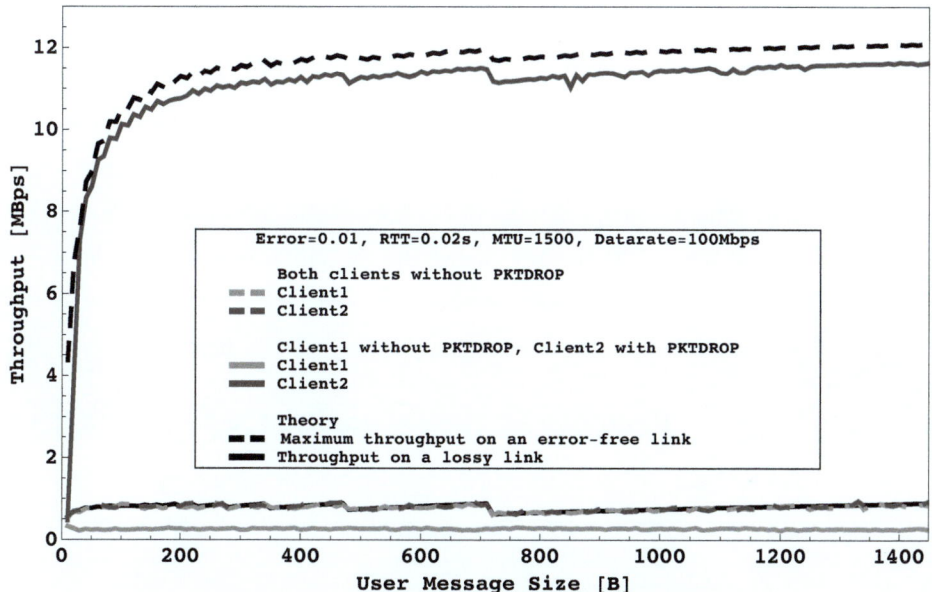

Figure 8.24: Throughput on a lossy bottleneck link

In the second case Client 2 and Server 2 apply PKTDROP. Sharing the link with an association that has to cope with many retransmissions lets the association with PKTDROP gain even more bandwidth. Thus the throughput of the association between Client 1 and Server 1 is reduced compared to the previous example, whereas the association with PKTDROP obtains the rest of the link, which is depicted in the lowest and the second highest graph of Figure 8.24. This is acceptable since `Client 1` is still misinterpreting packet loss as congestion indication.

8.5.3 Fairness when Lossy Link is not the Bottleneck

Sometimes one link of a path is faulty, whereas the rest is error-free. When packet drop reporting is provided, the connection could be more aggressive because the retransmission behavior of a connection applying PKTDROP reporting is different from one without this feature.

A scenario for this situation is shown in Figure 8.25. The link between `Client 2` and `Router 1` is configured with a packet error rate of 1%. The other links are error-free. The packet drop reports sent from `Server 2` to `Client 2` and the resulting retransmissions can lead to an unfair utilisation of the bottleneck link between `Router 1` and `Router 2` towards the association between `Client 1` and `Server 1`. The graphs in Figure 8.26 show the simulation results, the through-

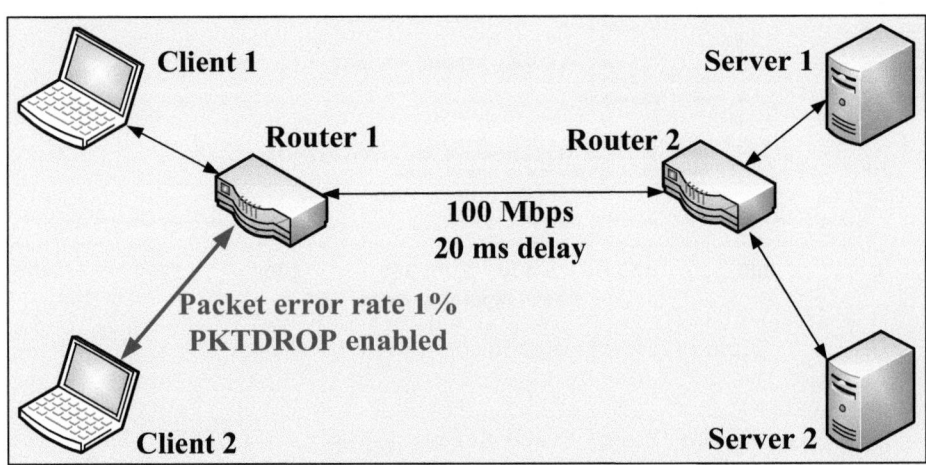

Figure 8.25: Lossy link is not the bottleneck

put on the application layer. Each simulation run was repeated 100 times with different seeds for the random numbers to ensure validity. The vertical bars rep-

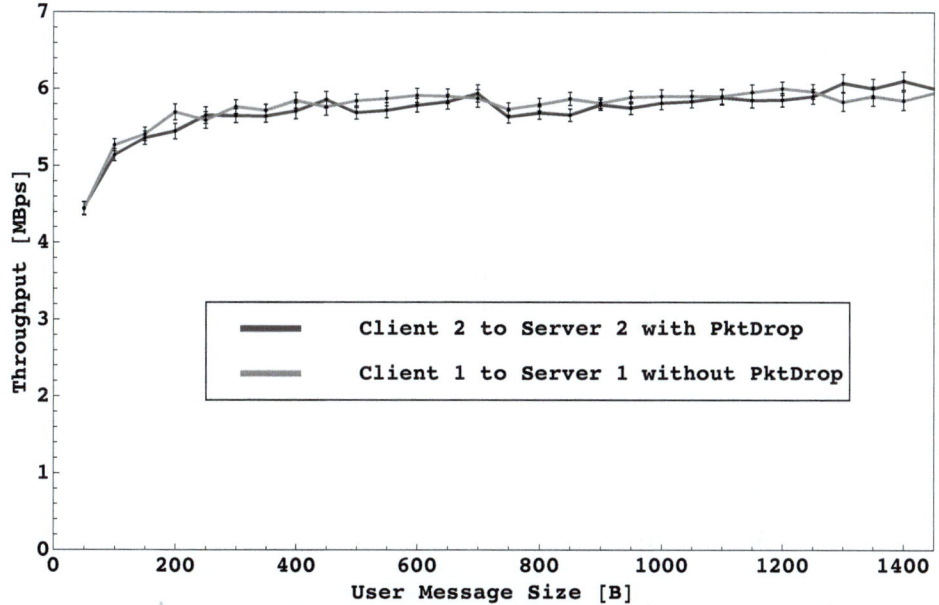

Figure 8.26: Throughput on a bottleneck link, if a tunnel link is configured with an error rate

resent the 95% confidence intervals. It is obvious that both connections share the bandwidth equally. They are fair towards each other. Hence, the application of packet drop reporting has no negative impact on other associations when sharing a bottleneck link.

8.6 Decreasing Duplicates by Reducing the Number of Fast Retransmissions

Multihoming and the ability to add new IP addresses make SCTP an ideal transport protocol in scenarios where handover becomes necessary. This can be the case in wireless LANs, when moving from one cell to the next, or when one path fails and the second one has to take over the load.

If the old and the new path have the same link properties, the handover performs as expected according to Equation 8.1. If the links are asymmetric, especially if the handover is carried out from a link with a long delay to one with a short delay, undesirable side effects might occur.

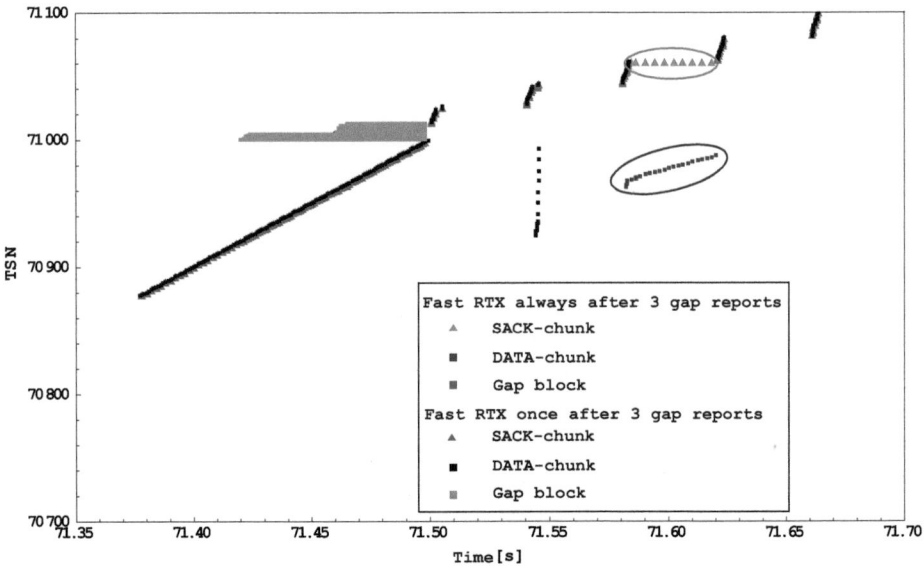

Figure 8.27: Handover with a different number of fast retransmissions

The test network consisted of a multihomed client and a multihomed server. The link delay of the primary path was 100 ms, of the second 20 ms. The handover was simulated by sending a packet containing an ASCONF chunk from the server to the client requesting to change the primary path. On reception of this packet, the client answers with an ASCONF_ACK chunk and starts sending new messages on the secondary path. As this path is faster, the new messages arrive ahead of the ones on the slow path. A gap ack block accumulates, which causes the sending of SACK chunks after each packet containing a DATA chunk. Therefore, fast retransmissions are sent. RFC 4960 [85] is not precise in stating, how often fast retransmissions should be sent. Therefore, two possibilities were chosen. At first, the sending of fast retransmissions was allowed always after the arrival of 3 SACK chunks indicating, that a specific TSN was still missing. Then only one fast retransmission per TSN was permitted. Figure 8.27 shows the two alternatives traced at the server side. On the left hand side of the figure, the `DATA` chunks (black) and the corresponding `SACK` chunks below are well to be seen. The region above the slope show the gap reports which resulted in the sending of fast retransmissions at about 71.55 seconds. So far the behavior in both scenarios is the same, indicated by the fact that the points of the second scenario cover those of the first one. Only the circled dots show that the sending of fast retransmissions always after 3 `SACK` chunks leads to the transmission of spurious duplicate TSNs and their corresponding acknowledgments. These extra messages not only have a negative influence on the network load but also on the congestion window since the window is always halved when a series of fast retransmissions occurs.

As a consequence, fast retransmissions should be sent at most once. This guarantees that a reaction from the receiver can occur, before the TSN is retransmitted, if necessary.

Chapter 9

Supporting Deployment through Network Address Translation for SCTP

The last chapter focused on the validation and improvement of SCTP. Yet, wide distribution of a protocol can only be achieved, if it can be used for a variety of applications. One obstacle on the way to a world-wide deployment is the fact, that SCTP messages, especially those from multihomed hosts, cannot pass through NAT middleboxes.

In this chapter NAT will be introduced, and it will be explained, why the existing algorithms are not suitable for SCTP. The approach to develop NAT middleboxes for SCTP in a multihomed environment will be described.

9.1 Introduction to NAT

Network Address Translation [82] is a common method for separating private networks from global networks by translating private IP addresses to public IP addresses. One reason is the shortage of public IPv4 addresses. By using NAT middleboxes the computers inside a LAN can have private IP addresses while only one public IP address is needed. Another reason is the wish to hide and protect the computers inside a LAN from direct access from the outside.

On passing through the NAT, the local computer's private IP address is substituted by one of the NAT's public IP addresses. To keep track of this address

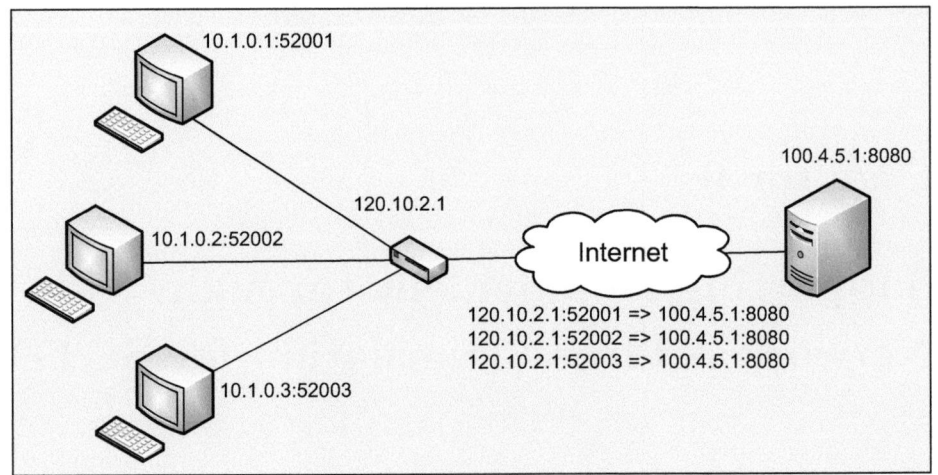

Figure 9.1: Using basic NAT

mapping a translation table is used, so that on the way back the responses can be mapped back to the originating address (see Figure 9.1). Thus, the address 'visible' to the remote endpoint of an association is only the public IP address that has been substituted for the real private IP address of the local endpoint.

This is a feasible method as long as the source ports of the clients connecting to the same server are different. The source port numbers are chosen dynamically from operating system dependent ranges. Some operating systems use the port numbers between 49152 and 65535. Since many clients can be located behind the same NAT middlebox and these clients might access a very popular server at about the same time, the chance that two clients get the same port is non-negligible. Therefore, the transport layer port number is also modified. This method is called Network Address and Port Number Translation (NAPT). NAT and NAPT have been in use for TCP and UDP for a long time, but SCTP as a fairly new transport protocol is not yet supported. Applying this method also to SCTP does not work for multihomed associations.

9.2 NAT for other Transport Protocols

9.2.1 NAT for TCP and UDP

Normally, TCP or UDP sessions are translated by changing the private IP address and additionally the private port number to a global IP address and port number in the TCP or UDP header, respectively. Thereby, the NAT middlebox chooses the port numbers from a pool and makes sure that two connections to the same server do not get the same port numbers.

As the transport layer checksum of the TCP and UDP packets covers the transport header which includes the port numbers, it has to be modified according to the port number change. However, the checksum used for TCP or UDP has the property that the change of the checksum can be computed from the change of the port numbers only. As a consequence, this can be done very efficiently by a simple set of additions and subtractions.

It should be noted that the behavior of NAT middleboxes varies dramatically because there were no standards describing how to build them. The Behavior Engineering for Hindrance Avoidance (BEHAVE) working group of the IETF develops Best Current Practice (BCP) documents giving requirements for NAT middlebox behavior and protocols to help applications to run over networks with NAT middleboxes.

9.2.2 Using Common NAT Middleboxes for Processing SCTP Associations

Considering only single homed SCTP clients and servers, it is possible to use this NAPT concept also for SCTP, since it has the same port number concept as TCP and UDP. However, the transport layer checksum used by SCTP is different from the one used by UDP and TCP. This checksum does not allow to compute the checksum change based only on the port number change. Therefore, the NAT middlebox has to compute the new SCTP checksum again based on the complete SCTP packet. This requires a substantial amount of computing power, which might be reduced when the computation is directly performed by hardware[1].

For multihomed SCTP clients and servers, reusing the techniques from TCP and UDP becomes much harder. Multihomed hosts can be attached to multiple networks. Therefore, the traffic of one SCTP association, in general, passes through different NAT middleboxes on different paths. Since each SCTP endpoint can only use one SCTP port number on all paths, the NAT middleboxes cannot change the port number independently. In order to apply the existing NAT concept, the NAT middleboxes involved would have to synchronize the port numbers in order to assign a common number for the association. This is very hard to achieve.

Based on this discussion it seems desirable to use a NAT mechanism for SCTP not requiring to change the SCTP header at all, and hence the port numbers, which avoids the synchronization among NAT middleboxes and the recomputation of the SCTP checksum.

Currently most NAT middleboxes only support protocols running on top of TCP or UDP. A standard technique for all other protocols is to encapsulate these packets into UDP instead of IP. Since both UDP and IP provide an unreliable packet delivery service, this is feasible. This also works for SCTP, as described in the draft [100], and is currently implemented in the SCTP kernel extension for Mac OS X.

It should be noted that NAT middleboxes on different paths are not synchronized, and therefore, the UDP port number might be different on different paths.

One drawback of using UDP encapsulation is that ICMP messages might not contain enough information to be processed by the SCTP layer. According to RFC 4960 SCTP has to react on ICMP messages like "Parameter Problem" or "Fragmentation needed". In order to interpret these messages correctly, the corre-

---

[1]Meanwhile, network adapters that provide checksum offloading are available

sponding association has to be found. An ICMP message containing an IP packet has to include at least the IP header and the first 8 bytes of the payload. If SCTP is directly encapsulated, 8 bytes are enough to identify the association, since the port numbers and the verification tag are provided. If SCTP is running over UDP, this is not possible.

Another drawback is that the simple peer-to-peer solution described in Sections 9.6 and 9.6.2 does not work, since the UDP port numbers might be changed by NAT middleboxes.

Tunneling SCTP over UDP has to handle the same problems as any other UDP based communication for NAT traversal. However, this is the only possibility for SCTP based communication through a NAT middlebox without modifying it to add SCTP support.

9.3 Specific NAT for SCTP

9.3.1 State of the Art

Currently, first NAT implementations are being developed that support SCTP in a way similar to TCP or UDP. Although this works fine for single homed SCTP associations, it does not work for multihomed SCTP associations. Therefore, these solutions are non-applicable for typical SCTP applications which require multihoming. However, also in these cases, some vendors and operators want to use NAT middleboxes for various reasons. Therefore, it is important to have NAT middleboxes which not only support SCTP in a limited way, but with all features, especially multihoming.

In [114] the authors describe an approach to integrate SCTP in network address translators for single homed client-server communication. A group of the Center for Advanced Internet Architecture at Swinburne University has implemented this method for the FreeBSD operating system [32]. After the single homed case is working, this project, SCTP over NAT Adaptation (SONATA), will now focus on the integration of the other scenarios provided in [90] and [98] to provide a fully functional SCTP NAT implementation.

In the remainder of this section the special needs for an SCTP NAT will be described and examples will be shown for single homed scenarios. The next sections will focus on the support of multihoming, transport layer mobility, and routing changes.

9.3.2 Using Verification Tags instead of Ports

In Subsection 2.2.2 the setup procedure of an association was described following the four way handshake shown on the left hand side of Figure 2.4.

For SCTP NAT the exchange of the verification tags in the handshake is of great importance. The verification tag in the common header is always the initiate tag sent by the peer in the `INIT` or `INIT_ACK` chunk during the association setup. Except for the initiation tag in the common header of the packet containing the `INIT` chunk, all others have to be a non-zero 32-bit number. It is noteworthy that most SCTP implementations use the verification tag for looking up the association when a packet is received. In Subsection 4.4.1 this method was already used when packets had to be assigned to associations and the combination of port number and address was not distinctive enough.

In the NAPT method described above, the NAT middlebox controls the 16-bit source port number of outgoing TCP connections in order to be able to distinguish multiple TCP connections of all clients behind the NAT middlebox to the same server. The basic idea for the SCTP specific method is to use the combination of the source port number and the verification tag instead. For single homed hosts this method is described in [90].

If NAT middleboxes use the verification tags together with the addresses and the port numbers to identify an association, the probability that two hosts end up with the same combination decreases to a tolerable level.

9.3.3 Creating and Modifying the NAT Table

The main task of a NAT middlebox is to substitute the source address of each packet with the public address used by the NAT middlebox and to keep the corresponding IP addresses in a table.

This NAT table consists of several entries. Each entry is a tuple comprising:

1. Local-Address

2. Global-Address

3. Local-Port

4. Global-Port

5. Local verification tag (Local-VTag)

6. Global verification tag (Global-VTag)

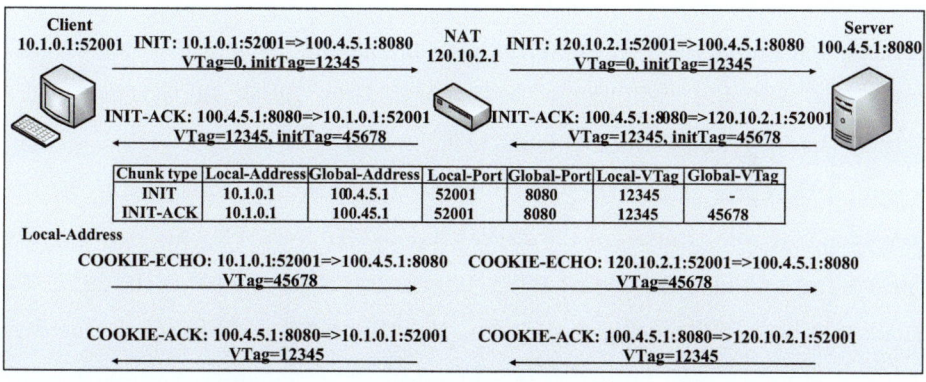

Figure 9.2: Setting up the NAT table during SCTP association setup

The message flow that leads to the initial entry during the handshake is shown in Figure 9.2. In the first message of the handshake, the verification tag in the common header must be set to 0, but the initiate tag (initTag) in the INIT chunk holds a 32-bit random number that is supposed to be the verification tag (VTag) of the incoming packets. Hence, at the beginning of the handshake, only one verification tag is known. The NAT middlebox keeps track of this information and takes the local private address (Local-Address) and the officially registered destination IP address (Global-Address) from the IP header of the SCTP packet and saves them in the NAT table. The local source port (Local-Port) and the destination port (Global-Port) are obtained in the same way.

The initiate tag of the INIT chunk, which the client has chosen for its communication, is also extracted from the INIT chunk header and saved as Local-VTag. The Global-VTag that eventually will be chosen by the communication partner is not known yet. Before forwarding the packet, the NAT middlebox exchanges the source address of the IP header with the NAT address (here: 120.10.2.1) and sends the packet toward the other endpoint. The other SCTP endpoint receiving the packet containing the INIT chunk answers the request with a message containing the INIT_ACK chunk. This message is addressed to the global address of the NAT middlebox and the Local-Port. Its verification tag in the common header must be identical to the initiate tag of the INIT chunk. The initiate tag of the INIT_ACK chunk will be used as the verification tag for all packets that are sent by the initiating endpoint (here: client 10.1.0.1) of the association. For an incoming INIT_ACK chunk, the NAT middlebox searches the table entries for the corresponding combination of Local-Port, Global-Address, Global-Port, and the Local-VTag and adds the Global-VTag. Thus, after the reception of the INIT_ACK chunk, both verification tags are known. Now the NAT middlebox sets the destination address to the Local-Address found in the table entry and delivers the packet. To complete the handshake, a packet with a COOKIE_ECHO chunk is sent that is acknowledged with a message containing a COOKIE_ACK chunk.

If the endpoints are single homed, the INIT and INIT_ACK chunk do not contain additional address parameters. If they are multihomed, they might announce all their addresses. In this case, an entry for each address will be added to the table. If an `ASCONF` chunk is received to add the wildcard address, an entry to the NAT table is made for that address. As both verification tags must be added, a parameter must be included in the `ASCONF` chunk that contains the verification tag that is not present in the common header.

In addition to rules to insert and modify entries, a timer has to be used to trigger the removal of entries that have not been used for a certain amount of time. This time should be long enough such that the SCTP path supervision procedure prevents the table entries from timing out, i.e. the timeout must be longer than twice the heartbeat interval timer to allow at least one retransmission of a `HEARTBEAT` chunk.

9.3.4 Code of Behavior for the Endpoints

As multiple clients behind the NAT middlebox might choose the same local port when connecting to the same server, it is possible that two different associations are started with the same address port combination. If a server receives an `INIT` chunk with the same address port combination as an already existing association, it assumes that the association has been restarted (see Subsection 2.2.2). To prevent such a misinterpretation, the `INIT` chunk sent by the clients should contain a parameter indicating that the server should not follow the restart procedure. Instead it should use the verification tag to distinguish between the associations. This is what most SCTP implementations already do. Furthermore, the SCTP endpoints must not include non-global addresses in the `INIT` or `INIT_ACK` chunk, because the peer cannot use these addresses which are not unique as destination addresses. If an SCTP endpoint is multihomed and has non-global addresses, it should set up the association single homed and then add the other addresses after the association has been established by sending an SCTP packet containing an `ASCONF` chunk for each address. To add such an address, the `ASCONF` chunk should contain only the wildcard address and the parameter providing the required verification tag. The source address of the packet containing the `ASCONF` chunk will be added to the association. To remove an address, an `ASCONF` chunk is sent with the wildcard address. Then, all addresses except the source address of the packet containing the `ASCONF` chunk are deleted from the association.

9.3.5 Code of Behavior for the NAT Middleboxes

If a NAT middlebox receives an `INIT` chunk that would result in adding an entry to the NAT table that conflicts with an already existing entry, it should not insert this entry and may send an `ABORT` chunk back to the SCTP endpoint. In the `ABORT` chunk, an M-Bit should be set that indicates that it has been generated by a middlebox. This happens if two different clients choose the same local port number and initiate tag and try to connect to the same server. On reception of such an `ABORT` chunk, the endpoint can try to choose a different initiate tag and try setting up the association again. If the NAT middlebox receives an SCTP packet that cannot be processed because it neither contains an `INIT` or `ASCONF` chunk nor is there an entry in the NAT table, the NAT middlebox should discard the packet and can send an `ERROR` chunk back. An M-Bit must be set to indicate that the chunk is generated by a middlebox, and an error cause should indicate that the NAT middlebox does not have the required information to process the packet. On reception of such an `ERROR` chunk, the endpoint should use an `ASCONF` chunk to provide the required information to the NAT middlebox.

9.3.6 New SCTP Protocol Elements

Clients require a new parameter to be included in the `INIT` chunk to indicate that they will use the procedures described in this chapter. This parameter is also included in the `INIT_ACK` chunk to indicate that the receiver also supports it. Another new parameter is required that can contain a verification tag and is included in an `ASCONF` chunk.

Both the ERROR chunk and the ABORT chunk must have an M-Bit indicating that the packet containing the chunk is generated by a middlebox instead of the peer. Two additional error causes are introduced, one to be included in the ERROR chunk to indicate that the NAT middlebox misses some state, and one to be included in the ABORT chunk to indicate a conflict in the NAT table.

After the structure and functioning of SCTP NAT has been outlined, example scenarios for different routing conditions will be described in the next sections, respecting single and multihomed hosts.

9.4 Associations with Stable Routing Conditions

In this section it is assumed that the routing conditions do not change during the lifetime of an association, i.e. neither a NAT middlebox nor a router is substituted by another one or changes its address.

9.4.1 Single homed Client to Multihomed Server

Most of the communication in the Internet happens between a client and a server in a way that the client requests a service that is provided by the server. To be able to contact the server, its address and port have to be known.

In Figure 9.3 the client initiates the association by sending a packet containing an INIT chunk to 100.4.5.1:8080. The NAT middlebox inserts an entry with all information except the Global-VTag in its table. The multihomed server announces all its global addresses in address parameters included in the INIT_ACK chunk. The packet crosses the NAT middlebox, which completes its first entry and adds a new one for each additional path. As a result, there will be a separate entry for each server address although there is only one association. When the client receives the chunk, it adds these addresses to its list of destination addresses.

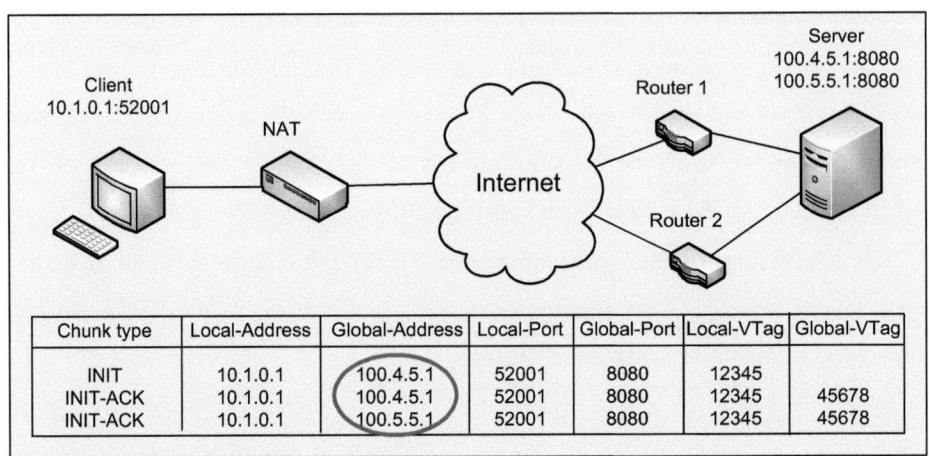

Figure 9.3: Building the NAT table for the single homed client with a multi-homed server

9.4.2 Multihomed Client and Server

The client sends an **INIT** chunk without a list of addresses to the server which responds with an **INIT_ACK** chunk including a list of all its addresses. As shown in Figure 9.4, this initial handshake uses the path via NAT 1.

After the association is established, the client adds its second address by sending an **ASCONF** chunk. If the packet containing this chunk is sent via the path containing **NAT 2**, both NAT middleboxes have the necessary state. If this packet is sent on the path via **NAT 1**, any packet sent from the client on the path via **NAT 2** will result in an **ERROR** chunk being sent back, and this will trigger the sending of an **ASCONF** chunk on the second path with the wildcard set. This chunk provides the necessary information to the NAT middlebox **NAT 2**.

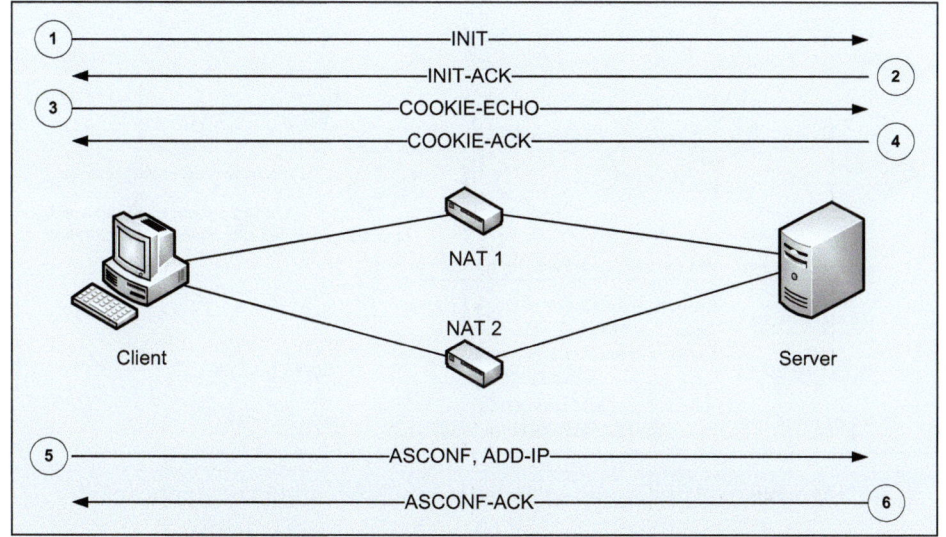

Figure 9.4: Multihoming through NAT middleboxes

9.5 Client-Server Communication with Changing Routing Conditions

9.5.1 Adding New NAT Middleboxes

After having set up an association, data can be exchanged between client and server. The packets are routed through the Internet. It cannot be disregarded that the routes are not stable and can change during the lifetime of an association, in particular if it has a long life span as expected for major SCTP application scenarios. Therefore, it may happen that a new NAT middlebox gets involved that has no knowledge of the properties of this association as depicted in Figure 9.5.

Passing through a new NAT middlebox also means, that the server will receive a packet with a new source address, which appears as if the client has got an additional IP address.

In Figure 9.5 the upper route shows the path where the association was set up initially. After the route was changed the packets travel on the lower route.

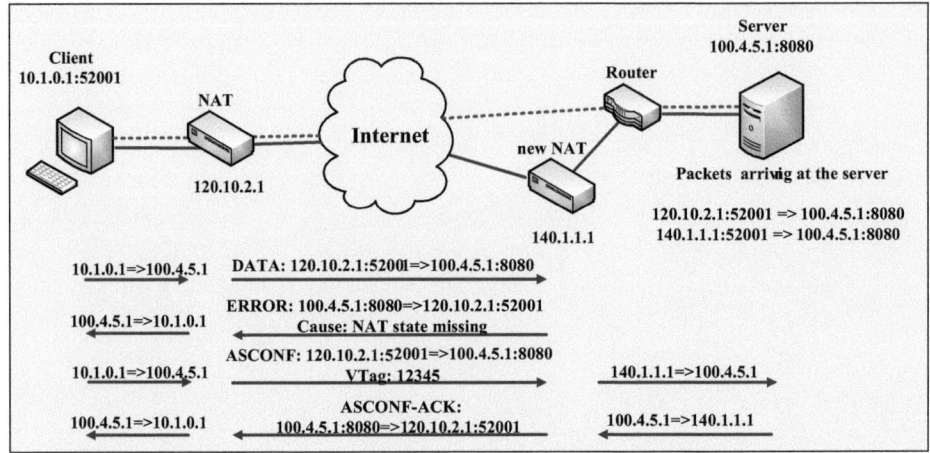

Figure 9.5: After a route change a new NAT middlebox appears

An example for the address/port combination for both routes is shown below the server.

If the new NAT middlebox receives the first packet from the client, it will send back a packet containing an ERROR chunk indicating that it misses the necessary NAT table entry. Therefore, upon reception of the ERROR chunk the client sends an ASCONF chunk on the new path with the necessary information, which prompts the new NAT middlebox to add a complete entry to its table.

This message can pass through the NAT middlebox and can be acknowledged by the server with an ASCONF_ACK message. Afterwards the communication can proceed as usual.

9.5.2 Client using Transport Layer Mobility

SCTP with its functionality of dynamic address configuration is well suited to be employed in an environment with host mobility. While all other parameters remain the same, the moving client will receive a new address. This not only results in a new source address for the packet, but also in a changing route, such that eventually another NAT middlebox has to be traversed which, again, initially has no knowledge of the association. As the situation is similar to the one described in the last subsection, the same actions should be taken. For more information on transport layer mobility see [73].

9.5.3 Multihomed Transport Layer Mobility

In the last subsection a scenario was discussed where a client moves and hence changes its source address and, as a consequence, the corresponding NAT middlebox as well. During the transition from one cell to another in a host mobility scenario, there is likely to be a zone where both cells are active and thus two addresses can be in use. Adding the new address results in a temporarily multihomed client. This situation can be handled similar to the case explained in the last section. The new address will be added via the sending of a message containing an `ASCONF` chunk. But as the old address will be completely replaced by the new one as soon as the previous cell is left, another parameter has to be added that indicates that the primary path should be set to the new address. This causes the server to send the next packets to the new address.

9.6 Peer-to-Peer Communication

With the introduction of file-sharing services peer-to-peer communication in the Internet increases. In contrast to the client-server model, the initiating host does not normally know the peer's 'real' address, because it is a private IP address, and thus, like the other host, hidden behind a NAT middlebox. The two peers need an agent to help them find their communication partner. This agent is usually called a rendezvous server. A detailed description for UDP and TCP handling peer-to-peer communication is given in [26].

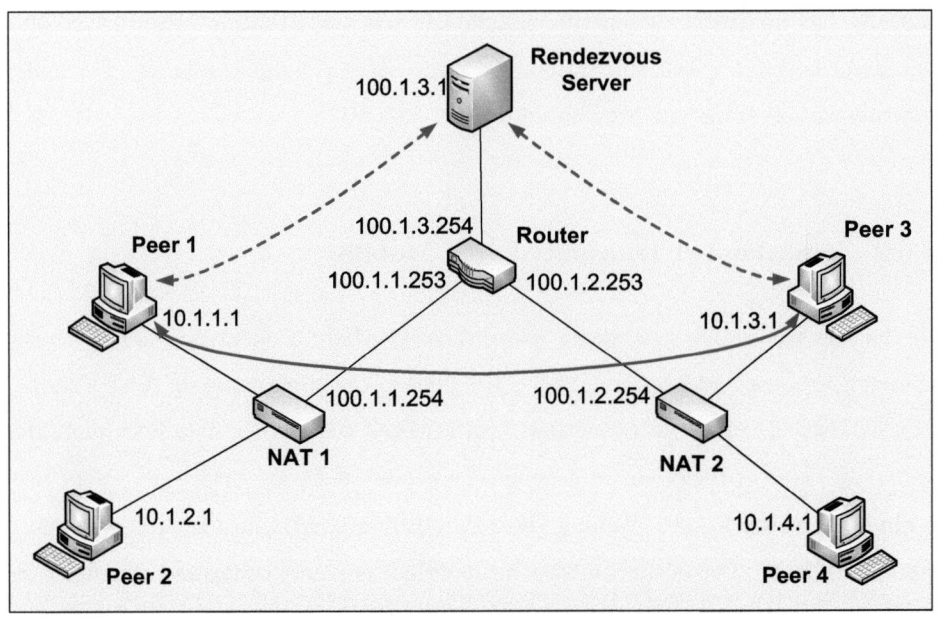

Figure 9.6: Peer-to-Peer communication with rendezvous server

9.6.1 Single homed Peer-to-Peer Communication

In the first scenario both peers are single homed. The corresponding network setup is shown in Figure 9.6. The communication process in this case consists of two phases. First, associations are initialized between the peers and the rendezvous server, then after retrieving the required information from the rendezvous server the peers can communicate with each other independent from the server.

Once both peers have retrieved the required information, the actual communication between the peers can start. As there is no server, both hosts have to be able to act as client and server. Thus both will start an association. If the message containing the INIT chunk of **Peer 1** reaches the NAT middlebox **NAT 2**, before **Peer 3**'s message could get through, it will be discarded. The retransmission of the INIT chunk will get through, if in the meantime **Peer 3** has sent an INIT chunk and thus has triggered the NAT middlebox to set up a table entry.

NAT 2 will find the entry and will allow the Peer 1's INIT chunk to pass. The best results for this 'hole punching' can be achieved, if the associations are started at the same time. From the perspective of SCTP the simultaneous sending of INIT chunks features a special case, because the INIT chunk is not followed directly by an INIT_ACK chunk, but by another INIT chunk. The SCTP collision handling procedure (compare Figure 2.4) will make sure that exactly one association between the peers will be established.

9.6.2 Multihoming with Rendezvous Server

The last step in increasing complexity of the NAT scenario is the communication between two multihomed peers that are behind different NAT middleboxes.

Just like in the single homed case, the rendezvous server has to gather the peers' information to fill its table. This time the table has to be enlarged by the additional addresses. The peers first set up an association with the rendezvous server. Using this server the peers can get each other's addresses and port numbers.

At this point, the peers have to set up an association via initialization collision to provide a path by using hole punching. In order to be able to also use the second path, the NAT middleboxes on the way have to get the necessary information. By sending messages containing ASCONF chunks almost simultaneously, the NAT middleboxes are notified to let packets arriving from the opposite direction pass through. Unfortunately, the mechanism described in Section 9.5.1 to ask for information by sending a message containing an ERROR chunk does not work when coming from the global side of the network, because only the host behind the NAT middlebox can provide the data to fill the NAT table. So when the message containing an ASCONF chunk arrives at the opposite NAT middlebox before an entry in the NAT table is present, the packet is discarded, but its retransmission might be successful. After both NAT tables got the appropriate entries the secondary paths can also be used.

9.7 Implementation of NAT for SCTP in INET

As pointed out in Subsection 3.2.4, INET supports the configuration of IP addresses and routing tables. Therefore, it is possible to simulate different subnetworks by applying public and private IP addresses to hosts and routers. Thereby, the distinction between different address levels like loopback, private, link-local, and global is necessary. Suitable routines according to [89] have already been implemented, when handling address parameters in the `INIT` and `INIT_ACK` chunk. Thus, important preconditions were already met.

9.7.1 Simulation of the NAT Middlebox

A NAT middlebox comprises features that are typical for routers like the forwarding of messages and the decision, on which path a packet has to be sent. Therefore, the routines that are the same in routers and NAT middleboxes can be taken from the already implemented modules.

New was the handling of the NAT table, the routines to create, modify and look up entries. In addition, SCTP messages had to be analyzed to retrieve information about the chunk type and relevant parameters therein.

To achieve this, the classes *NatTable*, *NatEntry*, *NatNetworkLayer*, and *NAT* were introduced. They were all combined in the compound module *NatDumpRouter*, which simulates a NAT middlebox (see Figure 9.7). In addition, a dump module was inserted between the link layer and the network layer to trace the traffic passing through the NAT middlebox. *NatTable* holds all the instances of the *NatEntries* together with methods to insert, search, and remove entries, and print the table. Methods to retrieve and set the contents of an entry belong to *NatEntry*.

NAT, which is part of the *NatNetworkLayer*, is the core module. It controls the traffic by analyzing the packets and taking actions according to chunk types.

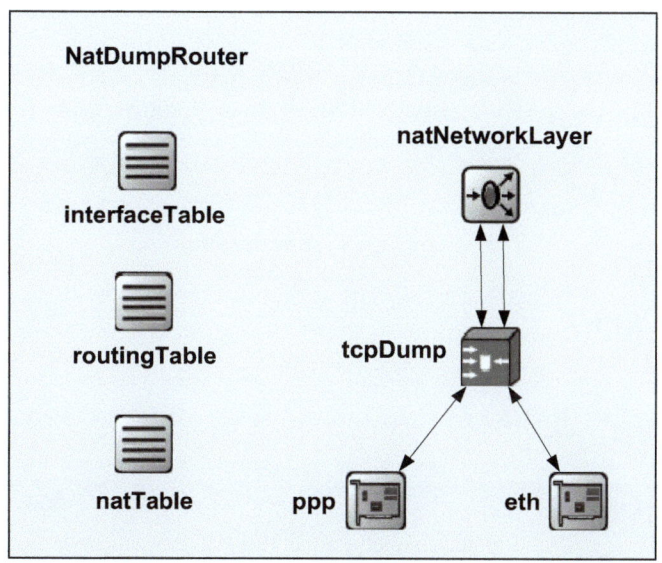

Figure 9.7: Components of the NAT module

It initiates table look-ups and triggers the transformation from local to global addresses and vice versa. Then it routes the packets to the right destination. Upon expiration of a timer, the timestamps of all the entries are controlled, and the entries that have not been in use for a sufficiently long time are removed. This time must be long enough that packets containing HEARTBEAT chunks that are important to confirm the paths are not rejected, even if they have already been retransmitted. As HEARTBEAT chunks are sent in intervals of $HB_{Interval} + RTO$ the timer was set to an expiration time of 63 seconds.

9.7.2 Changes on the Application Layer

On the application layer new modules for the peer-to-peer scenarios were needed. A simple protocol had to be introduced for the communication between the peers and the rendezvous server. The server needed a table to store the names of the communication partners, their global addresses and ports.

Figure 9.8 shows the multihomed version of Figure 9.6. To obtain both ad-

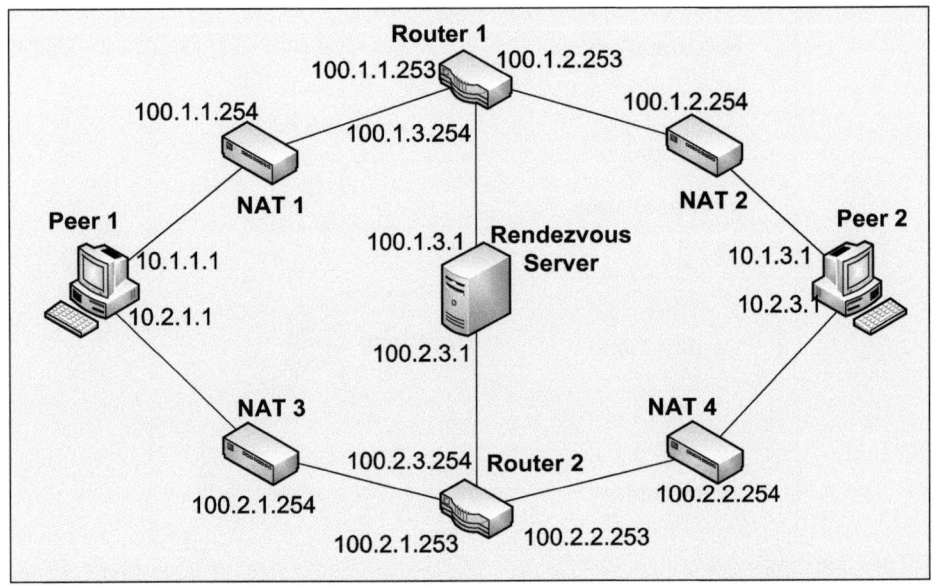

Figure 9.8: Communication with the rendezvous server in a multihomed scenario

dresses of the other peer, both peers have to set up an association to the **Rendezvous Server**. They send a message with the name of the peer, they want to connect to, and the information, whether they are multihomed or not, to the server. By passing through **NAT 1** or **NAT 2**, respectively, the addresses are changed to the global addresses of the NAT middleboxes. The server enters the information in a table. After the establishment of the association, the peers send packets with `ASCONF` chunks via **NAT 3** or **NAT 4**, respectively, to the server to inform it about their second addresses. Upon arrival of these messages, the server updates the table and answers with an `ASCONF_ACK` chunk. If it has gathered all the necessary data, it sends messages to both peers with the global addresses and ports of their communication partners. Then the server shuts down the association. Afterwards the peers set up a connection with the other peer as described in Subsection 9.6.2.

At the time, when the new NAT modules in the simulation were tested, there was no other implementation available. Therefore, the main target was to see whether the concept concerning the message flow, especially in the case of multihoming, could be verified.

It was started with the simplest scenario to set up the NAT table and the corresponding methods, and then the multihoming case was tested. The peer-to-peer networks were again more complex and had the testing of the INIT collision as main focus. At some points aspects of the concept had to be corrected, until finally the concept could be verified by the simulation.

Chapter 10

Conclusion and Outlook

10.1 Achieved Results

In this thesis the main concern was the evaluation, improvement, and extension of the Stream Control Transmission Protocol. To provide a research basis, the INET framework of the OMNeT++ simulation environment was extended [76] and the SCTP protocol was implemented according to RFC 4960. To enhance the simulation's functionality, the main protocol extensions, like Dynamic Address Reconfiguration (RFC 5061), Authenticating Chunks (RFC 4895), Partial Reliability Extension (RFC 3758), Packet Drop Reporting, and Stream Reset, the last two specified in internet drafts, were provided, too. For more realistic testing scenarios and to generate the necessary data, applications were added that operate as client, server, or peer (Chapter 6). The SCTP extension of the INET framework is publicly available and can be downloaded from the github website [34].

The validation of the simulation was improved and facilitated, after its features had been expanded by the ExtInterface [96] that enabled the communication between the simulation and real networks. The crucial module for the success of the connection was the real time scheduler, that had to synchronize the wall clock time of the real network with the simulation time (Section 5.1).

To analyze traces and make debugging easier, the network analyzer Wireshark was extended with a graphical tool that visualizes the data transfer of SCTP associations by plotting either TSNs, Cumulative TSN Acks, and gap ack blocks, or the advertised receiver window and received bytes. Statistical values concerning the association can be obtained, too. Together with the ExtInterface, whose methods to convert the messages from the simulation format into the network format can be used to generate traces in the pcap format, a powerful tool for testing and analyzing (Section 4.3) was provided. It is included in the latest Wireshark distribution.

To confirm the reliability of the simulation results, often hundreds or even thousands of runs are needed. The automation of the generation of Xgrid specification files and its integration in the OMNeT++ framework reduced the processing time linearly with the number of CPUs used [79] (Section 5.2).

One important value for judging the performance is the throughput. As SCTP is a message oriented protocol, where the bundling of DATA chunks can result in a high percentage of header bytes compared to user data, it cannot be handled like the byte stream oriented TCP. Therefore, SCTP specific formulae were needed. To obtain an upper bound for the throughput, one formula was developed for the throughput for associations under ideal conditions and one, when error-prone links with delays are present [78]. These equations could be verified by comparing them to simulation results (Chapter 7). Applying them to real associations showed that they are valid also in this environment.

Although SCTP adopted the algorithms for congestion control and flow control from TCP, SCTP's message orientation calls for a different treatment. Investigations revealed that the calculation of the outstanding bytes, which influences the size of the congestion window and thus the amount of data allowed to transmit, leads to unfairness towards TCP, if the DATA chunk header is not taken into account [77] (Section 8.3).

In the case of flow control the message orientation revealed unexpected problems, too. For the temporary storage of user messages the receiver has to allocate extra memory. This can lead to an exhaustion of the receive buffer before the advertised receiver window hits zero. In addition, a large number of unnecessary retransmissions is performed. To solve this problem, the arwnd should reflect the size of the receive buffer, and it should be reduced by the amount of data really needed by the receiver instead of just the user data [77] (Section 8.2).

A reliable transport protocol like SCTP requires the acknowledgment of received data. To increase the efficiency SACK-chunks are normally only sent for every other packet. It was shown that there are situations, like a DTLS handshake, short term associations, or a misconfiguration of parameters, when a delayed acknowledgment leads to an unnecessary extension of the processing time. Therefore, an additional flag was introduced in the DATA chunk header, called I-Bit, that informs the receiver that the acknowledgment should not be delayed, but sent immediately [97]. This flag leads to a reduction in the lifetime of short term associations and an increase of the throughput in long term connections (Section 8.4).

Lossy links, that play an important role in wireless LANs, lead to spurious retransmissions and a considerable decrease of the throughput. The SCTP extension PKTDROP overcomes this deficiency by informing the sender which messages have been corrupted. Simulations reveal that the otherwise negative impact of packet loss can be almost fully compensated when applying PKTDROP [78] (Section 8.5).

The possibility to change addresses in a wireless LAN is a common requirement. It was found out that handover from one destination address to another can lead to undesirable duplicate TSNs, if the delay on the second link is less than on the first one. A reduction of the duplicates can be obtained by decreasing the number of fast retransmissions to only one instead of retransmitting always after three gap reports (Section 8.6).

Deploying a new transport protocol is only possible, if it can be applied on all common operating systems and in any environment. As SCTP is implemented in all UNIX derivatives and a prototype for the Windows OS is available, the first prerequisite is almost met. For the second one it is necessary, that SCTP associations can be set up regardless of the network the peers are in. To achieve this, the traversal through NAT middleboxes must be guaranteed. As the common techniques for UDP and TCP cannot be applied for SCTP, an SCTP specific NAT had to be developed [90]. Multihoming required a special treatment, because messages belonging to the same associations have to pass through NAT middleboxes in different subnets. The Add-IP extension enables the addition of addresses in multihoming scenarios. In peer-to-peer networks INIT collisions are the typical variant of the four way handshake to set up an association. A rendezvous server has to provide the necessary information about the peer's connection data [98] (Chapter 9).

10.2 Future Work

The simulation described in this thesis establishes a basis for future research work. Currently two projects at Münster University of Applied Sciences and the University of Duisburg-Essen funded by the DFG deal with the analysis of SCTP features (see Section 1.1). To be able to conduct experiments they rely on the simulation. On the other hand, the simulation is an ongoing project as it will be enhanced by new features to meet the research demands.

The goal of a project with the University of British Columbia is the connection of the simulation with Message Passing Interface (MPI) applications. Therefore, the real time scheduler has been extended to also accept Inter-process Communication (IPC) sockets. Until then the simulation only supported one-to-one style sockets, one-to-many style sockets had to be realized to meet the needs of the application. A time factor was introduced to adapt the real time to the simulation time. After the feasibility has been shown [68], the next work concentrates on performance issues, scalability and different topologies.

A new approach for Wireshark will be the support for the dump file format *pcapng* [15], that, among other features, enables the capturing on multiple interfaces, which is of great interest for SCTP. The extension of the SCTP dissector and the graphical tool will be a future project.

The integration of SCTP NAT in the Linux kernel is a current project. To test parts of the implementation, the real network will be connected to the simulation to take advantage of the peer-to-peer functionality and the rendezvous server. As soon as an application is provided on the real computer, the NAT middlebox in the simulation can be tested against the real application, too.

Another research result of the University of British Columbia is the userland implementation of SCTP (see Section 1.1). A current project at Münster University of Applied Sciences is to port this stack to other operating systems that do not allow the implementation of kernel extensions, for instance the OS X iPhone. After the successful completion of the project, future work will focus on testing SCTP applications on mobile devices.

List of Figures

2.1	Transport of SS7 messages over SCTP	8
2.2	SCTP chunk format	10
2.3	SCTP message format	11
2.4	Variants of SCTP handshakes	12
2.5	SCTP DATA chunk format	14
2.6	SCTP SACK chunk format	16
2.7	Evolution of the congestion window	18
3.1	OMNeT++ simulation environment	31
3.2	Inside the modules	32
3.3	OMNeT++ integrated in the Eclipse IDE	33
3.4	Analyzing results of a vector file	34
3.5	Compound Module StandardHost	36
4.1	Data link access with a BPF device	38
4.2	*tcpdump* output for an SCTP association	40
4.3	Wireshark main window	43
4.4	Trace with several associations	46
4.5	*SCTP Analyse Association* window	47
4.6	Statistics of the chunk types	48
4.7	Start window for the graphical analysis of the data transfer of an endpoint	49
4.8	TSNs over time	50

4.9	Clipping of TSNs over time	51
4.10	Advertised Receiver Window and transmitted Bytes	52
5.1	Sending and receiving real packets	56
5.2	Message flow between simulation and real network	59
5.3	The compound module ExtRouter	61
5.4	Using traceroute to traverse a simulated network	62
5.5	Output of the *traceroute* command	64
5.6	Passing through a simulated network connecting real computers	65
5.7	Output of the *ping* command	66
5.8	The three Xgrid components	68
5.9	The Xgrid administration tool	69
5.10	Mapping of the original files to the Xgrid hierarchy	72
6.1	Extensions to the StandardHost module	77
6.2	Simulation Architecture of the simple module *sctp*	79
6.3	Hierarchy of the SCTP messages	81
6.4	Simulation State Machine	84
6.5	Flowchart for the calculation of the congestion window	89
6.6	Flowchart for the calculation of the peer's advertised receiver window	90
6.7	Class diagram of the simulation	92
6.8	Output of the dump module	97
6.9	Verifying the bandwidth-delay product	99
6.10	Network with five clients sharing a limited link	100
6.11	Five clients sharing a limited link	101
6.12	`Client1` sends data via `extRouter` to a real PC while internal traffic from `Client2` to `Server1` is passing through `extRouter`	103
6.13	Throughput of the SCTP association between `Client1` and a real PC	104

6.14	Throughput of the SCTP association between `Client1` and a real PC with varying number of routers	105
7.1	Maximum throughput for two different data rates	110
7.2	Evolution of the congestion window during a simulation	111
7.3	Evolution of a window cycle	114
7.4	Evolution of a window cycle, when the headers are taken into account	116
7.5	Comparison between Equation 7.10 with Equation 7.12	116
7.6	Comparison between simulation and theory for varying parameters	117
8.1	Outline of the test scenario	121
8.2	Throughput measurements version 1	123
8.3	Throughput measurements version 2	124
8.4	Throughput measurements version 3	125
8.5	Comparison between the performance of the real implementation and the optimal throughput	126
8.6	Path failure detection on FreeBSD, Linux and Solaris	129
8.7	FreeBSD: Reduction of the advertised receiver window with and without real memory utilization	133
8.8	Number of chunks accepted for a given arwnd	134
8.9	Ratio of retransmitted to delivered bytes for a varying amount of additional memory	136
8.10	Ratio of retransmitted to delivered bytes in the absence or presence of the SWS avoidance algorithm	137
8.11	Comparison of the course of the ratio of retransmitted to delivered bytes to the number of packets fitting in the arwnd	139
8.12	Ratio of retransmitted to delivered bytes, if the size of the real receiver window is announced	140
8.13	IP Datagrams containing SCTP `DATA` chunks	141
8.14	Testbed	146

8.15	Throughput on the transport layer	147
8.16	Goodput, if the header is not taken into account	148
8.17	Goodput, if the header is taken into account	149
8.18	Scenario with bottleneck link	151
8.19	Delayed SACKs with and without SACK-IMMEDIATELY option	151
8.20	Delayed SACKs with and without I-Bit on error-prone link	152
8.21	Retransmission behavior when parameters on sender and receiver do not match	154
8.22	DTLS handshake	156
8.23	Comparison of an association with and without packet drop reporting	158
8.24	Throughput on a lossy bottleneck link	159
8.25	Lossy link is not the bottleneck	160
8.26	Throughput on a bottleneck link, if a tunnel link is configured with an error rate	161
8.27	Handover with a different number of fast retransmissions	162
9.1	Using basic NAT	166
9.2	Setting up the NAT table during SCTP association setup	171
9.3	Building the NAT table for the single homed client with a multi-homed server	176
9.4	Multihoming through NAT middleboxes	177
9.5	After a route change a new NAT middlebox appears	178
9.6	Peer-to-Peer communication with rendezvous server	180
9.7	Components of the NAT module	183
9.8	Communication with the rendezvous server in a multihomed scenario	184
B.1	Testbed	221

List of Tables

4.1 Assigning addresses and verification tags to associations 45

8.1 Amount of bytes on the transport and application layer, when calculating the outstanding bytes with and without header for user message sizes of 30 and 60 bytes 144

Bibliography

[1] Project Akaroa.
Available at: http://www.cosc.canterbury.ac.nz/research/RG/net_sim/simulation_group/akaroa/about.chtml.

[2] M. Allman. TCP Congestion Control with Appropriate Byte Counting (ABC). *RFC 3465*, February 2003.

[3] M. Allman, V. Paxson, and W. Stevens. TCP Congestion Control. *RFC 2581*, April 1999.

[4] J. Banks. *Handbook of simulation: principles, methodology, advances, applications, and practice.* Wiley-Interscience, 1998.

[5] J. Banks, J. Carson, B. Nelson, and D. Nicol. *Discrete-event system simulation.* Prentice Hall Upper Saddle River, NJ, 2001.

[6] S. Bellovin, J. Ioannidis, A. Keromytis, and R. Stewart. On the Use of Stream Control Transmission Protocol (SCTP) with IPsec. *RFC 3554*, July 2003.

[7] L. Birta and G. Arbez. *Modelling and Simulation: Exploring Dynamic System Behaviour.* Springer-Verlag New York, Inc. Secaucus, NJ, USA, 2007.

[8] B. Braden, D. Clark, J. Crowcroft, B. Davie, S. Deering, D. Estrin, S. Floyd, V. Jacobson, G. Minshall, C. Partridge, L. Peterson, K. Ramakrishnan, S. Shenker, J. Wroclawski, and L. Zhang. Recommendations on Queue

Management and Congestion Avoidance in the Internet. *RFC 2309*, April 1998.

[9] R. Braden. Requirements for Internet Hosts - Communication Layers. *RFC 1122*, October 1989.

[10] B. Callaghan and R. Gilligan. Snoop Version 2 Packet Capture File Format. *RFC 1761*, February 1995.

[11] M. Carson and D. Santay. NIST Net: a Linux-based network emulation tool. *ACM SIGCOMM Computer Communication Review*, 33(3):111–126, 2003.

[12] G. Castagnoli, S. Brauer, and M. Herrmann. Optimization of cyclic redundancy-check codes with 24 and 32 paritybits. *IEEE Transactions on Communications*, 41(6):883–892, 1993.

[13] B. Chun, D. Culler, T. Roscoe, A. Bavier, L. Peterson, M. Wawrzoniak, and M. Bowman. PlanetLab: an overlay testbed for broad-coverage services. *ACM SIGCOMM Computer Communication Review*, 33(3):3–12, 2003.

[14] D. Clark. Window and Acknowledgement Strategy in TCP. *RFC 813*, July 1982.

[15] L. Degioanni and F. Risso. PCAP Next Generation Dump File Format, http://www.tcpdump.org/pcap/pcap.html (work in progress). March 2004.

[16] T. Dreibholz and E. Rathgeb. Reliable Server Pooling A Novel IETF Architecture for Availability-Sensitive Services. *Proceedings of the 2nd IEEE International Conference on Digital Society (ICDS)*, February 2008.

[17] T. Dreibholz and E. Rathgeb. A Powerful Tool-Chain for Setup, Distributed Processing, Analysis and Debugging of OMNeT++ Simulations. In *Proceedings of the 1st OMNeT++ Workshop*, pages 978–963, March 2008.

[18] L. Dryburgh and J. Hewitt. *Signaling System No. 7 (SS7/C7): Protocol, Architecture, and Services*. Cisco Press, 2005.

[19] Eclipse.
Available at: http://www.eclipse.org.

[20] emulab – total network testbed.
Available at: http://www.emulab.net.

[21] U. Esbold, E. P. Rathgeb, and A. Jungmaier. Secure SCTP: A versatile secure transport protocol. *Telecommunication Systems*, 27(2–4):273–296, 2004.

[22] K. Fall and K. Varadhan. The ns Manual.
Available at: http://www.isi.edu/nsnam/ns/ns-documentation.html, 2008.

[23] R. Ferrús, A. Brunstrom, K. Grinnemo, R. Fracchia, G. Galante, and F. Casadevall. Towards transport-layer mobility: Evolution of SCTP multihoming. *Computer Communications*, 31(5):980–998, 2008.

[24] J. Fitzpatrick, S. Murphy, M. Atiquzzaman, and J. Murphy. Using cross-layer metrics to improve the performance of end-to-end handover mechanisms. *Computer Communications*, 32(15):1600–1612, 2009.

[25] S. Floyd and V. Jacobson. On traffic phase effects in packet-switched gateways. *Internetworking: Research and Experience*, 3(3):115–156, 1992.

[26] B. Ford, P. Srisuresh, and D. Kegel. Peer-to-peer communication across network address translators. *USENIX Annual Technical Conference*, April 2005.

[27] T. George, B. Bidulock, R. Dantu, H. Schwarzbauer, and K. Morneault. Signaling System 7 (SS7) Message Transfer Part 2 (MTP2) — User Peer-to-Peer Adaptation Layer (M2PA). *RFC 4165*, September 2005.

[28] GNU General Public License.
Available at: http://www.gnu.org/licenses/gpl.html.

[29] Guile.
Available at: http://www.gnu.org/software/guile/guile.html.

[30] S. Guruprasad, R. Ricci, and J. Lepreau. Integrated network experimentation using simulation and emulation. *Testbeds and Research Infrastructures for the Development of Networks and Communities, 2005. Tridentcom 2005. First International Conference on*, pages 204–212, 2005.

[31] M. Handley and E. Rescorla. Internet Denial-of-Service Considerations. *RFC 4732*, November 2006.

[32] D. Hayes and J. But. Alias sctp Version 0.1: SCTP NAT implementation in IPFW. *CAIA, Swinburne University, Tech. Rep. 080618A, Jun*, 2008.

[33] C. Hohendorf, E. P. Rathgeb, E. Unurkhaan, and M. Tüxen. Secure end-to-end transport over SCTP. *JCP*, 2(4):31–40, 2007.

[34] github social coding - inet-framework.
Available at: http://github.com/inet-framework/inet.

[35] ITU-T Recommendation Q.2210:. Message Transfer Part Level 3 functions and messages using the services of ITU Recommendation Q.2140. *International Telecommunication Union, Geneva*, July 1996.

[36] ITU-T Recommendation Q.700:. Introduction to CCITT Signalling System No. 7. *International Telecommunication Union, Geneva*, March 1993.

[37] ITU-T Recommendation Q.701-Q.705:. Signalling System No. 7 (SS7) - Message Transfer Part (MTP). *International Telecommunication Union, Geneva*, March 1993.

[38] ITU-T Recommendation Q.706:. Signalling System No. 7 - Message Transfer Part Signalling Performance. *International Telecommunication Union, Geneva*, March 1993.

[39] ITU-T Recommendation Q.711-Q.715:. Signalling System No. 7 (SS7) - Signalling Connection Control Part (SCCP). *International Telecommunication Union, Geneva*, July 1996.

[40] ITU-T Recommendation Q.731:. Digital Subscriber Signalling System No. 1 (DSS 1) - ISDN user-network interface layer 3 - General aspects. *International Telecommunication Union, Geneva*, May 1998.

[41] ITU-T Recommendation Q.761-Q.767:. Signalling System No. 7 (SS7) - ISDN User Part (ISUP). *International Telecommunication Union, Geneva*, July 1996.

[42] J. Iyengar, P. Amer, and R. Stewart. Concurrent multipath transfer using SCTP multihoming over independent end-to-end paths. *IEEE/ACM Transactions on Networking (TON)*, 14(5):951–964, 2006.

[43] J. Iyengar, K. Shah, P. Amer, and R. Stewart. Concurrent Multipath Transfer Using SCTP Multihoming. *SPECTS 2004*, 2004.

[44] A. Jungmaier. sctplib Implementation.
Available at: http://www.sctp.de/sctp-download.html.

[45] A. Jungmaier. *Das Transportprotokoll SCTP–Leistungsbewertung und Optimierung eines neuen Transportprotokolls*. PhD thesis, University of Duisburg-Essen, August 2005.

[46] A. Jungmaier and E. Rathgeb. A Novel Method for SCTP Load Sharing. *Lecture notes in computer science*, pages 1453–1456, 2005.

[47] A. Jungmaier and E. Rathgeb. On SCTP multi-homing performance. *Telecommunication Systems*, 31(2):141–161, 2006.

[48] A. Jungmaier, E. Rathgeb, and M. Tüxen. On the Use of SCTP in Failover-Scenarios. *Proceedings of the SCI 2002*, 10:363–368, 2002.

[49] A. Jungmaier, E. Rescorla, and M. Tüxen. Transport Layer Security over Stream Control Transmission Protocol. *RFC 3436*, December 2002.

[50] H. Kamal, B. Penoff, and A. Wagner. SCTP-based middleware for MPI in wide-area networks. In *Communication Networks and Services Research Conference, 2005. Proceedings of the 3rd Annual*, pages 157–162, 2005.

[51] H. Kamal, B. Penoff, and A. Wagner. SCTP versus TCP for MPI. In *Proceedings of the 2005 ACM/IEEE conference on Supercomputing*. IEEE Computer Society Washington, DC, USA, 2005.

[52] J. Loughney, G. Sidebottom, L. Coene, G. Verwimp, J. Keller, and B. Bidulock. Signalling Connection Control Part User Adaptation Layer (SUA). *RFC 3868*, October 2004.

[53] M. Mathis, J. Semke, and J. Mahdavi. The macroscopic behavior of the TCP congestion avoidance algorithm. *ACM SIGCOMM Computer Communication Review*, 27(3), July 1997.

[54] S. McCanne and V. Jacobson. The BSD packet filter: A new architecture for user-level packet capture. In *Proc. WinterÂŠ93 USENIX Conference*, 1993.

[55] K. Morneault, R. Dantu, G. Sidebottom, B. Bidulock, and J. Heitz. Signaling System 7 (SS7) Message Transfer Part 2 (MTP2) — User Adaptation Layer. *RFC 3331*, September 2002.

[56] K. Morneault and J. Pastor-Balbas. Signaling System 7 (SS7) Message Transfer Part 3 (MTP3) — User Adaptation Layer (M3UA). *RFC 4666*, September 2006.

[57] K. Morneault, S. Rengasami, M. Kalla, and G. Sidebottom. Integrated Services Digital Network (ISDN) Q.921 — User Adaptation Layer. *RFC 4233*, January 2006.

[58] A. Mosig. Net Simulator 2. Routing-Seminar.
Available at: http://www.uni-koblenz.de/steigner/seminar-routingsim/mosig.pdf, 2004.

[59] J. Nagle. Congestion Control in IP/TCP Internetworks. *RFC 896*, January 1984.

[60] P. Natarajan, F. Baker, and P. Amer. Multiple TCP Connections Improve HTTP Throughput Myth or Fact? *TR2008-333, Department of Computer & Information Sciences, University of Delaware, USA*, 2008.

[61] The Network Simulator NS-2.
Available at: http://nsnam.isi.edu/nsnam/index.php.

[62] OMNET++ User Manual Version 4.0.
Available at: http://omnetpp.org/doc/omnetpp40/manual/usman.html.

[63] L. Ong, I. Rytina, M. Garcia, H. Schwarzbauer, L. Coene, H. Lin, I. Juhasz, M. Holdrege, and C. Sharp. Framework Architecture for Signaling Transport. *RFC 2719*, October 1999.

[64] OpenSSL - Cryptography and SSL/TLS Toolkit.
Available at: http://www.openssl.org.

[65] The OPNET Modeler.
Available at: http://www.opnet.com.

[66] H. Park, M. Kim, S. Lee, S. Kang, and Y. Kim. A mobility management scheme using SCTP-SIP for real-time services across heterogeneous networks. In *Proceedings of the 2009 ACM symposium on Applied Computing*, pages 196–200. ACM New York, NY, USA, 2009.

[67] V. Paxson and M. Allman. RFC2988: Computing TCP's Retransmission Timer. *RFC Editor United States*, 2000.

[68] B. Penoff, A. Wagner, M. Tüxen, and I. Rüngeler. MPI-NeTSim: A network simulation module for MPI . *15th IEEE International Conference on Parallel and Distributed Systems (ICPADS'09), Shenzhen, CHINA*, December 2009.

[69] J. Postel. Internet Protocol. *RFC 791*, September 1981.

[70] J. Postel. Transmission Control Protocol. *RFC 793*, September 1981.

[71] E. Rathgeb, C. Hohendorf, and M. Nordhoff. On the Robustness of SCTP against DoS Attacks. In *Convergence and Hybrid Information Technology, 2008. ICCIT'08. Third International Conference on*, volume 2, 2008.

[72] E. Rescorla and N. Modadugu. Datagram transport layer security. *RFC 4347*, April 2006.

[73] M. Riegel and M. Tüxen. Mobile SCTP transport layer mobility management for the Internet. In *Proc. SoftCOM 2002, International Conference on Software, Telecommunications and Computer Networks*, pages 305–309, 2002.

[74] M. Riegel and M. Tüxen. Mobile SCTP, draft-riegel-tuexen-mobile-sctp-09 (work in progress). *IETF*, November 2007.

[75] L. Rizzo. Dummynet: a simple approach to the evaluation of network protocols. *ACM SIGCOMM Computer Communication Review*, 27(1):31–41, 1997.

[76] I. Rüngeler, M. Tüxen, and E. Rathgeb. Integration of SCTP in the OMNeT++ simulation environment. In *Proceedings of the 1st international conference on Simulation tools and techniques for communications, networks and systems & workshops table of contents*. ICST (Institute for Computer Sciences, Social-Informatics and Telecommunications Engineering) ICST, Brussels, Belgium, Belgium, 2008.

[77] I. Rüngeler, M. Tüxen, and E. Rathgeb. Congestion and Flow Control in the Context of the Message-Oriented Protocol SCTP. In *Proceedings of the 8th International IFIP-TC 6 Networking Conference*, page 481. Springer-Verlag, 2009.

[78] I. Rüngeler, M. Tüxen, and E. Rathgeb. Considerations on Handling Link Errors in SCTP. *ICB Research Reports, University of Duisburg-Essen*, August 2009.

[79] R. Seggelmann, I. Rüngeler, M. Tüxen, and E. Rathgeb. Parallelizing OMNeT++ Simulations using Xgrid. *2nd International Workshop on OMNeT++ (OMNeT++ 2009)*, March 2009.

[80] D. Smith and R. Bellcore. Effects of Feedback Delay on the Performance of the Transfer-Controlled Procedure in Controlling CCS Network Overloads. *Selected Areas in Communications, IEEE Journal on*, 12(3):424–432, 1994.

[81] Snoop Man Page.
Available at: http://docs.sun.com/app/docs/doc/819-2240/snoop-1m.

[82] P. Srisuresh and K. Egevang. Traditional IP Network Address Translator (Traditional NAT). *RFC 3022*, January 2001.

[83] W. Stevens, B. Fenner, and A. Rudoff. *Unix Network Programming: The Sockets Networking API*. Addison-Wesley, 2004.

[84] M. Stewart, R. Ramalho, Q. Xie, M. Tüxen, and P. Conrad. Stream control transmission protocol (SCTP) Partial Reliability Extension. *RFC3758, May*, 2004.

[85] R. Stewart. Stream Control Transmission Protocol. *RFC 4960*, September 2007.

[86] R. Stewart, P. Lei, and M. Tüxen. Stream Control Transmission Protocol (SCTP) Stream Reset, draft-stewart-sctpstrrst-04 (work in progress). *IETF*, January 2007.

[87] R. Stewart, P. Lei, and M. Tüxen. Stream Control Transmission Protocol (SCTP) Packet Drop Reporting, draft-stewart-sctp. pktdrprep-08 (work in progress). *IETF*, October 2008.

[88] R. Stewart, K. Poon, M. Tüxen, and V. Yasevich. Sockets API Extensions for Stream Control Transmission Protocol (SCTP), draft-ietf-tsvwg-sctpsocket-19 (work in progress). *IETF*, February 2009.

[89] R. Stewart and M. Tüxen. Stream Control Transmission Protocol (SCTP) IPv4 Address Scoping, draft-stewart-tsvwg-sctp-ipv4-00 (work in progress). *IETF*, May 2002.

[90] R. Stewart, M. Tüxen, and I. Rüngeler. Stream Control Transmission Protocol (SCTP) Network Address Translation, draft-ietf-behave-sctpnat-01 (work in progress). *IETF*, February 2009.

[91] R. Stewart and Q. Xie. *Stream control transmission protocol (SCTP)—A Reference Guide*. Addison-Wesley Longman Publishing Co., Inc. Boston, MA, USA, 2001.

[92] R. Stewart, Q. Xie, M. Tüxen, S. Maruyama, and M. Kozuka. RFC5061: Stream Control Transmission Protocol (SCTP) Dynamic Address Reconfiguration. *Internet RFCs*, 2007.

[93] SCTP Testtool.
Available at: http://sctp.fh-muenster.de/sctp-testtool.html.

[94] TShark Man page.
Available at: http://www.wireshark.org/docs/man-pages/tshark.htm.

[95] M. Tüxen. Stream Control Transmission Protocol, Errata ID 1440. Technical report, July 2008.

[96] M. Tüxen, I. Rüngeler, and E. P. Rathgeb. Interface connecting the inet simulation framework with the real world. In *Simutools '08: Proceedings of the 1st international conference on Simulation tools and techniques for communications, networks and systems & workshops*, pages 1–6, ICST, Brussels, Belgium, Belgium, 2008. ICST (Institute for Computer Sciences, Social-Informatics and Telecommunications Engineering).

[97] M. Tüxen, I. Rüngeler, and R. Stewart. SACK-IMMEDIATELY extension for the Stream Control Transmission Protocol, draft-tuexen-tsvwg-sctp-sack-immediately-00 (work in progress). *IETF*, July 2008.

[98] M. Tüxen, I. Rüngeler, R. Stewart, and E. Rathgeb. Network Address Translation for the Stream Control Transmission Protocol. *IEEE Network*, 22(5):26–32, 2008.

[99] M. Tüxen, R. Seggelmann, and E. Rescorla. Datagram Transport Layer Security for Stream Control Transmission Protocol, draft-ietf-tsvwg-dtlsfor-sctp-00 (work in progress). *IETF*, October 2008.

[100] M. Tüxen and R. Stewart. UDP Encapsulation of SCTP Packets, draft-tuexen-sctp-udp-encaps-02 (work in progress). *IETF*, November 2007.

[101] M. Tüxen, R. Stewart, P. Lei, and E. Rescorla. RFC4895: Authenticated Chunks for the Stream Control Transmission Protocol (SCTP). *Internet RFCs*, 2007.

[102] C. Van Jacobson, C. Leres, and S. McCanne. Tcpdump Man Page. Available at: http://www.tcpdump.org/tcpdump_man.html.

[103] C. Van Jacobson and S. McCanne. libpcap, Initial public release 1994. *Available at http://www.tcpdump.org*, 1994.

[104] A. Varga et al. INET Framework Documentation. *Available at: http://inet.omnetpp.org*, 2009.

[105] A. Varga et al. OMNeT++ Discrete Event Simulation System. *Available at: http://www.omnetpp.org*, 2009.

[106] A. Varga and R. Hornig. An overview of the omnet++ simulation environment. In *Simutools '08: Proceedings of the 1st international conference on Simulation tools and techniques for communications, networks and systems & workshops*, pages 1–10, ICST, Brussels, Belgium, Belgium, 2008. ICST (Institute for Computer Sciences, Social-Informatics and Telecommunications Engineering).

[107] M. Welzl. Passing Corrupt Data Across Network Layers: An Overview of Recent Developments and Issues. *EURASIP Journal of Applied Signal Processing*, 2005(2):242–247, 2005.

[108] M. Welzl, M. Rossi, A. Fumagalli, and M. Tacca. TCP/IP over IEEE 802.11 b WLAN: the challenge of harnessing known-corrupt data. In *IEEE International Conference on Communications, 2008. ICC'08*, pages 280–284, 2008.

[109] D. Wetherall and C. Lindblad. Extending Tcl for dynamic object-oriented programming. In *Proc. of the 3rd conference on USENIX. Third Annual Tcl/Tk Workshop*. USENIX Association Berkeley, CA, USA, 1995.

[110] Windows Kernel Driver for SCTP, 2009.
Available at: http://www.co-conv.jp /en/product/sctpDrv/20081224.

[111] Wireshark protocol analyzer.
Available at: http://www.wireshark.org.

[112] G. Wright and W. Stevens. TCP/IP illustrated. Vol. 2: The implementation. *Addison-Wesley Professional Computing Series, Reading, Mass.: Addison-Wesley*, 1995.

[113] Xgrid Programming Guide, 2007.
Available at: http://developer.apple.com/documentation/MacOSXServer /Conceptual/Xgrid_Programming_Guide/Xgrid_Programming_Guide.pdf.

[114] Q. Xie, R. Stewart, M. Holdrege, and M. Tüxen. SCTP NAT Traversal Considerations, draft-xie-behave-sctp-nat-cons-03 (work in progress). *IETF*, November 2007.

Appendix A

Configurable Parameters of the Simulation

In order to be able to test the network under different conditions numerous protocol specific parameters are provided. The user can easily configure them by editing a text file, which is *omnetpp.ini* by default. The parameters are divided into those concerning the transport layer and those specifying the applications.

A.1 Protocol Parameters

A.1.1 Parameters for the basic SCTP functionality according to RFC 4960

The parameters concerning the transport layer can be configured for each host's SCTP stack individually. In RFC 4960 a number of parameters with their default values are listed, that can be set by the user. They have their equivalents in the following alphabetically ordered list.

- assocMaxRetrans: Maximum number of consecutive unacknowledged heartbeats and retransmissions, before the peer is considered to be unreachable (default: 10).

- hbInterval: Interval between two heartbeats (default: 30 s).

- maxInitRetrans: Maximum number of retransmissions for an INIT chunk (default: 8).

- pathMaxRetrans: Maximum number of consecutive unacknowledged heartbeats and retransmissions on a certain path, before the path is set inactive default: 5).

- rtoAlpha: Needed to calculate RTO (default: 0.125).

- rtoBeta: Needed to calculate RTO (default: 0.250).

- rtoInitial: Initial retransmission timeout (default: 3 s).

- rtoMin: Minimum of the retransmission timeout (default: 1 s).

- rtoMax: Maximum of the retransmission timeout (default: 60 s).

- validCookieLifetime: Lifespan of the State Cookie (default: 10 s).

Most implementations provide the user with additional SCTP kernel parameters. We made the following attributes configurable.

- sctpAlgorithmClass: Subclassed from SCTP Algorithm (default: "SCTPAlg").

- arwnd: Advertised receiver window to be announced in the `INIT_ACK` or `INIT` chunk (default: 65535).

- maxBurst: Maximum number of packets that may be sent at once (default: 4).

- nagleEnabled: Indicates whether the Nagle algorithm is used or not (default: true).

- naglePoint: Number of bytes when a packet is considered to be full and can be sent, when the Nagle algorithm is enabled (default: 1468). The value should be adjusted to configured MTU.

- numGapReports: Number of `SACK` chunks that have to report this TSN to be missing before it is fast retransmitted (default: 3)

- reactivatePrimaryPath: Indicates whether the original primary path should be activated after it has lost its status and has come up again (default: false).

- sackFrequency: Number of chunks to arrive before a `SACK` chunk is sent (default: 2).

- sackPeriod: Time after which the Sack-timer expires and a `SACK` chunk has to be sent (default: 200 ms).

- ccModule: Indicates which congestion control model should be used (default: 0 means that the algorithm suggested in RFC4960 is taken).

- ssModule: Indicates which stream scheduling model should be used (default: 0 means that the ROUND_ROBIN scheduling is used).

- swsLimit: Silly window syndrome avoidance limit. For advertised receiver windows smaller than swsLimit, a window of 1 is announced (default: 3000).

- sendQueueLimit: Maximum size of the send queue (default: 0).

A.1.2 Parameters for special purposes

Parameters that can be used with any extension

- osbWithHeader: Indicates whether the outstanding bytes should be counted including the header (default: false).

- padding: Indicates whether the outstanding bytes should be counted including the padding bytes (default: false).

- RTXMethod: Method how often fast retransmission can occur (default: 0).

    0 once after 3 gap reports

1 once per RTT

2 once per RTO

3 always after 3 gap reports

- fairStart: Start time, if the throughput for a predefined time interval should be computed (default: 0).

- fairStop: Stop time, if the throughput for a predefined time interval should be computed by counting the data being delivered to the upper layer and dividing them by the difference between fairStop and fairStart (default: 0).

- sackNow: Flag to use the I-Bit in the last `DATA` chunk of the cwnd (default: false).

- natFriendly: Indicates that the sender is behind a NAT middlebox and, therefore, no private addresses should be included in the `INIT` or `INIT_ACK` chunk (default: false).

Parameters to test flow control

- bytesToAddPerRcvdChunk: Memory needed by the OS for an incoming chunk (default: 0).

- bytesToAddPerPeerChunk: Memory needed by the peer for an incoming chunk (default: 0). This is the number of bytes that is additionally subtracted from the peer a_rwnd.

- tellArwnd: Indicates, that the sender of the `SACK` chunk should set the arwnd parameter to the real value (default: false).

- messageAcceptLimit: The receiver is limited by a certain number of messages (default: 0).

Parameters to test SCTP extensions

- auth: Indicates whether AUTH is activated (default: false).

- chunks: Chunk types that have to be authenticated. Several chunks are separated by a comma (default: "").

- addIP: Indicates whether AddIP is activated (default: false).

- addTime: Sets the time when an address should be added or deleted (default: 0 s).

- addAddress: The address to be added or deleted (default: "").

- addIpType: The value of the AddIp-Parameter type (default: "")

    49153 ADD_IP_ADDRESS

    49156 SET_PRIMARY_ADDRESS

    49154 DELETE_IP_ADDRESS

    Several parameters are separated by a comma.

- packetDrop: Indicates whether packet drop reporting is activated (default: false).

Special Parameters

- testing: Indicates whether debug output should be enabled.

- timeout: If testing is true, it sets the time when debug output should be started.

A.2 Application Parameters

In addition to those parameters that are needed for every connection like destination address or message length, some parameters are provided that allow to change the sending behavior. As a host can start several applications so that for instance a server can have associations with numerous clients, the application parameters can be configured independently for every application. Parameters that influence the sending and receiving behavior are

- delayFirstRead: The receiver waits delayFirstRead seconds before the first incoming message is read.
- thinkTime: Time between two consecutive send calls.
- echoDelay: In case of an *echoserver* the time waited before the data is sent back.

Other parameters are specific to SCTP like

- outboundStreams: Number of outbound streams the host wants to use.
- ordered: Indicates whether the messages should be ordered or unordered.
- address: As the host can be multihomed, all addresses can be bound or just the ones specified.

To allow more predictable and longer testing times, the following parameters can be configured.

- queueSize: Size of sendqueue before the upperlayer is notified to send new data.
- startTime: Time when the client application starts the handshake.
- stopTime: If greater than 0, time when a `SHUTDOWN` chunk will be sent.

Parameters to test NAT:

- ownName: Name included in the NAT message to the rendezvous server.
- peerName: Name of the peer the sender of the NAT message wants to communicate with.

- rendezvous: Indicates whether the peer is still in the rendezvous phase.
- multi: Indicates whether the peer is multihomed.

Appendix B

Configuration Examples

B.1 Fairness Test of Section 8.3

B.1.1 Setting up the network

In the ned file of the example, the network of Figure 8.14, which we repeat here for convenience, has to be defined with all the submodules. We need four **Standard-**

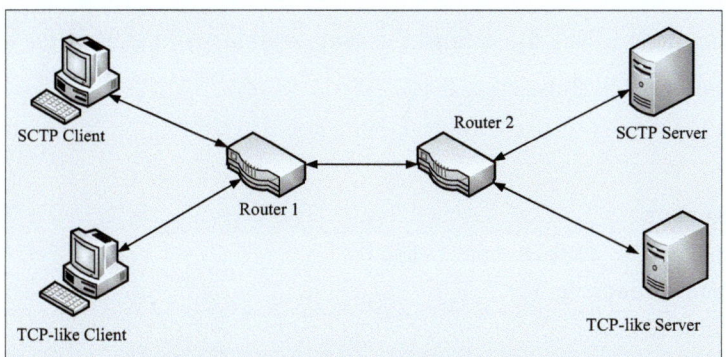

Figure B.1: Testbed

Hosts and two **Routers**. Two channels have to be defined, one for the unlimited and one for the bottleneck link.

First the location of the necessary modules has to be declared:

```
package inet.examples.sctp.fair;
import inet.nodes.inet.StandardHost;
import inet.nodes.inet.Router;
```

```
import ned.DatarateChannel;
```

Then the channels can be configured. Only the values that are different from the default have to be specified.

```
channel BottleneckPath extends DatarateChannel
{
    parameters:
        datarate = 1Mbps;
}

channel NormalPath extends DatarateChannel
{
    parameters:
        datarate = 1Gbps;
}
```

Finally, the network is assembled. For each module the **routingFile** parameter is set to the name of the file defined for that module. An example for a routing file has been given in Subsection 5.1.4.

```
network fair
{
    parameters:
        volatile double testTimeout;
        bool testing;
    submodules:
        sctp_client: StandardHost {
            parameters:
                routingFile = "sctp_client.mrt";
                @display("i=laptop3;p=128,317");
            gates:
                pppg[1];
        }
        sctp_server: StandardHost {
            parameters:
                routingFile = "sctp_server.mrt";
```

```
            @display("i=laptop3");
        gates:
            pppg[1];
    }
    tcp_client: StandardHost {
        parameters:
            routingFile = "tcp_client.mrt";
            @display("i=laptop2;p=302,398");
        gates:
            pppg[1];
    }
    tcp_server: StandardHost {
        parameters:
            routingFile = "tcp_server.mrt";
            @display("i=laptop2");
        gates:
            pppg[1];
    }
    router1: Router {
        parameters:
            routingFile = "router1.mrt";
            @display("i=abstract/router;p=270,293");
        gates:
            pppg[4];
    }
    router2: Router {
        parameters:
            routingFile = "router2.mrt";
            @display("i=abstract/router");
        gates:
            pppg[4];
    }
connections:
    sctp_client.pppg[0]  <-->    NormalPath
                         <--> router1.pppg[0];
```

```
        router2.pppg[0]      <-->   NormalPath
                             <-->   sctp_server.pppg[0];
        tcp_client.pppg[0]   <-->   NormalPath
                             <-->   router1.pppg[1];
        router2.pppg[1]      <-->   NormalPath
                             <-->   tcp_server.pppg[0];
        router1.pppg[2]      <-->   BottleneckPath
                             <-->   router2.pppg[2];
}
```

B.1.2 Configuring the Parameters

The *omnetpp.ini* is the configuration file of the example. Here, the values for the parameters are set and configurations are defined:

```
[General]
network = fair
fair.testing = false
**.testTimeout = 0

# UDP and TCP apps (off)
**.numUdpApps = 0
**.numTcpApps = 0


# TCP like client
**.tcp_client.numSctpApps = 1
**.tcp_client.sctpAppType = "SCTPClient"
**.tcp_client.sctpApp[0].address = "10.1.2.1"
**.tcp_client.sctpApp[0].port = 0
**.tcp_client.sctpApp[0].connectAddress = "10.1.4.1"
**.tcp_client.sctpApp[0].connectPort = 8888
**.tcp_client.sctpApp[0].numRequestsPerSession = 100000000
**.tcp_client.sctpApp[0].queueSize = 1000
**.tcp_client.sctpApp[0].requestLength= 1452
**.tcp_client.tcpdump.dumpFile = "tcp_client.pcap"
```

```
# TCP like server
**.tcp_server.numSctpApps = 1
**.tcp_server.sctpAppType = "SCTPServer"
**.tcp_server.sctpApp[0].address = "10.1.4.1"
**.tcp_server.sctpApp[0].port = 8888
**.tcp_server.tcpdump.dumpFile = "tcp_server.pcap"

# SCTP client
**.sctp_client.numSctpApps = 1
**.sctp_client.sctpAppType = "SCTPClient"
**.sctp_client.sctpApp[0].address = "10.1.1.1"
**.sctp_client.sctpApp[0].connectAddress = "10.1.3.1"
**.sctp_client.sctpApp[0].connectPort = 6666
**.sctp_client.sctpApp[0].requestLength= 1452
**.sctp_client.sctpApp[0].numRequestsPerSession = 100000000
**.sctp_client.sctpApp[0].queueSize = 1000
**.sctp_client.tcpdump.dumpFile = "sctp_client.pcap"

# SCTP server
**.sctp_server.numSctpApps = 1
**.sctp_server.sctpAppType = "SCTPServer"
**.sctp_server.sctpApp[*].address = "10.1.3.1"
**.sctp_server.sctpApp[0].port = 6666
**.sctp_server.tcpdump.dumpFile = "sctp_server.pcap"


# NIC configuration
**.ppp[*].queueType = "REDQueue"

**.vector-recording = false

[Config fairnessTest]
**.sctp_client.sctpApp[0].requestLength = ${12..204 step 12}
**.sctp.osbWithHeader = true
```

```
**.sctp.padding = true
**.sctp_client.sctpApp[0].startTime = truncnormal(1s,0.2s)
**.sctp_client.sctpApp[0].stopTime = truncnormal(600s,10s)
**.sctp_client.sctp.fairStart = 50s
**.sctp_client.sctp.fairStop = 450s
**.tcp_client.sctpApp[0].startTime = truncnormal(5s,0.2s)
**.tcp_client.sctpApp[0].stopTime = truncnormal(500s,10s)
**.tcp_client.sctp.fairStart = 50s
**.tcp_client.sctp.fairStop = 450s
**.sctp_server.tcpdump.countStart = 50s
**.sctp_server.tcpdump.countStop = 450s
**.tcp_server.tcpdump.countStart = 50s
**.tcp_server.tcpdump.countStop = 450s
```

In this example we only enabled one SCTP application per host, although it is possible to have several applications, even from different transport protocols. The sctp_client is connected to the sctp_server and the tcp_client to the tcp_server. The start and stop times are chosen randomly according a normal distribution with a given mean and standard deviation. Other start and stop times are configured to measure the throughput on the application layer (*fairStart* and *fairStop*) and on the network layer (*countStart* and *countStop*). The UMS of the SCTP client is iterated from 12 to 204 bytes in steps of 12. Thus, the configuration *fairnessTest* comprises 17 runs. The dump module is set to record the traces.

B.2 Changing Error Rate and Delay

In this example a new configuration aspect is the changing of the error rate and the delay in the *omnetpp.ini*, which has not been possible prior to OMNeT++ version 4.0.

The network consists of a client and a server, which are connected via two routers. The link between the two routers is configured with a packet error rate (*per*) and a delay.

```
package inet.examples.sctp.matt;
import inet.nodes.inet.StandardHost;
import inet.nodes.inet.Router;
import ned.DatarateChannel;

channel bottleNeck extends DatarateChannel
{
    delay = 0.1s;
    datarate = 100Mbps;
    per = 0.005;
}

channel unlimited extends DatarateChannel
{
    datarate = 1 Gbps;
}

network ClientServerWithRouter
{
    parameters:
        double testTimeout @unit(s) = default(0s);
        bool testing = default(false);
    submodules:
        client: StandardHost {
            parameters:
                routingFile = "client.mrt";
                @display("p=37,182;i=laptop3");
            gates:
                pppg[1];
        }
        server: StandardHost {
            parameters:
                routingFile = "server.mrt";
                @display("p=448,175;i=server1");
            gates:
```

```
                pppg[1];
        }
        router1: Router {
            parameters:
                routingFile = "router1.mrt";
            gates:
                pppg[2];
        }
        router2: Router {
            parameters:
                routingFile = "router2.mrt";
            gates:
                pppg[2];
        }
    connections:
        client.pppg[0]   <--> unlimited  <--> router.pppg[0];
        router1.pppg[1]  <--> bottleNeck <--> router2.pppg[0];
        router2.pppg[1]  <--> unlimited  <--> server.pppg[0];
}
```

To configure the packet error rate for the bottleneck link, both directions have to be distinguished. To set the error rate for instance to 0.01, the link from **router1** to **router2** has to be set to

`**.router1.pppg$o[1].channel.per=0.01`

for the outgoing and

`**.router1.pppg$i[1].channel.per=0.01`

for the incoming direction. To iterate over the values, a variable has to be defined which can be referred to when configuring the opposite direction:

`**.router1.pppg$o[1].channel.per=${N=0.005..0.01 step 0.001}`
`**.router1.pppg$o[1].channel.per=${N}`

Otherwise, the configuration would result in 36 instead of 6 runs, because the iterations over parameter spaces are realized as nested loops.

Die VDM Verlagsservicegesellschaft sucht für wissenschaftliche Verlage abgeschlossene und herausragende

Dissertationen, Habilitationen, Diplomarbeiten, Master Theses, Magisterarbeiten usw.

für die kostenlose Publikation als Fachbuch.

Sie verfügen über eine Arbeit, die hohen inhaltlichen und formalen Ansprüchen genügt, und haben Interesse an einer honorarvergüteten Publikation?

Dann senden Sie bitte erste Informationen über sich und Ihre Arbeit per Email an *info@vdm-vsg.de*.

Sie erhalten kurzfristig unser Feedback!

VDM Verlagsservicegesellschaft mbH
Dudweiler Landstr. 99   Telefon +49 681 3720 174
D - 66123 Saarbrücken   Fax   +49 681 3720 1749
www.vdm-vsg.de

Die VDM Verlagsservicegesellschaft mbH vertritt

Printed by Books on Demand GmbH, Norderstedt / Germany